AIRBORNE FORCES AT WAR

From Parachute Test Platoon
to the 21st Century

VOICE FOR THE ARMY . . . SUPPORT FOR THE SOLDIER

Since 1950, the Association of the United States Army has worked to support all aspects of national security while advancing the interests of America's Army and the men and women who serve.

AUSA is a private, non-profit educational organization that supports America's Army—Active, National Guard, Reserve, Civilians, Retirees and family members. AUSA provides numerous professional development opportunities at a variety of events both local and national.

Association of
The United States Army
2425 Wilson Blvd.
Arlington, Virginia 22201
Tel. 800.336.4570
www.ausa.org

Many persons assisted the authors and producers in creating this book. They wish to express special thanks to the persons listed here.

82d Airborne Division War Memorial Museum:
    John Aarsen
82d Airborne Division: *Maj. Amy Hannah,*
    MSgt. Chris Fletcher, Sgt. Mike Pryor
Airborne and Special Operations Museum:
    John S. Duvall, Ph.D.
American Battle Monuments Commission:
    Michael G. Conley
Association of the United States Army:
    Roger Cirillo, Ph.D.
Do You Graphics photo researchers:
    Cyndy and Mike Gilley, Dottie Siders
National Infantry Museum: *Z. Frank Hanner*
Photo researcher: *Michael Dolan*
Program Executive Office Soldier: *Debi Dawson,*
    Maj. Shawn P. Lucas, Erin Thomas
Soldier System Center, Natick: *Janice Rosado*
U.S. Army Center of Military History: *Deena Everett,*
    Joseph Frechette, Lenore Garder, Renée Klish, Frank Shirer
XVIII Airborne Corps: *Donna Barr Tabor,*
    Maj. Richard Patterson

Production team for the book:
Editor: *Nina D. Seebeck, One Hundred Proof Editorial Services*
Designer: *Liz Weaver, Paprika Creative*
Indexer: *Amy B. Thompson*
Coordinator: *Simone Hammarstrand*
Producer: *F. Clifton Berry, Jr., FCB Associates LLC*

Jeep is a registered trademark of Chrysler LLC.

AIRBORNE FORCES AT WAR

From Parachute Test Platoon to the 21st Century

Robert K. Wright Jr., Ph.D. ■ John T. Greenwood, Ph.D.

Presented by the

Association of the United States Army

Washington, D.C.

Naval Institute Press

Annapolis, Maryland

Naval Institute Press
291 Wood Road
Annapolis, Maryland 21402
www.usni.org

Library of Congress Cataloging-in-Publication Data

Wright, Robert K., 1946–
  Airborne forces at war : from parachute test platoon to the 21st
century / Robert K. Wright, Jr., John T. Greenwood.
      p. cm.
  Includes bibliographical references and index.
  ISBN 978-1-59114-028-3 (alk. paper)
  1. United States. Army—Airborne troops—History. I. Greenwood, John
T. II. Title.
UD483.W75 2008
356'.1660973—dc22
                            2007041012

Printed in the United States of America.

12 11 10 09 08 07   9 8 7 6 5 4 3 2
First Printing

To the men and women of the
Army's airborne forces: past, present, and future.
They descend from the skies to execute the Nation's missions.

Contents

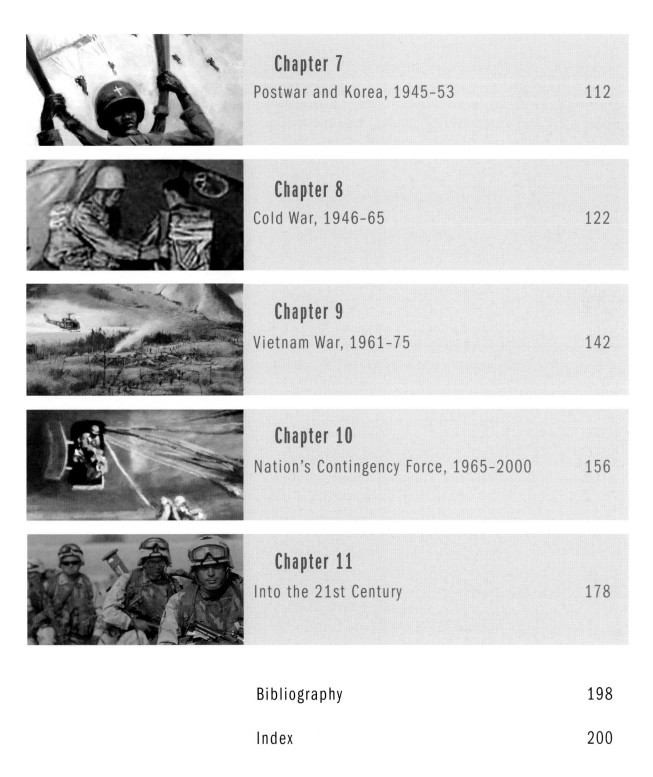

Foreword

Gen. Gary E. Luck.
Photo courtesy
XVIII Airborne Corps
Historian.

The men and women who have worn jump wings, a maroon beret, and the airborne tab are part of a proud community. From the moment Lt. Bill Ryder led the Test Platoon on its first jump it has taken an exceptional soldier to be Airborne.

To be part of the airborne community is to show courage every single day. When the Green Light comes on only the brave can go out the door. This is true whether the drop zone is at Fort Bragg or in some distant country.

Every member chose the hard way. Each accepted the challenge to meet only the highest standards. Whatever the Military Occupational Specialty, whatever the job, airborne soldiers have always been professionals taking pride in the quality of their performance.

Each paratrooper has been dedicated to defending America and bringing freedom and hope to the rest of the world. This was true in major conflicts from World War II to the Gulf. It shows in contingency operations in places like Lebanon and Haiti, or in the response to a hurricane or other natural disaster. And it is especially true today in places like Afghanistan and Iraq where terrorists are the enemy.

Taken together these qualities form the Airborne Spirit instilled from day one by leaders like William Lee, Matthew Ridgway, and James Gavin. It is something passed on by every leader who followed, and at every level. From commanding general to squad leader the Airborne soldier has always been led from the front and has always willingly followed.

These pages describe the units and individuals who made up the airborne community. It shows their sacrifices and accomplishments. In these pages you can see the continuity of the mission and the flexibility and agility needed to do it better.

Whether by parachute, by glider, or by helicopter airborne soldiers have always taken the fight behind enemy lines. They have always been the country's best. This book tells their story.

"Airborne . . . All the Way!"

Gary E. Luck
General, U.S. Army (Retired)

Preface

Why would someone want to jump out of a perfectly good airplane in flight? It's a valid question. Paratroopers learn to expect the question and to have their own responses ready. "Because they're nuts"; or "To earn jump pay"; or a similar jest. The real reason is to join with like-minded soldiers; buddies who also put their "knees in the breeze" and build the bonds of shared perils and achievements in peace and war.

The U.S. Army's paratroopers and glider soldiers performed admirably from their first combat in World War II. Their descendants have continued the tradition of exemplary service. The airborne units of today build upon the heritage, and constitute a potent element of national power in the 21st Century.

This book is an illustrated survey of the airborne forces of the United States Army from inception to the present day. It focuses on airborne units who used parachutes and gliders in service to the nation. It presents highlights of combat actions and peacetime developments involving airborne units.

Ranger units and Special Operations Forces share the use of parachutes to travel from sky to earth. Air assault forces may not employ parachutes, but they are experts at using helicopters to conquer time and distance. Those units appear here in context, but are not covered in detail. Each of those exceptional forces deserves its own singular fuller coverage.

A note on unit designations. The designations of Army units vary as the Army organizes, reorganizes, and transforms itself. The lineage of an Army unit is more complex than a genealogical family tree. This book uses the designation of the unit at the time it is mentioned.

F. Clifton Berry, Jr.
Former trooper in the 82d Airborne Division
and producer of the book

Chapter 1
Concept Becomes Reality, 1940–41

GENESIS OF A CONCEPT

Frenchman André-Jacques Garnerin is credited with making the first successful parachute descent. On October 22, 1797, using a parachute of his own design, he jumped from a balloon at an altitude of about 3,000 feet over Paris.

More than 114 years after Garnerin's feat, U.S. Army Capt. Albert Berry performed the world's first successful parachute jump from an airplane in flight. On March 1, 1912, Berry used a cumbersome parachute apparatus designed by A. Leo Stevens, a balloonist and parachutist, to leap from a Benoist biplane over Jefferson Barracks near St. Louis, Missouri. Spectators were impressed, but the Army was not and did not exploit the military potential of his achievement. Berry's jump was more of a stunt than an exploration of a new combination of emerging technologies. Soon thereafter, daredevils—both male and female—were delivering crowd-pleasing performances parachuting from soaring airplanes in air shows across the United States.

During World War I, observers in balloons on both sides had access to parachutes for emergency use. Late in the war, German pilots also were outfitted with parachutes. U.S. and other Allied airplane pilots were not so fortunate. However, in the postwar years, parachutes eventually became standard issue for U.S. air crews.

Toward the end of the war, the first great leap of imagination on the potential employment of large airborne forces came from Brig. Gen. William "Billy" Mitchell, U.S. Army Air Service, who headed American air operations in the St. Mihiel and Meuse-Argonne offensives of 1918. Mitchell, of course, later gained fame as a forward-looking but outspoken advocate of airpower who was court-martialed in 1925 and subsequently resigned. In October 1918, Mitchell received the approval of Gen. John J. Pershing, commander of the American Expeditionary Forces, to plan a massive aerial offensive that included a parachute drop of the 1st Division at Metz behind the German lines. With heavy fighter and bomber support, aerial resupply, and a closely coordinated ground offensive, Mitchell described his plan as "a simultaneous attack in front and rear, and on both flanks from overhead, a fire which no body of troops could have withstood." The Armistice of November 11, 1918, intervened and ended the war.

German parachute troopers with machine gun. Copied from print received from *Infantry Journal*, which obtained it from the German Military Attaché in Washington, October 30, 1940. *National Archives.*

While Mitchell's grandiose scheme was never put into action, it clearly foreshadowed airborne operations of World War II. He had envisioned a massive airborne vertical envelopment to jump the trench lines and break into the enemy's rear to turn the course of the ground battle and the war. It was upon such innovative and often revolutionary thinking that the development and use of airborne forces would always depend.

In experiments in the late 1920s, the U.S. Army dropped a few soldiers and machine guns from airplanes by parachute, but it did not seriously pursue the notion of airborne forces then or in the 1930s. Meanwhile, the military in other nations were doing so, notably the Soviet Union and Germany.

The Soviet Union's Red Army conducted test drops of a dozen men, equipped with machine guns and rifles, in August and September 1930. By 1931 the Red Army was testing the tactics of seizing airfields with parachute forces followed by air-landed units carried in transport airplanes. The Red Army continued expansion of its parachute and air-landing forces throughout the 1930s. The popularity of civilian sport parachuting and gliding, with a resultant accumulation of trained personnel for military purposes, greatly aided this growth.

The Red Army's maneuvers in 1935 and 1936 included parachute drops and air landings of

units of more than a thousand men. British and German military officers observed the successful activities. While the British military was as uninterested in airborne forces as its U.S. counterparts, the Germans were already experimenting, quietly and on a small scale.

In the first half of the 1930s, the Treaty of Versailles still tightly restricted the growth and development of German military forces. Nevertheless, Germany began to build a reservoir of trained pilots and support personnel through commercial airline endeavors and sport glider clubs. When Adolf Hitler repudiated the treaty in March 1935, German military expansion quickly leaped ahead. Freed of restrictions and with conscripts flowing into the ranks, German forces experimented with—and created—parachute, glider, and air-landing units.

ACTION ACCELERATES

Before 1940, the U.S. War Department General Staff had been discussing internally (but unhurriedly) the possibilities of pursuing the development of an airborne force. The pace picked up early in 1940 when Gen. George C. Marshall, Chief of Staff, directed Maj. Gen. George A. Lynch, Chief of Infantry and a strong supporter of forming an airborne force, to push the development of "air infantry." Maj. William C. Lee, then serving on Lynch's staff, became the project officer. Having served

From left to right, Lt. Col. Harris M. Melasky, soon to become commander of the 550th Infantry Airborne Battalion in Panama; Maj. Gen. George A. Lynch, Chief of Infantry (in civilian clothes); Air Corps Brig. Gen. Frank M. Andrews, Assistant Chief of Staff, G-3, U.S. War Department; Parachute Test Platoon leader 1st Lt. William T. Ryder; and members of the platoon observe Pvt. Leo Brown being readied for a jump from a tower at the Safe Parachute Company at Hightstown, New Jersey. August 1, 1940.
National Archives.

with and observed European armies in the mid-1930s, he had gained an appreciation of German developments and already believed in the vast potential of airborne forces.

By April 1940, the War Department approved plans for formation of a test platoon of airborne infantry under the Infantry Board at Fort Benning, Georgia. That decision, and Lee's central role, started an accelerated process to test the airborne concept and led to creation of airborne forces within the Army. Lee's achievements then—and in ensuing years—rightly earned him the title "Father of the Airborne."

Hitler's attack on Poland in September 1939 unveiled none of his new airborne forces. However, the strike in the West that began in April 1940 featured the first extensive wartime use of airborne forces in history in a series of meticulously planned, daring, and stunningly effective operations. On April 9, 1940, a parachute regiment of Gen. Kurt Student's Fliegerdivision 7 (7th Parachute Division) dropped at Aalborg, Denmark, to secure bases and at Oslo and Stavanger, Norway, to seize airfields and to clear the way for follow-on forces in the strike against Norway and Denmark.

A month later, the German invasion of the Netherlands and Belgium that began the campaign in the West against France and Britain on May 10 saw the use of parachute, glider, and air-landing forces on an unprecedented scale. Especially noteworthy were the 7th Parachute Division's parachute drops that seized airfields

near Rotterdam and The Hague for the air-landing units and secured the strategic bridges at Rotterdam, Dordrecht, and Moerdijk for the invading ground forces. The predawn glider assault that took the supposedly impregnable Fort Eben Emael guarding the Albert Canal in Belgium was a particularly audacious feat that was critical to luring the British and French forces northward into the strategic trap in Belgium and Holland and away from the German main armored thrust through the Ardennes toward Sedan.

The devastating employment and swift successes of the airborne forces in the spring of 1940 were part of an overwhelming display of German military prowess and power in the blitzkrieg of air, airborne, armored, and ground forces. The incredible German victory in the West in May 1940 stunned American civilian and military leaders and infused a sense of extreme urgency into the U.S. Army's experimental plans for an airborne force.

PARACHUTE TEST PLATOON FORMED

On June 25, 1940, only days after the fall of France, Lynch directed the Commandant of The Infantry School at Fort Benning to form the Parachute Test Platoon. Selected as platoon leader was 1st Lt. William T. Ryder from the 29th Infantry Regiment at Fort Benning with 2nd Lt. James A. Bassett as assistant platoon leader. Ryder then chose 48 enlisted volunteers from the 29th Infantry to form the rest of the platoon. By July 11, the mission began.

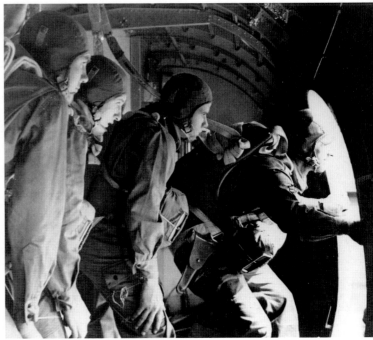

The soldiers of the Parachute Test Platoon set up shop next to Lawson Field, Fort Benning's airfield. An abandoned hangar became a training hall and parachute packing site. The Army Air Corps provided airplanes and parachutes for the endeavor. Air Corps Warrant Officer Harry "Tug" Wilson and a group of noncommissioned officers, all experienced parachutists and parachute riggers, were detailed to Fort Benning to share their unique and invaluable knowledge. Ryder and Bassett led their men on a full schedule to learn about parachutes and parachuting, plus pursuing a rigorous physical conditioning regime that became an essential part of the paratroopers' ethos.

Lee arranged for the platoon's training to include a week on 150-foot parachute drop towers located on the premises of the Safe Parachute Company at Hightstown, New Jersey. Towers like them, although taller at 250 feet, had been a popular feature of the 1939 New York World's Fair. The platoon's training on the towers familiarized them with landing by parachute and built confidence and readiness for the real thing. During the training, Lynch, who never wavered in his support for the parachute troops, visited the platoon and even made a controlled jump to the delight of the platoon.

Training intensified after the Parachute Test Platoon returned to Fort Benning. Over succeeding weeks they worked to enhance soldier skills while also learning to pack and maintain their main parachutes and reserve chutes. The platoon members made their first jump on August 16, 1940. As the jump aircraft made repeated passes over Lawson Field, Wilson tapped each man on the leg as a signal to make the jump. Ryder led, and jumped first. The first enlisted man to jump was Pvt. William N. "Red" King. More jumps followed in the next two weeks.

The platoon jumped as a unit on August 29 at Fort Benning, making its fifth jump on the occasion. The Secretary of War, Henry L. Stimson, plus Marshall and other senior officers, flew down from Washington to witness the jump followed by the platoon's mock assault on an objective. The event marked successful culmination of two intense months of experimentation and training that provided the catalyst for further progress.

With that milestone, the members of the Parachute Test Platoon did more than validate the parachuting concept for the Army. They established standards for all who later followed them out the door of an aircraft in flight. Their esprit, willingness to experiment, intense physical conditioning, and attention to the mission have inspired their successors in peace and war in the decades since.

top left
Paratroopers of the 501st Parachute Battalion ready to board the aircraft. *National Archives.*

top right
Paratroopers preparing to jump. *National Archives.*

501ST PARACHUTE BATTALION ACTIVATED

The success of the Parachute Test Platoon's
work triggered existing War Department
plans to form parachute infantry units. The
501st Parachute Battalion was activated at Fort
Benning on October 1, 1940, with Maj. William
M. Miley as its first commanding officer.

Miley and his leaders of the 501st faced and
surmounted many challenges. They had to
form the flow of volunteer officers and men
into a real battalion with squads, platoons, and
companies organized and ready to train for
assigned missions. Of course, all were required
to qualify as parachutists. Parachute Test
Platoon veterans (including Ryder) became
instructors and mentors in those endeavors.
In addition, the 501st was to be prepared to
expand into three more parachute battalions

when directed. The unit would first coalesce;
then on order, it would divide and form new
units in its own likeness.

Senior officials from Washington continued to
visit Fort Benning to observe the new airborne
capability with their own eyes. Photos from
the airborne demonstration conducted on
January 17, 1941, appear in sequence on the
facing page and this page.

PROVISIONAL PARACHUTE GROUP

Activation of the 501st Parachute Battalion constituted a major step forward. Miley and his officers and men applied themselves to the tasks
assigned. However, if the newborn airborne
were to become a combat force, many other
activities beyond their existing capabilities had
to be conducted concurrently. Common sense
prevailed. The Provisional Parachute Group
was created under the Chief of Infantry to take
on those responsibilities.

The Provisional Parachute Group became
operational at Fort Benning in March 1941
with now Lt. Col. William C. Lee (promoted in
September 1940) as its commander. Lee had
driven airborne developments successfully
from his position on the staff of the Chief of
Infantry. Now he was given the opportunity
to lead from the scene of the action. And lead
he did.

PARACHUTIST BADGE

Capt. William P. Yarborough, 501st Parachute Battalion, designed the first Parachutist Badge. In early March 1941, Maj. William M. Miley, commander of the 501st, sent Yarborough to Washington on temporary duty with the Chief of Infantry for the purpose. The mission, as Yarborough wrote in a memo afterward, was "procurement of a suitable parachutist badge which would meet with the approval both of the War Department and the Commanding Officer of the 501st Parachute Battalion."

Miley and the Chief of Infantry both gave Yarborough full authority to approve any design that he considered acceptable. Arriving in Washington, he sketched the design in the G-3 office, and hand-carried it to the appropriate offices for coordination and approval. The Quartermaster General's office helped prepare a finished copy of the design and placed a rush order with the Bailey Banks & Biddle Company in Philadelphia.

By March 14, 1941, Bailey Banks & Biddle had produced 350 badges that were already in Miley's hands, ready for presentation to the paratroopers of the 501st.

Yarborough wrote in his April 1941 memo about the mission, "This is believed to have been an all-time speed record for War Department Procurement."

The Parachutist Badge is received upon successful completion of the three-week Basic Airborne Course, including five parachute jumps.

Source: The Quartermaster Foundation.

Army leadership expected the Provisional Parachute Group to perform several major missions at the same time. Jump training had to be organized and conducted to provide qualified parachutists for the additional battalions to be activated soon. Implicit in that mission was the requirement to devise an efficient curriculum with qualified instructors and appropriate equipment. When the new battalions were activated, the Provisional Parachute Group would oversee their training, as it did with the 501st.

Other critical missions included creation of tables of organization and equipment for the various airborne units. Many questions arose and answers were sought. For example, what were the limits on the size and weight of weapons, ammunition, and equipment that parachute units needed immediately upon landing? Would the weapons be dropped in rolls like the Germans did and picked up after landing, or would they be carried down by each man? What kinds of fire support would be organic to the units?

Lt. Col. William C. Lee, "Father of the Airborne," in command of the Provisional Parachute Group at Fort Benning, Georgia, 1941. *National Archives.*

GERONIMO!

Among the more enduring and widespread traditions of the Army paratroopers that has reached far into American culture itself was the use of the jump yell "GERONIMO!" Gerard M. Devlin in his book *Paratrooper!* tells the story of how this tradition was born. After completing two individual jumps, the members of the Parachute Test Platoon readied for their first mass jump in the summer of 1940. Naturally, they were apprehensive, so Pvts. John Ward, Aubrey Eberhardt, Lester McLaney, and Leo Brown went to the post theater to watch Paramount Pictures' *Geronimo* in which the U.S. Cavalry chased the Apache chief Geronimo and his band all over the screen.

While consuming more than a few beers after the movie and discussing the next day's mass jump, Eberhardt noted he was not concerned about the jump. The others kidded him that he would be so scared that he would not remember his own name. This angered Eberhardt, who was by far the tallest member of the platoon and not someone to anger. He retorted: "All right, dammit! I tell you jokers what I'm gonna do! To prove to you that I'm not scared out of my wits when I jump, I'm going to yell 'Geronimo' loud as hell when I go out that door tomorrow!"

Before the plane carrying Eberhardt and his group of jumpers even got off the ground everyone in the platoon knew of his boast, and they were waiting to see if he carried through on it. Not only did he yell his now legendary

"Geronimo!" as he exited the aircraft, so did all the other jumpers. Devlin continues the story:

> With jumpers continuing to spill from the plane, a loud "Geronimo!" shout accompanied by an Indian war whoop, could be heard like a clap of thunder. Without knowing it at the time, Private Aubrey Eberhardt had just originated what was to be the jumping yell of the American paratroopers.

"Geronimo" quickly entered the airborne vocabulary and lore. When designing the 501st Parachute Battalion's new insignia and pocket patch, Miley incorporated "Geronimo" into both. The 501st Parachute Battalion later assumed "Geronimo" as the unit motto for its insignia and pocket patch, and it remains the regiment's motto on its distinctive unit insignia today. The 509th Parachute Infantry Battalion also incorporated "Geronimo" into its wartime pocket patch.

Distinctive unit insignia of 501st Infantry. *U.S. Army Center of Military History.*

Doctrine for their employment in combat had to be thought out and approved. What sorts of missions might be assigned? How long should parachute units be expected to remain in combat after jumping in for a mission and before meeting with friendly forces? Three days? A week? What organic supporting units—such as engineer, ordnance, and medical—would be required? The task lists were long and formidable, but Lee and his group of innovators were equal to the challenges.

Through the Parachute Test Platoon, 501st Parachute Battalion, and the Provisional Parachute Group, in less than a year the U.S. Army had planted the seeds for a brand-new fighting arm. Whether the crop would flourish or fail remained to be seen, but the men cultivating it were determined to succeed.

Chapter 2
One Battalion to Five Divisions: Building the Airborne Force, 1941–45

PREPARING FOR WAR: THE LESSONS OF CRETE

Two months after the Provisional Parachute Group began pressing ahead with its multiple tasks at Fort Benning, the Germans conducted the world's largest airborne operation to date— Operation MERCURY, the seizure of Crete.

On April 6, 1941, Adolf Hitler attacked into the Balkans, swiftly overran Yugoslavia, and pushed into Greece to confront Greek and arriving British Commonwealth forces. Greece fell to the rapidly advancing Germans by the end of April 1941. British forces withdrew to Egypt and to the strategic island of Crete in the eastern Mediterranean, to which the Germans now turned their attention. British Commonwealth and Greek forces held the island now, and the Royal Navy controlled the Mediterranean waters around it. If Hitler wanted Crete, he would have to use his airborne forces to get it.

The mission of taking the heavily defended island was assigned to Gen. Kurt Student's new XI Fliegerkorps (XI Air Corps) that combined the Luftwaffe's parachute troops and air transport squadrons. Flying from Greece early on May 20, 1941, the Luftwaffe's 7th Parachute Division and glider units launched the first large-scale airborne invasion ever attempted with an orchestrated attack on the town of Chania and the airfields at Maleme, Rethymnon, and Heraklion to seize airheads for following air-landing units. The defenders exacted a heavy toll on the initial assault forces as well as on the parachute and air-landed reinforcements. By May 28 the German forces had defeated the British, and Crete was theirs.

The seizure of Crete was a strategic but Pyrrhic victory for Germany that was bought at the price of future German airborne operations. Casualties in the elite parachute units approached 40 percent. The Germans later officially reported 6,580 men as killed, wounded, or missing out of the total force of 23,000, while unofficial estimates went much higher. More than 170 of the 500-plus Junkers Ju-52 transports in the operation were lost or severely damaged. Such drastic losses crippled German airborne capabilities and dampened the German high command's enthusiasm for any future large-scale missions. In July 1941, Hitler, now committed to his all-out war against the Soviet Union, told Student that "Crete proved that the days of the parachute troops are over." After Crete, the Germans never mounted an airborne operation of larger than battalion size. Student later lamented that Crete was "the graveyard of Germany's parachutists."

Across the Atlantic, U.S. airborne planners reached exactly the opposite conclusion than Hitler and drew different lessons from Crete. They saw the days of the paratroopers as just dawning, not ending. Crete was an impetus for creating units larger than battalions, adding glider units, and planning operations of greater scale rather than small raids. Their next step was to generate more battalions. Once in existence, they would constitute the basis for producing new regiments for use in limited special task force-type missions. Much like the Germans and British, American planners envisioned three types of airborne forces: parachute, glider, and air-landing units.

MORE BATTALIONS, THEN REGIMENTS

From July through October 1941, the experienced 501st Parachute Battalion provided the cadres for activation of the 502d, 503d, and 504th Parachute Battalions at Fort Benning. In the new units, they guided the flow of carefully selected volunteers through jump training and then the individual and unit training that forged them into functioning combat units. This expansion brought in many of the field- and company-grade officers who would later lead the parachute infantry units during the war and play prominent roles in the Army thereafter.

In the Panama Canal Zone, the 550th Infantry Airborne Battalion was activated in July 1941 as an air-landing unit. Maj. William M. Miley's 501st Parachute Battalion moved its Company C to the Canal Zone in September to carry out maneuvers with the 550th to develop techniques for parachute and air-landing operations. So successful were these exercises that another air-landing unit, the 88th Infantry Airborne Battalion, was activated at Fort Benning in October 1941. While the parachute and air-landing battalions were being formed and trained, plans were under way for creating glider-borne units.

After the Japanese attack on Pearl Harbor on December 7, 1941, any existing limitations on the expansion of the U.S. armed forces were swiftly lifted. For the budding parachute battalions, the expansion meant dividing and multiplying again. Thus, the 502d Parachute Infantry under George Van Horn Moseley, Jr., the 503d initially under Miley, and the 504th under Theodore H. Dunn were activated at Fort Benning in March and May 1942.

Between July and December 1942, five more regiments were activated and began service: the 505th at Fort Benning in July under Col. James M. Gavin; the 506th and 507th at Camp Toccoa, Georgia, some 175 miles to the north, in July under Robert F. Sink and George V. Millett, Jr., followed by the 501st under Howard R. Johnson in November; and the 508th (Roy E. Lindquist) at Camp Blanding, Florida, in October. Camp Toccoa's legendary Mt. Currahee, meaning "Stand Alone" in the local Native American dialect, soon became firmly fixed in paratrooper lore and myth and was engraved in the motto and distinctive unit insignia of the 506th Parachute Infantry, which was forged there.

Of the eight regiments formed in 1942, the 502d was assigned to the 82d Airborne Division upon its activation and the 504th to the 101st. The 501st, 503d, 505th, 506th, 507th, and 508th were all initially separate regiments that could become regimental combat teams with augmentation and could be attached to larger combat elements, such as divisions or corps, as operational requirements dictated. The Army's operational thinking was still focused more in terms of airborne task forces rather than full divisions.

In 1943, the remaining wartime parachute infantry regiments were organized. In January 1943, Orin D. Haugen's 511th was activated at Camp Toccoa and the 513th (James W. Coutts) at Fort Benning, intended respectively for the new 11th and 13th Airborne Divisions. The last four parachute infantry regiments formed were the 517th (Louis A. Walsh), originally assigned to the 17th Airborne Division, at Camp Toccoa in March 1943; the 515th

top left
Jumpers descend from three-plane formation over Fort Benning, April 8, 1941. *National Archives.*

top right
Distinctive unit insignia of 506th Parachute Infantry. *U.S. Army Center of Military History.*

(Julian B. Lindsay) at Fort Benning in May 1943 as an administrative holding unit for the Parachute School (later assigned to the 13th Airborne Division in March 1944); and the separate 541st (Ducat M. McEntee) in August and 542d (William T. Ryder of the Test Platoon) in September 1943 at Fort Benning, neither of which saw action during the war. The 513th and 517th regiments eventually swapped assignments, ending up in the 17th and 13th Airborne Divisions, respectively.

As a grueling physical training and conditioning program whittled down the initial groups of volunteers, each of these regiments developed a distinct identity, traditions, cohesion, and esprit all its own. In each instance, the unique and legendary commanders, such as Reuben H. Tucker who assumed command of the 502d in December 1942, Gavin of the 505th, Sink with the 506th, Johnson with the 501st, Haugen with the 511th, and others, were the dynamic forces that molded the units and their personalities. Mostly in their thirties, these regimental commanders were hard-driving, dedicated, and determined leaders who focused on physically and mentally toughening the officers and men for the rigors of airborne and combat operations and hammering them into cohesive fighting units. These men were larger than life, but, then again, so were the elite paratroopers they commanded who were selected in the first place for their "demonstrated soldierly qualities; agility; athletic ability; intelligence; determination; and daring."

Much the same happened with the glider infantry regiments that were organized in 1942 and 1943. The 88th Glider Infantry was formed in June 1942 at Fort Bragg from the 88th Infantry Airborne Battalion and was intended to test glider and air-landing concepts and train other glider units. Four more regiments came with the activation of the two airborne divisions on August 15, 1942—the 325th and 326th with the 82d and the 327th and 401st with the 101st Airborne Division. The 326th was transferred from the 82d in February 1943 and later assigned to the 13th Airborne Division, where it joined the 88th. The 187th and 188th Glider Infantry of the 11th Airborne Division were activated in February 1943, and the 193d and 194th of the 17th Airborne Division in April 1943.

During the war, some separate battalions were also organized or redesignated. The 550th Infantry Airborne Battalion was redesignated as a glider infantry battalion. The 551st was organized on November 1, 1942, in the Canal Zone to replace the 501st after it departed with the 503d for Australia. In the segregated Army of the war years, the War Department organized the African-American 555th Parachute Infantry Company on December 30, 1943, at Fort Benning and authorized its expansion into a battalion in November 1944. Nicknamed the "Triple Nickles," the 555th never left the United States but was sent to the Pacific Northwest in the summer of 1945 to fight forest fires caused by incendiary bombs carried across the Pacific by Japanese balloons. That gained them another nickname, the "Smoke Jumpers."

UNITY OF COMMAND

Confronted with the requirements of fighting a world war after Pearl Harbor, the War Department was reorganized on March 9, 1942, into the Army Air Forces (AAF), Services of Supply (later Army Service Forces or ASF), and Army Ground Forces (AGF). Less than two weeks later, William C. Lee, a colonel since December 1941, was promoted to brigadier general with the Provisional Parachute Group's redesignation as the Airborne Command on March 21 as part of the newly established AGF under Lt. Gen. Lesley J. McNair.

Under Lee's leadership, the group had achieved much during its first hectic year. By March 1942, Fort Benning and its surrounding training areas were overcrowded with units being mobilized and trained. Lee recommended moving the Airborne Command and its activities to a suitable location with an adjacent airfield and more room for training and maneuvering its airborne units. Approval came promptly. Fort Bragg, North Carolina, became the home of the Airborne Command in April 1942. The U.S. Army Parachute School, a vital part of the

African-American soldiers of the 555th Parachute Infantry Company, Fort Benning, Georgia, in a C-47 transport plane preparing to make one of the required five qualifying jumps for obtaining the coveted Parachutist Badge of a U.S. Army paratrooper. March 1944. *National Archives.*

Airborne Command, remained at Fort Benning where the necessary infrastructure now existed, including four 250-foot free descent jump training towers.

The Airborne Command (later redesignated the Airborne Center in February 1944) was given authority to unify myriad activities relating to the Army's airborne forces. Its missions included those performed by the former group and much more. Additional missions ranged from activating and training new units, providing trained replacements for units overseas, and developing doctrine in closer collaboration with the AAF on the use of its resources for airborne developments.

In May 1942, the AAF redesignated the Air Transport Command as the I Troop Carrier Command at Stout Field, Indianapolis, Indiana, and gave it the mission of organizing and training all troop carrier wings, groups, and squadrons. The new command soon stationed troop carrier units at Laurinburg-Maxton Army Air Base, North Carolina, near Fort Bragg, and at Pope Army Airfield on the post, which significantly enhanced collaboration and training with the Airborne Command and its units.

Throughout the war, the I Troop Carrier Command remained the AAF's primary organization for training troop carrier units and crews for airborne operations.

The establishment of I Troop Carrier Command's bases near the Airborne Command and Fort Bragg significantly simplified joint planning between airborne and troop carrier forces. The two commands planned and conducted joint field exercises which enhanced and evaluated readiness levels of the troop carrier and airborne units, and also provided opportunities to test operational concepts. From their inception to the end of the war, these two commands worked together to cope with persistent shortages of troop carrier airplanes and gliders, and trained air crews to operate them. They developed joint procedures for planning and executing operations, exchanged liaison officers for mutual coordination, and applied lessons learned from combat experiences.

By the end of 1942, a vastly expanded Airborne Command required additional space, so the Hoffman Airborne Camp, 40 miles west of Fort Bragg, was acquired and construction of temporary buildings began in November 1942. Soon the Airborne Command moved its activities to the new site where it oversaw the activation of the 11th and 17th Airborne Divisions as well as the training of the last three airborne divisions and their glider infantry units. On May 1, 1943, the area was renamed Camp Mackall, named for Pvt. John Thomas "Tommy" Mackall, 2d Battalion, 509th Parachute Infantry, who was wounded on November 8, 1942, in the initial operations in Algeria and died of his wounds four days later. For the rest of the war, Camp Mackall was the principal training center for the airborne as well as the troop carrier and glider units stationed at Laurinburg-Maxton, less than 20 miles to the south.

Airborne field artillerymen use their 75-mm pack howitzer to support the paratroopers' seizure of an airfield in a military demonstration at Fort Bragg in September 1942. *Library of Congress.*

A paratrooper's life was not easy, even on the best of days. This artilleryman from the 456th Parachute Field Artillery Battalion, 82d Airborne Division, smacked onto a North Carolina cornfield during maneuvers. An airborne medic immediately rushed to his assistance. Serious, often disabling, injuries resulted from landings like this one. Camp Mackall, North Carolina, Airborne Center. Date not given. *82d Airborne Division War Memorial Museum.*

THE AIRBORNE DIVISIONS

Lee's position at the Airborne Command gave him wide latitude to recommend changes in the airborne force and its organization. Even before Crete, in an article that appeared in the April 1941 issue of *Infantry Journal*, Lee had proposed creating "air landing divisions" at a time when the Army's official airborne vision was fixed no higher than the battalion level. Despite Lee's vision, it was his visit in May 1942 to the United Kingdom with Lt. Gen. Dwight D. Eisenhower, the American theater commander, to study British airborne doctrine, organization, and operations that pushed American plans beyond battalion- or regimental-sized operations.

The British airborne division had two parachute brigades and supporting glider elements that could be used for a wide variety of missions. British paratroopers had already concluded that seizing heavily defended airfields and landing areas where gliders and transports could land was now prohibitively expensive in men and equipment, as the German experience in Crete had shown. After seeing the British airborne divisions, Lee returned and recommended to McNair similar airborne divisions with two parachute units and one glider unit.

In June 1942, McNair accepted Lee's recommendation but reversed Lee's ratio of parachute and glider units. In proposing activation of two airborne divisions, he insisted that "An airborne division should be evolved with a stinginess in overhead and in transportation which has absolutely no counterpart this far

in our military organization." Contrary to Lee, who was envisioning much larger airborne operations, McNair was still thinking along the earlier lines of small parachute units jumping to secure appropriate landing areas or airheads, followed by the flow of larger forces of glider-borne troops or air-landed units brought in by transports. The later airborne divisions created in 1943 followed the same pattern when they were organized.

The creation of the two new divisions should have been relatively simple. However, it was not, because forces within the War Department opposed using any of the existing Regular Army or National Guard division designations for this "experimental force." As a result, two Organized Reserve divisions were selected, the 82d Infantry Division that had been mobilized under Maj. Gen. Omar N. Bradley in March at Camp Claiborne, Louisiana, and the 101st Infantry Division that was still inactive. Thus it was that two divisions judged to be acceptable for an "experimental force" became the two great American airborne divisions of World War II and two of the most distinguished divisions in the history of the U.S. Army.

The 82d ("All American") Airborne Division had been one of the Army's best fighting divisions in World War I. It had been ordered into active World War II service in March 1942, with Bradley in command and Brig. Gen. Matthew B. Ridgway as assistant division commander. When Bradley was reassigned in late June to command of the 28th Infantry Division, Ridgway succeeded to command and was promoted to major general. For a brief time in July the 82d began to convert to a motorized division. Then Ridgway received the word that his command would become the first airborne division of the U.S. Army, and on August 15 would be reorganized and redesignated as the 82d Airborne Division.

The same day the 82d was redesignated it was split, with half of its officers and men forming the cadre for the new 101st ("Screaming Eagle") Airborne Division. With a proud heritage tracing back to the Wisconsin "Iron Brigade" of the Civil War, the 101st Division was only briefly activated in World War I and between the wars was an Organized Reserve unit headquartered in Milwaukee, Wisconsin. On August 15 at Camp Claiborne, the 101st became an airborne division and Lee, newly promoted to major general, became its first commander. Working closely together, Ridgway and Lee equitably distributed the 82d's senior leaders and personnel so that both divisions, which shared the same birthday and parent unit, had the same firm basis for future development.

Brig. Gen. Don Pratt, the 82d's assistant division commander, moved to the 101st in the same role. Miley now replaced Pratt, was promoted to brigadier general, and brought his wealth of experience in airborne operations to the new division. Brig. Gen. Joseph M. Swing remained as division artillery commander, and Anthony C. McAuliffe was promoted to brigadier general and took over the 101st divisional artillery. Col. Maxwell D. Taylor, who became the 82d's chief of staff in July, was promoted to brigadier general in December when he replaced Swing who took command of the 11th Airborne Division.

As activated, the 82d and 101st Airborne Divisions were "triangular," like the other infantry divisions of the time. That is, a division's primary combat power came from three regiments of infantry reinforced by division artillery and supported by units such as engineers, signal, medical, ordnance, and others, and with their own organic transportation. The new airborne divisions retained two of their infantry regiments (each reduced to two battalions), which were redesignated as glider infantry, and received a parachute infantry regiment that had completed its initial training. The 504th was assigned to the 82d and the 502d to the 101st. A similar 2:1 ratio applied to the artillery, with two glider and one parachute field artillery battalions of 75-mm pack howitzers, and to other arms as well.

In line with McNair's guidance, the 82d and 101st had "streamlined" glider and parachute infantry regiments. Although the airborne divisions of 1942–43 had the triangular structure, their overall troop strength of 8,505, of which only about 2,400 were actually paratroopers, was just slightly more than half that of the standard 1942 infantry divisions of 15,514 officers and men. McNair's emphasis on a light, mobile, air transportable division meant no weapons heavier than .30-caliber machine

top left
The shoulder sleeve insignia of the 82d ("All American") Airborne Division.

top right
The shoulder sleeve insignia of the 101st ("Screaming Eagle") Airborne Division.

right

Brig. Gen. William M. Miley, Assistant Division Commander, 82d Airborne Division, at desk. A long-time paratrooper and former commander of the 501st Parachute Battalion and 503d Parachute Infantry, Miley was intimately involved in many aspects of developing the Army's airborne forces. He assumed command of the brand-new 17th Airborne Division at Camp Mackall, North Carolina, on April 15, 1943.
82d Airborne Division War Memorial Museum.

top left

The shoulder sleeve insignia of the 11th ("The Angels") Airborne Division.

top center

The shoulder sleeve insignia of the 13th Airborne Division.

top right

The shoulder sleeve insignia of the 17th ("Thunder from Heaven") Airborne Division.

guns, 60- and 81-mm mortars, the ineffective 2.36-inch bazookas, and 75-mm pack howitzers. One of the most glaring weaknesses of these divisions once they were on the ground was in antitank defense, so effort was devoted to developing an air-transportable airborne tank, the T9E1 of some 15,000 pounds, that could pick up this mission. The 28th Airborne Tank Company was even activated in 1944 before the experiment was abandoned as impractical.

The airborne divisions were tough, flexible, and well-trained, but they lacked the strength to absorb heavy casualties once committed to combat and required reinforcement, fire support, and transportation for any sustained operations. This inherent flaw in design would show up in the initial divisional airborne operations.

Three more airborne divisions were activated at Camp Mackall within the next year: the 11th ("The Angels") Airborne Division under now Maj. Gen. Joseph M. Swing on February 25, 1943; two months later, the 17th ("Thunder from Heaven") Airborne Division under now Maj. Gen. William M. Miley on April 15; and then the 13th Airborne Division under Maj. Gen. George W. Griner (later Maj. Gen. Elbridge G. Chapman, Jr.) on Friday, August 13. This completed the building of the wartime divisional airborne force.

MEANS TO AN END

All three types of airborne units (parachute, glider, and air-landing) required transport aircraft, both powered and glider, and qualified crews to lift them from departure airfield to their destination.

The Douglas C-47 Skytrain (nicknamed "Gooney Bird") transport performed the multiple roles of carrying cargo and air-landed units, dropping parachutists, and towing gliders. The C-47 was the military version of the ubiquitous DC-3 civilian airliner of the immediate prewar years. Deliveries of C-47s began in early 1942, and by war's end more than 10,000 had been produced for U.S. and allied forces.

The C-47, crewed by two pilots and a crew chief and two other crew members for troop transport duties, carried up to 24 combat-equipped parachutists. Its allowable cargo load of 6,000 pounds could include a 1/4-ton truck (the "Jeep") or a 105-mm howitzer loaded through a large cargo door in the left side of the fuselage into which the jump door was integrated. Maximum range of the C-47 was 1,500 miles.

The other main workhorse of the troop carrier fleet after 1944 was the twin-engined Curtiss C-46 Commando. Capable of carrying 10,500 pounds of cargo or 36 paratroopers, the C-46 had the advantage of doors on both sides of the fuselage, which allowed the jumpers to exit more quickly. But it had other disadvantages. Like the C-47, it had not been designed for airborne troop or cargo missions.

Both the AAF and airborne forces pushed for the development of an aircraft better suited to the requirements of airborne missions, and finally settled on the Fairchild C-82. Dubbed the "Packet" because of its boxlike center cabin, it had all the features desired: a cargo load of 15,000 pounds or 42 fully loaded paratroopers, was low to the ground, and had front and rear ramps that made for easy loading and unloading. However, higher wartime priorities for fighters and bombers prevented any substantial production. During the war no operational troop carrier units were converted to the C-82 which would see extensive service in the early postwar years.

top left
The Douglas C-47 Skytrain transport airplane, derived from the civilian DC-3, was the workhorse of the troop carrier fleet during the war. *Library of Congress.*

top right
Waco CG-4A glider in flight. *U.S. Air Force.*

bottom right
One of the 34-foot towers at jump school, Fort Benning, Georgia, during World War II. The floor height of the original towers was dictated by the length of utility poles available at Fort Benning at the time of construction. All succeeding towers used in airborne training have retained the 34-foot height. *82d Airborne Division War Memorial Museum.*

The Waco CG-4A glider also entered service in 1942. It was a high-wing monoplane with a fuselage of tubular steel covered by fabric. The nose section pivoted upward for loading and unloading. The CG-4A carried 15 troops, including two pilots, or a cargo load of 3,750 pounds. Its size allowed for loading a Jeep and trailer or a 75-mm pack howitzer with crew.

To make the journey from transport aircraft to the drop zone, parachutists required parachutes. The origin and expansion of parachute units created demands that the existing parachute production base, managed by the Air Corps, was unable to meet. The continuing shortage of parachutes impeded training in 1941 and 1942. Production eventually picked up in 1943, but the early shortages posed challenges to individual qualification and unit training.

In an equation that remained constant over the years, the limitations of the existing transport airplanes and gliders that would deliver the airborne forces and their supplies and equipment to combat restricted the number and size of vehicles and artillery in the airborne divisions. This equation had two limiting aircraft factors—heavy transport aircraft which could swiftly carry the troops and equipment to the theater of operations and the tactical transports which delivered them to their landing zones in the theater. The former was on the way to solution with the arrival of the four-engined Douglas C-54 Skymaster, the military version of the commercial DC-4, in 1944. A new generation of transports, such as the C-82, offered the potential to solve the tactical delivery problem.

THE 34-FOOT TOWERS

During World War II, the 34-foot towers at Fort Benning and Camp Toccoa were an essential element in training parachutists in basic jump techniques.

Students climb steps to the structure representing a mock airplane with its floor 34 feet above the ground. Its doors are mockups of airplane doors. Each student wears a parachute harness with a training reserve parachute in front. A trolley above the student's head dangles two riser straps that a jumpmaster-instructor connects to the harness. The trolley rides on a cable to a mound 400 feet away. Four trolleys and cables serve each door.

At the jumpmaster's command the student stands in the door, then exits and immediately assumes the correct body position for a real jump. The student falls to the end of the risers, and then gets a sharp jolt approximating a parachute's opening shock. Riding to the distant mound, the student practices canopy checks and prepares to land. At the end of the ride the student is unhooked, graded, and critiqued, and double-times back to the tower for another repetition.

Over the years, the infamous "34-foot towers" were probably responsible for washing out more fledgling Army paratroopers than the 250-foot towers.

Photo courtesy 82d Airborne Division War Memorial Museum.

PARACHUTE QUALIFICATION

For parachute units to be created, parachutists had to be trained to fill them. The basic parachutist qualification course conducted at Fort Benning during World War II evolved from the experiences of the Parachute Test Platoon, the 501st Parachute Battalion, and the work of the Provisional Parachute Group. The course consisted of four stages, each lasting one week.

The first week, or "A Stage," was designed to bring the volunteers to peak physical condition. Calisthenics, rope climbing, and cross-country running enhanced endurance. Jumping from platforms four to six feet high taught the techniques of landing to absorb shock while minimizing injury. In addition, the parachute landing fall technique was introduced to reduce the numerous jump injuries by absorbing and distributing the landing impact over a larger area of the jumper's body through landing on the balls of the feet and rolling onto the calf, thigh, and buttocks.

"B Stage" in the second week built elementary skills needed for parachuting. The 34-foot mock towers, an idea borrowed from the Germans, taught proper exit techniques from an airplane door, but also acted as a psychological screening mechanism that washed out many an aspiring paratrooper. The swing landing trainer simulated an actual parachute landing. Students also learned to pack and care for their main and reserve parachutes during this and later stages.

The highlights of "C Stage" week included parachute drops from the four 250-foot towers erected in 1941 and 1942. Students developed greater proficiency in proper landing skills. The wind machine helped students learn to recover from landing, collapse their opened parachute, get out of the harness, and join their unit.

The fourth week of training culminated in "D Stage," consisting of five qualifying jumps from an airplane and award of the Parachutist Badge. The qualified parachutists then joined their battalions for individual and unit training and preparation for deployment.

HEADED FOR COMBAT

The first airborne unit to complete training and head for action was the 2d Battalion of Miley's 503d Parachute Infantry (Separate) under Lt. Col. Edson D. Raff. Later redesignated as the 2d Battalion, 509th Parachute Infantry (Separate) on November 2, 1942, it sailed for Scotland from New York on June 6, 1942. Now under Col. Kenneth Kinsler, the 503d itself left for Gen. Douglas MacArthur's Southwest Pacific Area (SWPA) theater on October 20, 1942, stopped in the Panama Canal Zone to pick up the 501st Parachute Battalion to replace Raff's 2d Battalion, and arrived in Australia on December 2.

top left
U.S. Army Parachute School soldiers clamber through the pipes of the "trainasium," a physical conditioning and training device lifted from the Germans and nicknamed the "plumber's nightmare," at Fort Benning, Georgia, January 1942. *National Archives.*

top right
Airborne students of an early class practice landing by tumbling. Landing injuries led to development of the "parachute landing fall." *National Infantry Museum.*

top left
In the suspended harness apparatus, jump school students practice control of the parachute and how to prepare to land correctly. Fort Benning, Georgia, January 26, 1941. *National Archives.*

top right
The wind machine taught airborne students how to recover after landing, get out of their harness, and join their unit. No date. *National Infantry Museum.*

By the autumn of 1942, both the 82d and the 101st moved from Camp Claiborne to Fort Bragg. There, under control of the Airborne Command and working with I Troop Carrier Command, they built the parachute and glider capabilities inherent in their organization. They continued unit training and participated in joint maneuvers to prepare for the combat missions that lay ahead, refined doctrine, and developed new techniques, including dropping of equipment and supplies by parachute. The 82d departed the United States first, on April 29, 1943, headed for French Morocco where it arrived on May 10 to prepare for its combat debut in July in Operation HUSKY, the invasion of Sicily. Meanwhile, the 101st arrived in the United Kingdom in September and October 1943 to begin training for the invasion of France slated for 1944.

In the short span of a few years, the U.S. Army's airborne forces had mushroomed from a concept to a test platoon to a handful of parachute infantry battalions to five divisions. The initial units had deployed to the United Kingdom and Australia in 1942 and 1943 fully ready for combat operations in which they were soon engaged. The 11th Airborne Division shipped out to the SWPA theater on May 8, 1944, to join the 503d Parachute Infantry Regiment. Miley's 17th Airborne Division was next, departing for Europe in August 1944. The last airborne division to leave the United States was the 13th, which moved to Europe in January 1945.

CHALLENGES OF ORGANIZATION AND STRENGTH

Although the airborne divisions were barely operational by early 1943, circumstances soon forced a change in the divisional structure. As originally organized, the 82d had the 325th and 326th Glider Infantry and only the 504th Parachute Infantry. While planning the 82d's use in the Sicilian operation, the War Department realized that the continuing lack of gliders and especially severe limitations on the shipment of the bulky crated gliders due to the lack of shipping space required a change if the 82d was to see combat. To give the division greater combat power that could be more quickly employed in the tactical zone, in February 1943 the planners transferred the 326th Glider Infantry to the Airborne Command (it later went to the new 13th Airborne Division) and assigned Gavin's 505th Parachute Infantry (Separate) in its place. The 82d now consisted of two parachute regiments—the 504th and 505th—and only one glider infantry regiment—the 325th—as Lee had originally preferred.

As the restructured 82d shipped off to North Africa, the 101st participated in the Carolina maneuvers in May and those in Tennessee in June and July 1943. McNair was not impressed with its performance in either of the maneuvers or its readiness for ground combat. He noted that "These trick outfits practically without exception emphasize their tricks to the exclusion of sound basic and other training for everyday fighting." On top of this came word from Sicily of the problems that the 82d Airborne

Division and troop carrier units had encountered in Operation HUSKY in July (see Chapter 3). McNair and his staff were convinced "of the impracticability of handling large airborne units . . . and that the airborne effort be restricted to parachute units of battalion size or smaller."

THE SWING BOARD, TC 113, AND THE KNOLLWOOD MANEUVERS

The performance of the 82d Airborne Division in Sicily sparked a major crisis that could have ended the existence of the airborne division in the U.S. Army. Not pleased with what he had heard, in September 1943 Gen. George C. Marshall decided to look into the matter more deeply. He directed Maj. Gen. Joseph M. Swing, commander of the 11th Airborne Division and just returned from the Mediterranean where he had acted as Eisenhower's American airborne advisor during Operation HUSKY, to convene a board at Camp Mackall to examine the airborne division.

Members of the Swing Board completed a thorough review of both Allied and Axis airborne operations. As they met, news of the highly successful jump of the 503d Parachute Infantry at Nadzab, New Guinea, in the SWPA in early September provided valuable input for their deliberations. The board found the current concept sound but recommended a number of improvements in training and coordination.

Above all, it pushed for publication of a training circular that would lay out all aspects of planning and conducting airborne operations. The Airborne Command then authored the only comprehensive statement of airborne doctrine during the war when Training Circular No. 113 (TC 113), *Employment of airborne and troop carrier forces*, was issued under Marshall's signature on October 9, 1943. In eight short pages, the circular encapsulated the strengths and weaknesses, the theory of employment, and what had been learned to date about the tactics and techniques of airborne and troop carrier operations.

TC 113 quickly became the doctrinal foundation for subsequent airborne training, planning, and operations. It laid out 11 specific missions, which have consistently remained the objectives of airborne operations:

(1) To seize, hold or otherwise exploit important tactical localities in conjunction with or pending the arrival of other military or naval forces.

(2) To attack the enemy rear and assist a break-through or landing by the main force.

(3) To block or delay enemy reserves by capturing and holding critical terrain features, thereby isolating the immediate battlefield.

Tennessee Maneuvers 1943. Soldiers of the 101st Airborne Division's 490th Quartermaster Company pack .30-caliber ammunition boxes into canvas wrappers for parachute resupply from aircraft, June 1943, Camp Campbell, Kentucky. *National Archives.*

(4) To capture enemy airfields.

(5) To capture or destroy vital enemy establishments, thereby paralyzing his system of command, communication, and supply.

(6) To create diversions.

(7) To assist the tactical air force in delaying a retreating enemy until the main forces can destroy him.

(8) To reinforce threatened or surrounded units.

(9) To seize islands or areas which are not strongly held and which the enemy cannot easily reinforce.

(10) To create confusion and disorder among the hostile military and civil personnel.

(11) As a constant threat by their mere presence in the theater of operations thereby causing the enemy to disperse his forces over a wide area in order to protect vital installations.

The appearance of TC 113 did not end the matter. Marshall and McNair still had doubts and demanded a test to prove that an airborne division could indeed operate as successfully in combat as contended in TC 113. McNair directed Swing to plan and conduct a massive five-day airborne maneuver involving glider, paratroop, air-landing, and troop carrier units in early January 1944 to capture the Knollwood Airport in North Carolina. So impressed with the entire maneuver was McNair, who attended it with Secretary of War Henry L Stimson, that he wrote to Swing:

The successful performance of your division has convinced me that we were wrong, and I shall now recommend that we continue our present schedule of activating, training, and committing airborne divisions.

For several contentious months, the entire American concept of an airborne division and its role in large-scale combat operations had hung by a very thin thread. Joe Swing's board and his masterfully executed maneuver had saved it.

STRENGTHENING THE AIRBORNE DIVISION

As the Airborne Command and leadership fought through the crisis of 1943, the initial results of operations showed that airborne divisions were high attrition units. To increase their fighting and staying power, they needed not only replacements for losses but also augmentation with separate parachute infantry regiments. This process began with the virtually permanent attachment of the 506th to the 101st in June 1943. When the 501st Parachute Infantry arrived in the United Kingdom in January 1944, it was also attached to the 101st. The same fate awaited the Airborne Command's 2d Airborne Infantry Brigade with the 507th and 508th Parachute Infantry which also arrived in January 1944. In preparation for the planned invasion, in January Eisenhower attached both regiments to the 82d, leaving the 2d to a training role until it was inactivated in January 1945. The 507th first replaced for the 504th, which remained in Italy until March 1944, and was later transferred to the 17th Airborne Division in August 1944 when the refreshed 504th rejoined the division. The 508th remained with the 82d through March 30, 1945.

Parachute Infantry Regiments Assigned by Division

	11th	13th	17th	82d	101st
1942–43	511th	513th	517th	504th 505th	502d
1945	188th 511th	515th 517th	507th 513th	504th 505th	502d 506th

Glider Infantry Regiments Assigned by Division

	11th	13th	17th	82d	101st
1942–43	187th 188th	88th 326th	193d 194th	325th	327th 401st
1945	187th	326th	194th	325th	327th

In addition to the need for more combat strength in the airborne divisions, shortages of essential equipment, wartime experience, and changes in doctrine eventually reversed the ratio of parachute to glider forces in the airborne divisions in a major organizational change in 1944–45. Doctrinal shifts now envisioned broader airborne missions of multiregimental and even multidivisional size. Another compelling reason for this reorganization was the persistent shortage of gliders and glider pilots for both training at home and combat operations overseas that had appeared as early as 1942.

Wartime experience clearly showed that the airborne division required reorganizing and strengthening. The restructured airborne division of December 16, 1944, effective March 1, 1945, had 12,979 officers and men, with two 2,482-man parachute infantry regiments, one glider infantry regiment of 3,114 with three battalions, an added parachute field artillery battalion, and increased numbers of supporting troops. Some former attachments were made permanent, such as the 506th with the 101st,

the 507th with the 17th, and the 517th with the 13th. However, these changes were all bought at the cost of disbanding existing airborne units because no additional personnel were available to underwrite the reorganization—thus the separate 509th, 550th, and 551st Parachute Infantry Battalions and the 88th, 193d, and 401st Glider Infantry disappeared. The 11th Airborne Division in the Pacific changed somewhat later and in a different manner (see Chapter 6). These changes put the finishing touches on the Army's five airborne divisions of World War II.

A CONSIDERABLE ACHIEVEMENT

By the time the war in Europe ended on May 8, 1945, the Army had raised, trained, and sent overseas an airborne force that had grown to an airborne corps, five airborne divisions, 14 parachute infantry regiments, and four separate battalions, and many battalions and companies of supporting troops, including artillery, signal, ordnance, quartermaster, engineers, and medical. Before the organizational changes in early 1945, the force had also included 10 glider infantry regiments, 15 glider field artillery battalions, and other glider units. Supporting these units were numerous troop carrier and glider squadrons of the AAF. Indeed, this was a considerable achievement that was seriously tested and successfully but bloodily confirmed on airborne battlefields from North Africa to Europe to the rocky crags of Corregidor Island in the Philippines.

top right
Pvt. Louis Homoki, Richmond, Virginia, of 2d Battalion, 503d Parachute Infantry, wearing jumpsuit and jump boots, negotiates obstacle course during training at Hungerford, England, August 1942. *National Archives.*

bottom right
Maj. Gen. Matthew B. Ridgway, Commanding General, 82d Airborne Division, nattily attired in his dress "pinks and greens" with his jump boots and trousers neatly bloused, on the steps of an English manor in Leicester, England, May 1944. *82d Airborne Division War Memorial Museum.*

BOOTS AND SUITS

Standard Army footgear and field clothing proved inadequate for the needs of parachute troops. The Provisional Parachute Group and the battalions at Fort Benning worked with the Quartermaster Corps to design and field appropriate new gear. Two examples were especially important: suitable jump boots and a two-piece parachute suit with suspenders.

Regular Army issue shoes lacked the support to minimize foot and ankle injuries. The shoes were unsuitable for parachutists, leading to fractures and other injuries. Parachutists required boots that provided sturdier support for feet and ankles to minimize injuries upon landing and serve the wearer well on long marches. Capt. William P. Yarborough, designer of the Parachutist Badge, also provided some ideas for appropriate jump boots and a parachute suit for Quartermaster consideration.

Parachute units at Fort Benning then conducted field trials of numerous boot designs developed in consultation with the Quartermaster Corps and orthopedic physicians at the post's station hospital. The final version was approved in the summer of 1942, and the Quartermaster Corps initiated production. Laced 10-inch jump boots served the intended practical purposes to reduce injuries and wear well in the field. They also created a positive morale factor. In 1941, then Maj. William Miley, commanding the 501st Parachute Infantry Battalion, had directed his men to wear their jump boots with their dress uniforms rather than the regulation low-cut shoes and to blouse their trouser legs into the tops of the boots. This immediately distinguished paratroopers from other soldiers, much to the troopers' delight, and boosted their egos well beyond reason, thus provoking innumerable fights along with an image of an elite fighting man.

The parachutist jumpsuit was developed concurrently. Air Corps coveralls, which served well during the early experimental days, were unsuitable for field training and combat wear. As adopted in 1942, the new two-piece parachutist jumpsuit (M42) was made of cotton twill fabric. Its jacket had four patch pockets fastened with snaps. Suspenders held up the trousers which sported large external pockets on the outside of each thigh. The pockets enabled parachutists to carry essential items such as grenades, first aid packets, and combat rations on their persons, ensuring immediate accessibility.

Extract from QMC Historical Studies, No. 5, February 1944, and Gerard M. Devlin, Paratrooper!

Chapter 3

Blood Upon the Risers: Airborne Operations in the Mediterranean, 1942–44

OPERATION TORCH

FIRST INTO THE FIGHT

Since arriving in England in June 1942, Lt. Col. Edson D. Raff and his paratroopers of the 2d Battalion, 503d Parachute Infantry, had been training rigorously, but with no apparent mission except to continue training. The Allies' decision to fight "Germany first" placed the priority on their most dangerous enemy, but no agreement on how to do this had been reached. The United States wanted a cross-Channel attack in 1942 or 1943, but Prime Minister Winston S. Churchill and the British preferred an offensive in the Mediterranean.

Until this strategic debate was resolved, Raff and the 2d Battalion trained with British paratroopers and commandos. After August 17, the battalion also began training closely with the Army Air Forces' (AAF's) 60th Troop Carrier Group, including day and night jumps, and continued to prepare for combat, whenever and wherever that might come.

Late in July the decision was made to postpone the cross-Channel attack and go ahead with Operation TORCH, the invasion of Northwest Africa. This would place an Allied force in the rear of Field Marshal Erwin Rommel's Afrika Korps, then fighting Lt. Gen. Bernard Law Montgomery's British Eighth Army in Egypt. On November 8, the Allies would strike French North Africa (Morocco, Algeria, and Tunisia) from the United Kingdom with combined British-U.S. forces, and directly from the United States with Maj. Gen. George S. Patton's Western Task Force. In August, Maj. Gen. Mark W. Clark became Lt. Gen. Dwight D. Eisenhower's deputy commander at the new Allied Force Headquarters (AFHQ) and the chief planner for Operation TORCH.

The Allies decided to land in French Morocco and Algeria, rather than strike deep into the Mediterranean directly to Tunisia, for fear of possible German and Italian interference. This meant that the ground forces would have to push quickly into Tunisia to seize the main port cities of Bizerte and Tunis before the Germans and Italians could move in reinforcements from Sicily and Italy. This situation was ideal for the use of airborne forces that could seize key objectives deep in the enemy's rear areas and hold them until ground forces arrived. Unfortunately, only the 2d Battalion and the three battalions of the British 1st Parachute Brigade, 1st Airborne Division, were trained and ready to go.

Another mission soon took priority. One of the most difficult tasks facing Clark was how to neutralize two Vichy French Air Force airfields at Tafaraoui and La Senia, south and east of the Algerian port city of Oran. If done, this would prevent any hostile fighters and bombers from attacking the invasion fleet carrying

the Center Task Force and also free the fields for use by Allied land-based aircraft waiting at Gibraltar. Clark had an appreciation of the potential that airborne troops brought to the planner since his days on Lt. Gen. Lesley J. McNair's staff. He had come to London in June as commander of II Corps, which was slated for the invasion of Europe, and had brought with him as his airborne advisor now Maj. William P. Yarborough. When Clark decided to employ Raff's battalion for this mission, he turned to Yarborough and Raff to solve the problem.

And a major problem it was: the airfields were at the extreme range of the C-47, more than 1,100 flying miles from England, across the Bay of Biscay, Spain, and the western Mediterranean. The C-47 crews, who had little experience in night formation flying and long-range navigation, would find this a most challenging mission. After the drops, the aircraft would have to land on the flats south and west of Oran before they ran out of fuel.

A recently developed British radar guidance system, Rebecca-Eureka, offered the hope of

guiding the C-47s to the objectives. While the systems were installed and training begun, one set was smuggled into French North Africa to pinpoint the landing zone (LZ) for Tafaraoui, the initial objective. Another was positioned on a Royal Navy ship in the invasion force.

Despite obvious problems, the French airfields were suitable targets for an airborne battalion. For the mission, the Paratroop Task Force was formed, comprising the 60th Troop Carrier Group and the 2d Battalion. Air Corps Col. William C. Bentley would command before the mission and until the jump; then Raff would take over. Exactly when the changeover would occur was fuzzy—could the air commander make the jump decision despite the airborne commander's input? This policy became standard in subsequent airborne operations, but was not without faults.

Yarborough was assigned to the task force's planning staff and would also go along on the mission as its executive officer. A critical question was whether the French would resist the invasion or lay down their arms when the Allies appeared. That uncertainty compelled

Paratroopers of the 2d Battalion, 503d Parachute Infantry, pulling in their parachutes after landing in a training jump in England, September 19, 1942. *National Archives.*

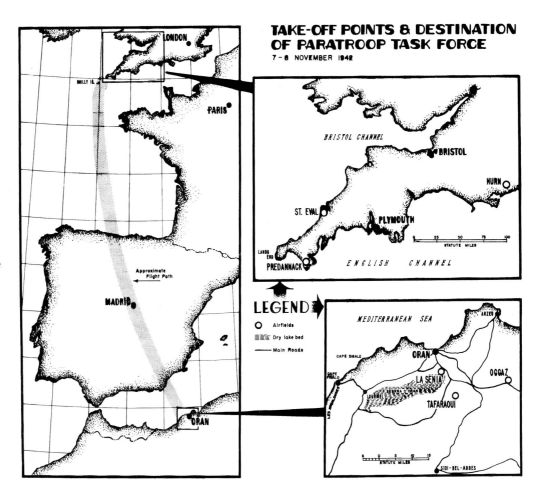

TAKE-OFF POINTS & DESTINATION OF PARATROOP TASK FORCE
7 – 8 NOVEMBER 1942

LEGEND
○ Airfields
▦ Dry lake bed
— Main Roads

Map of the Raff airborne operation to Tafaraoui and La Senia air bases near Oran, Algeria. *U.S. Air Force.*

Yarborough to plan two operations—one for peace and one for war. Moreover, there would be no air support, no follow-on air-landed or air-dropped troops or supplies, no firm plans for linking up with the Allied landing force, and little intelligence about the objectives. But there was a lot of one thing, and that was uncertainty.

Some Allied planners objected to the mission, believing that the Allies should save their limited airborne assets to seize objectives ahead of the ground push into Tunisia. On top of this, Raff doubted the battalion could succeed in a daylight attack and Bentley doubted the troop carriers could reach Oran in sufficient strength at night. Thus, serious questions persisted about the mission before it ever left the ground.

On November 2, the 2d Battalion, 503d Parachute Infantry, was officially redesignated the 2d Battalion, 509th Parachute Infantry. No other battalions were ever formed, so in December 1943 the unit was redesignated again as the 509th Parachute Infantry Battalion, which it remained until March 1, 1945.

At 2130 on the night of November 7, 39 C-47s and 556 paratroopers of the Paratroop Task

Force took off from their bases in western Cornwall for the long flight down the Bay of Biscay, across Spain, and to their objectives. Continuous practice and training did not prevent a confused and disjointed mission. Not much went right from the start. They departed thinking the French would not resist. That changed but communications went awry, and word never reached the aircraft that they would receive a hostile reception. The weather over Spain was bad. Planes were scattered—some landing in Spanish Morocco, another at Gibraltar, and others in French Morocco—completely missing their objectives. On top of that, the Rebecca-Eureka system did not work properly.

By 0900 on November 8, only 33 aircraft had reached the area of Oran, 27 of them grouped in the vicinity of Lourmel, well to the southwest of Oran and to the west of the two airfields. Raff's group indeed jumped, and Raff himself was injured and later turned over command of operations to Yarborough. A series of misadventures and encounters now ensued with Allied forces, as well as French ground and air forces, which produced the airborne's first wartime killed-in-action casualties, including Pvt. John Thomas "Tommy" Mackall, Pvt. Ira L. Brookins, and Lt. David C. Kunkle.

Yarborough finally flew and marched overland to Tafaraoui on the morning of November 9. The rest of the battalion reached his group that afternoon in commandeered trucks and buses. The C-47s were there to greet them, having landed on the field on November 8 despite some opposition and linked up with American forces that took the base that day. For elite American paratroopers, their first combat jump was not an auspicious debut.

In their initial combat action, troopers of the 509th established another enduring tradition of airborne forces. Although widely scattered, they joined with other troopers nearby and carried out the mission as best they could. Beginning with the operations in North Africa, these "little groups of paratroopers," or LGOPs, have contributed to mission success (or averting disaster) in virtually every airborne mission since.

TUNISIA

The mixed-up scrum at Lourmel, La Senia, and Tafaraoui only marked the beginning of the 509th's operations in North Africa. By November 10, the Germans and Italians were pushing aircraft, troops, and equipment into Tunisia and the Allies had begun "the race for Tunis." Two days later Raff was ordered to jump and seize the airfield at Tébessa, near the Tunisian border, to forestall the Germans. Hurriedly preparing the parachutes and equipment from the Lourmel jump, Raff readied his

Companies D and E for the mission slated for November 15.

While Raff was getting ready, British paratroopers took the city of Bône. Then, in coordination with Raff's attack, they took the airfield at Souk el Arba in Tunisia on the road to Tunis on November 16.

Upon learning of a larger French airfield at Youks-les-Bains to the west of Tébessa, Raff switched his objective. After a successful, unopposed landing and a friendly welcome from the French 3d Zouave Regiment that was defending the airfield, Raff quickly took Tébessa. Never one to hesitate, the aggressive Raff added arriving American and British units to his now Franco-American team. Within a week he had built the "Raff Force" that was hitting the German and Italian units all along the Tunisian border as far south as Gafsa and penetrating as far east as Sidi bou Zid and the Faid Pass.

Higher headquarters soon curtailed Raff's adventures, fearing that the Axis would cut off and destroy his unit. Nonetheless, Eisenhower in his *Crusade in Europe* praised Raff's aggressiveness:

> The story of his operations in that region is a minor epic in itself. The deceptions he practiced. The speed with which he struck, his boldness and his aggressiveness, kept the enemy confused during a period of weeks.

President Franklin D. Roosevelt and Prime Minister Winston S. Churchill sit with their staffs during a summit conference at Casablanca, Morocco, January 1943. The Allies decided at the conference to advance from North Africa to Sicily in midsummer 1943. *National Archives.*

top left
Paratroopers of the 80th Antiaircraft Artillery Battalion, 82d Airborne Division, loading Jeep into a Waco CG-4A glider at Oujda, French Morocco. June 16, 1943. *82d Airborne Division War Memorial Museum.*

top right
Paratroopers of Battery A, 319th Parachute Field Artillery Battalion, 82d Airborne Division, loading a 75-mm pack howitzer into a Waco CG-4A glider during training in the Fifth Army Training Area at Oujda, French Morocco. June 11, 1943. *82d Airborne Division War Memorial Museum.*

Allied operations soon ground to a halt with the onset of the cold and wet winter in northern Tunisia and especially the arrival of thousands of German and Italian troops who blunted the drive for Tunis. Stalemate followed and Raff's 509th was soon parceled out piecemeal to fight as infantry along the thin Allied lines. A major British airborne raid at Pont du Fahs and Depienne airfields on November 29 only resulted in the paratroopers being surrounded, suffering heavy losses, and having to fight their way more than 60 miles back to the Allied lines.

The final airborne mission for Raff's paratroopers was a late December attempt to blow up the coastal railroad bridge at El Djem. The mission failed to blow up the bridge, but the team did destroy some of the tracks to the south of it. Raff stayed in command through the remaining months of fighting until the Axis forces surrendered early in May 1943. Yarborough left in January to become assistant G-3 on Clark's staff planning for the upcoming Sicilian and Italian operations. Then he returned to Fort Bragg and in March assumed command of the 2d Battalion, 504th Parachute Infantry, which was slated for shipment to North Africa. With the Axis capitulation, the 509th moved to the flat, treeless desert at Oujda in far eastern French Morocco to refit and prepare for its next mission. It would share this harsh training area with the arriving 82d Airborne Division, to which it was soon attached.

ON TO SICILY: OPERATION HUSKY

GETTING READY
President Franklin D. Roosevelt and Churchill and their Combined Chiefs of Staff convened in Casablanca, Morocco, on January 14, 1943, to plan for the next offensive operations against the Axis. Allied forces had been in North Africa for two months and were still fighting in Tunisia and Libya. Much hard fighting remained. However long that might take, they wanted to maintain the offensive pressure, both in Europe and the Pacific.

A cross-Channel invasion of the continent was not feasible before 1944. Thus, after Operation TORCH, they decided to seize Sicily by midsummer 1943 and move on to the Italian mainland. Removing Italy from the Axis in 1943 would help set the stage for the invasion of France in 1944. It would also keep German forces engaged and away from concentrating on the Eastern Front against the Soviet Union.

Planning began immediately for Operation HUSKY, the invasion of Sicily. For this operation, the 82d Airborne Division was now trained, reorganized, and ready for shipment to the theater. A large part of the British 1st Airborne Division was already in North Africa and more trained units were coming. Allied planners counted on the American and British airborne divisions to play significant roles in the invasion so that it would now be possible to test what large airborne forces could actually do in major combat operations.

The 82d arrived at Casablanca on May 10 and quickly moved to the desolate Oujda in Clark's Fifth Army Training Area. The 52d Troop Carrier Wing with which the 82d would go to war was located in the same area to facilitate training. The unrelenting heat and sun tortured the paratroopers during the day, forcing training to be moved to the cooler night hours. There would be no distractions.

Within days of arriving at Oujda, Maj. Gen. Matthew B. Ridgway informed Col. James M. Gavin and Col. Reuben H. Tucker that the 82d's job on Sicily was to prepare the way for the American seaborne assault forces of Patton's Seventh U.S. Army that were to land on July 10. Ridgway selected Gavin's 505th Parachute Infantry, reinforced with one of the 504th's battalions, for the initial jump late on

the evening of July 9. The 504th would be the follow-on force to drop late on D-Day, July 10.

While the 1st Airborne Division's 1st Airlanding Brigade would lead off the British landings with a glider-borne assault south of Syracuse, the 505th would spearhead the American invasion of Sicily with a massed airborne assault. In the first regimental-sized airborne operation in American military history, Gavin's 3,400 paratroopers were to land on four main drop zones (DZs) arranged like a string of pearls from southeast of Gela to a point south of Niscemi. They were to seize two critical junctions on the Gela-Niscemi road, protect the landings of the 1st and 45th Infantry Divisions, disrupt communications, confuse the enemy as to American objectives, and block key roads. These operations would prevent German and Italian reserves from attacking the landing beaches. Teaming with the 1st Infantry Division, the 505th would then take Ponte Olivo airfield between Gela and Niscemi.

The 505th and 504th were both built into regimental combat teams (RCTs) with the addition of parachute field artillery, engineers, signal, and medical elements. After a dispute with the British over the allocation of troop carriers, Eisenhower confirmed that the 52d Troop Carrier Wing with five groups and 250 C-47s would support the 82d. Three additional parachute and glider lifts beginning on D+1 would bring in the remaining combat elements of the division over the next several days, including the two remaining battalions of the 504th and the 325th Glider Infantry.

top left
Paratroopers of the 505th Parachute Infantry, 82d Airborne Division, conduct a massed demonstration parachute drop for Lt. Gen. George S. Patton, Jr., commanding general, Seventh U.S. Army, at Oujda, French Morocco, on June 3, 1943. *National Archives.*

bottom left
Paratroopers of Col. James M. Gavin's 505th Parachute Infantry climb aboard a C-47 for a training jump at Oujda, French Morocco, on June 2, 1943. *National Archives.*

top right
Lt. Gen. George S. Patton, Jr., commanding general of Seventh U.S. Army, addresses the 82d Airborne Division at Oujda, French Morocco, on June 3, 1943, during a visit before the invasion of Sicily.
National Archives.

bottom right
A rare color photograph shows soldiers of the 320th Glider Field Artillery Battalion, 82d Airborne Division, loading a Jeep into a glider through the nose opening at Kairouan, Tunisia, in preparation for the airborne assault on Sicily.
82d Airborne Division War Memorial Museum.

82D AIRBORNE DIVISION'S BAPTISM OF FIRE

The invasion forces concentrated on the southeastern corner of the island, with the point of the corner dividing Montgomery's Eighth Army from Patton's Seventh U.S. Army. For the first time, each army had airborne support—the 1st Airborne Division with the Eighth Army aiming for objectives on the eastern shore; the 82d Airborne Division with the Seventh U.S. Army assaulting the southern shore to the west. By early July the 82d had flown forward to the airfields around Kairouan, Tunisia, to make its final preparations.

As the men of Gavin's combat team anxiously relaxed in the shade of their C-47s awaiting

takeoff, each paratrooper was given a mimeographed note from Gavin telling them of their mission and exhorting them:

> The term American Parachutist has been synonymous with courage of a high order. Let us carry the fight to the enemy and make the American Parachutist feared and respected through all his ranks. Attack violently. Destroy him wherever found.

Within hours in the early evening of July 9, the 226 transports lifting the 505th RCT plus 3d Battalion, 504th, took off for Sicily. The course plotted for the C-47s was difficult for crews not proficient in night formation flying and navigation over water—it hooked them around Malta and then back toward the southern tip of Sicily before turning northwest and making two more turns to reach the DZs. Flying at 500 feet to avoid detection, the transports were buffeted throughout by strong northwest winds exceeding 25 to 30 miles per hour, twice the velocity considered safe for any parachute drop.

But this was a combat operation, not a training jump. The transports flew on and were blown well off course and scattered, especially those groups at the end of the stream. Only sporadic and light enemy fire greeted the confused transports as they crisscrossed the Sicilian coast and circled to locate their DZs and unload their planeloads, or "sticks," of paratroopers. Returning troop carrier pilots reported dropping 80 percent of the paratroopers within the designated DZs. In reality, less than 20 percent actually landed anywhere near their DZs.

The result was that the 505th was scattered all over southern Sicily rather than concentrated between Gela and Niscemi. Some paratroopers landed as far away as Syracuse, 65 miles from their planned DZs, and others ended up joining with the British to carry on the fight. The 2d Battalion, 505th, landed pretty much concentrated and intact, but near Donnalucara on the coast, more than 25 miles from its DZ. The paratroopers who landed behind the 1st Infantry Division's beaches were only a small percentage of the number planned. On the other hand, many more than planned ended up behind the 45th Infantry Division's beaches, providing an unintended but welcome assist. Gavin himself landed about five miles south of Vittoria, some 20 miles from his intended DZ, uncertain until the next morning if he was even in Sicily.

Not all of the paratroopers missed their DZs and failed in their assigned missions. Capt. Willard "Bill" Follmer's Company I, 3d Battalion, 505th landed nearly squarely on its DZ. Quickly forming up, Follmer took his objective, the high ground to the south and overlooking the key road junction east of Gela where the road from Niscemi met Highway 115 from Vittoria. Meanwhile, Company A, 1st Battalion, 505th, under Capt. Ed Sayre, whose task it was actually to take the junction, landed several miles from its DZ. Sayre collected enough men to fight off a strong attack by elements of the western Kampfgruppe (battle group) of the Hermann Goering Panzer Division that was pushing toward the beaches from Niscemi. He then took and held the intersection. Both companies completed their missions successfully

and linked up with the 1st Division on July 10. For his leadership and bravery, Sayre received a Distinguished Service Cross (DSC).

Gavin gathered what troopers he could but largely laid low on July 10. That evening he headed for his objectives and early on July 11 ran into elements of the 45th Infantry Division that had already penetrated inland. Now knowing his location, Gavin headed off along Highway 115 toward Gela and the area where his main force should have landed.

Where the highway crossed the Biazza Ridge, Gavin and his ragtag force of paratroopers and infantrymen from the 45th ran into the Hermann Goering Panzer Division's second Kampfgruppe. With 60-ton Mark VI Tiger I heavy tanks and plenty of infantry, the Germans were driving from Biscari toward the beaches. Without antitank weapons, paratroopers manhandled two of the 456th Parachute Field Artillery Battalion's 75-mm pack howitzers into position on the ridge in time to duel the Tigers and knock one out. Gavin's force was hard-pressed in this uneven fight until naval gunfire and heavy artillery support stopped the German attack. Gaining 11 Sherman M-4 tanks from the 45th, Gavin's growing combat team cleared the Germans from the ridge, consolidated their position, and established contact with Ridgway in Gela late on July 11. In the process, Gavin's fight at Biazza Ridge seriously disrupted the German attack on the beaches and even led to its withdrawal.

Although much of the 505th was badly dispersed, Gavin's relentless training in the

top left
Regimental staff and radio operators of the 505th Parachute Infantry on Biazza Ridge, Sicily, on July 11, 1943, as Col. James M. Gavin and his combat team took on Tiger tanks and panzer grenadiers of the Hermann Goering Panzer Division. *National Archives.*

top right
Paratroopers of the 82d Airborne Division fully loaded and awaiting takeoff from Tunisia for their first combat jump into Sicily in Operation HUSKY. July 9, 1943. *U.S. Air Force.*

top left

Col. James M. Gavin, commander of the 505th Parachute Infantry, talks with war correspondent Jack M. "Beaver" Thompson of the *Chicago Tribune* on July 11, 1943, below the Biazza Ridge where Highway 115 crossed the rail line from Vittoria to Gela. *National Archives.*

top right

This map from James M. Gavin's *Airborne Warfare* clearly reflects the confused nature of the 82d Airborne Division's actual airborne landings in Sicily during the night of July 9–10, 1943, in Operation HUSKY. *Infantry Journal.*

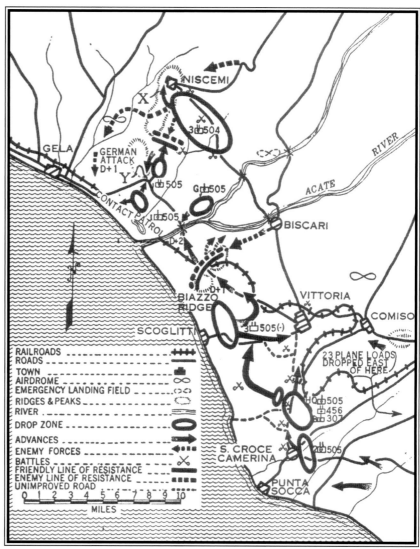

Moroccan desert paid off. Acting on Gavin's departing message to "Attack violently. Destroy him wherever found," the troopers banded together and carried out their assigned missions as best they could. They harassed and attacked German and Italian forces when and where they found them, effectively disrupting the defenses and blocking the enemy forces from the beachheads in many places. Perhaps in landing seemingly all over Sicily, the American paratroopers had caused so much general confusion that the Germans and Italians badly overestimated their numbers and intentions.

The 504th's mission was postponed until the night of D+1, July 11. Patton, Ridgway, and airborne planners had reservations about flying this reinforcement mission over the invasion fleet. Although the fleet and ground forces knew the aircraft were coming, they had been attacked repeatedly by enemy aircraft during the last two days. Despite concerns, the drop at Farello airstrip northeast of Gela went ahead as planned.

Everything went well until the initial aircraft had dropped their paratroopers and the troop carriers reached the fleet. Trigger-happy gunners on the ground and in the invasion fleet found the transports flying low on a moonlit night simply too threatening. Of the 144 C-47s with 2,300 paratroopers on board, 23 were shot down, 37 severely damaged, and others hit by friendly fire that killed and wounded both aircrew members and paratroopers. That night the 504th suffered 229 casualties—81 dead, 132 wounded, and 16 missing—and the troop carriers had 37 casualties and 53 missing. Other transports dropped their paratroopers early or turned away. Among those missing after the mission was Brig. Gen. Charles L. Keerans, Jr., the 82d's assistant division commander, who was riding along as an observer.

Some transports got through the antiaircraft fire to their DZs. There, both planes and descending paratroopers became targets for the 1st Infantry Division, which thought it was being attacked by German paratroopers. The

mission was a disaster for the 504th at a time that the unit was badly needed as reinforcements.

By July 14, Ridgway only had under his command slightly more than 3,000 of the more than 5,300 men of the 82d who were involved in the two airborne missions to Sicily. Despite these awful initial setbacks, the 82d spent 13 days in the line and another 28 in reserve during the Sicilian Campaign. It fought well throughout and ended the campaign at Trapani at the far western end of the island, more than 150 miles from where it started.

After the war, German Gen. Kurt Student rendered his conclusion on the role of the 82d in Sicily:

> The Allied airborne operation in Sicily was decisive despite widely scattered drops which must be expected in a night landing. It is my opinion that if it had not been for the Allied airborne forces blocking the Hermann Goering Armored Division from reaching the beachhead, that division would have driven the initial seaborne forces back into the sea.

LESSONS OF OPERATION HUSKY

After North Africa and Sicily, some senior Army commanders expressed serious doubts about the large American airborne force. Eisenhower questioned even having airborne divisions. Writing to Gen. George C. Marshall on September 30, he commented that "I do not believe in the airborne division. I believe that airborne troops should be reorganized into self-contained units, comprising infantry, artillery, and special services, all of about the strength of a regimental combat team."

Although also disappointed in the overall performance of the airborne forces, Ridgway countered that they had to be committed and fought as divisions, not piecemeal as smaller units. The size of the airborne force was not the problem. At the highest levels, naval, ground, and air planning had to do a much better job of coordinating the airborne aspects within the overall framework of operations.

In Ridgway's view, many senior commanders saw the airborne divisions as "a brand new toy" and a "magic key which would open many tactical doors, whenever an assault operation was planned." In reality, such commanders knew little about how to employ the airborne force or

Maj. Gen. Matthew B. Ridgway, commanding general, left, and Brig. Gen. Maxwell D. Taylor, commanding the division artillery, seated in the Jeep, and staff members of the 82d Airborne Division confer overlooking battlefield just outside Ribera, Sicily, on July 26, 1943. *National Archives.*

When Col. James M. Gavin's lightly armed paratroopers ran into the Germans' Mark VI Tiger I tanks mounting 88-mm guns on July 11, they were seriously overmatched until help arrived. 1st Lt. Harold H. Swingler, Headquarters Company, 505th, came across this Tiger stopped on the road on the western side of Biazza Ridge with the crew outside talking. He tossed a hand grenade among them, killing them all, and thus captured the 82d's first Tiger tank. *National Archives.*

bottom right
Maj. Gen. Matthew B. Ridgway, center, is flanked by his aide Capt. Don C. Faith, left, and Lt. Col. Charles W. Billingslea of the 325th Glider Infantry. Ribera, Sicily, July 26, 1943. *National Archives.*

what limitations it had once it was engaged in ground combat operations.

In Operation HUSKY, the airborne force confronted problems that were many and serious because this was its initial large-scale combat experience. In a classic understatement, Gavin commented in his postwar *Airborne Warfare* that "Sicily was a sobering experiment for all of the troopers and staffs of the US 82d Airborne Division." Much was learned, but that experiment carried a stiff price for the division: 206 troopers killed, 810 wounded (474 of whom never returned to the division), 48 missing, and 172 taken prisoners of war.

With daylight operations not deemed feasible due to enemy antiaircraft and fighter defenses, night operations were the only alternative. Troop carriers required much more thorough training in day and night formation flying and navigation and had to train with the airborne units they would support in combat. Course planning for the transports had to be simplified and to steer wide of any naval forces in future operations. The C-47s needed self-sealing gas tanks to prevent fires and explosions when hit by antiaircraft fire. Clearly, special pathfinder units had to be set up who could land early at the DZs and glider LZs, mark them, and set up guidance systems and beacons for the main force to follow.

After Sicily revealed serious weaknesses in the airborne division as organized in 1942, Ridgway began his campaign to enlarge the airborne division so that it had more fighting and support personnel, artillery, and transportation. The airborne divisions certainly needed more fighting power, especially heavier weapons to

fight tanks, as Gavin's joust with the Tigers in Sicily proved. Ridgway saw the answer to this problem in close and continuous tactical air support throughout airborne operations.

A change was also required in the weapons that the individual paratroopers carried. The troopers had to jump ready to fight, and stocked with whatever supplies they needed to continue fighting for several days. Less reliance had to be placed on air-dropped containers with weapons and ammunition that might land nowhere near the soldiers, who could not afford the time to search for these loads.

ITALY SURRENDERS, BUT THE GERMANS DON'T

Unfortunately, the war didn't stop so that the airborne and AAF leaders could work out the problems so evident in Operation HUSKY. With Sicily secured in August, the Allies pressed on to Italy to knock out Benito

Mussolini. Two airborne operations were planned—one at Capua north of Naples to assist Operation AVALANCHE, the landing at Salerno south of Naples planned for September 9; and another to capture Rome. Ridgway opposed them both because "they would result in the destruction of my division." Both were eventually scrubbed. When the 82d's planned drop on Rome was canceled, Eisenhower released the division for Clark's use, if needed. The Italian government surrendered on September 8, and Clark's Fifth Army landed at Salerno the next day.

SALERNO

While the Italians now largely gave up the fight, the Germans certainly did not. They pressured the Salerno beachhead so heavily that Clark called for immediate help. On September 13 he sent an urgent personal letter to Ridgway in Sicily that was carried by a fighter pilot. Clark's request was terse: "I want you to make a drop within our lines on the beachhead and I want you to make it tonight. This is a must."

Working closely with now Lt. Col. William Yarborough, who was once again the assistant G-3, Fifth Army, Ridgway's staff hurriedly pulled together this priority mission. That night, newly trained pathfinder teams using Eureka beacons for Rebecca-equipped aircraft and ground markers guided the troop carrier aircraft to the DZ near the Sele River. Tucker led two battalions of his 504th Parachute Infantry to jump near Paestum. The operation testified to the cohesion and readiness of the regiment as well as of the entire 82d and the troop carrier units. Only eight hours had elapsed from the receipt of the warning alert for the operation to the jump into the darkness and 15 hours since Clark had penned his letter.

The 504th was quickly thrown into the line facing Altavilla and Albanella to blunt the German drive. Gavin's entire 505th Parachute Infantry jumped in on the next night, September 14. The 325th Glider Regimental Combat Team and Tucker's 3d Battalion came in by landing craft on September 15. Ridgway now had most of his 82d Airborne Division consolidated in the beachhead and fighting.

Troopers of the 82d Airborne Division suit up and prepare for the short-notice jump into the Salerno beachhead on September 13, 1944. *National Archives.*

Paratroopers of the 504th Parachute Infantry wind their way up a steep hillside following mules carrying mortar ammunition and supplies to forward positions in the fighting in the difficult terrain of the Venafro sector near San Pietro Infine, Italy. December 12, 1943. *National Archives.*

Tucker was soon driving the Germans back in his sector. After capturing Albanella, Tucker got into a nasty scrap at Altavilla and Hill 424 on September 16–18. The 504th found itself in a dire situation and threatened with encirclement. When VI Corps advised Tucker to withdraw, he responded "Retreat Hell! Send me my other battalion!" The corps did. The timely arrival of his recently landed 3d Battalion along with the 1st Battalion, 325th Glider Infantry, tilted the balance in Tucker's favor. For his intrepid leadership and heroism in the fight for Altavilla and Hill 424, Tucker was awarded the first of his two wartime DSCs.

On the night of September 14, the 509th was committed much farther inland, in a revival of a previously canceled mission. Jumping near the town of Avellino, 15 miles behind the front and surrounded by 4,000-foot mountains, their job was to distract the Germans and block the movement of German reinforcements toward the beachhead. In contrast to the two Sele River missions, this mission was marred by widespread drops that scattered the 509th's troopers over more than 100 square miles of mountainous terrain around Avellino. Again, LGOPs, no single group larger than 80, achieved some impromptu feats of arms that disrupted the Germans who were already beginning to pull back from Salerno. Gavin later appropriately called it "the ill-fated battalion operation of Avellino."

The 82d was in the midst of action for the rest of September and into October that pushed the Germans back from the bridgehead and took Naples. The 505th, 325th Glider Infantry, and especially the 504th all had conspicuous roles in these operations. On October 1, the 82d occupied Naples and took over the mission of restoring order. The Germans left booby traps and mines all over the city, and the 307th Airborne Engineer Battalion had been deactivating and collecting the explosives and mines. On Sunday, October 10, a massive explosion blew apart the Italian Army barracks the 307th occupied and left 18 dead and 56 wounded. It was the result either of a tragic accident with the stored explosives or of a German mine that the engineers did not locate in their own quarters.

Meanwhile, on September 30, the 505th was attached to the 23d Armoured Brigade, British X Corps, and pushed triumphantly through Naples and on to the north to the Volturno River in pursuit of the withdrawing Germans. As the troopers reached the river, on October 4 Ridgway summoned Gavin to division headquarters and made him assistant division commander. On October 10, Gavin took up his new job and was promoted to brigadier general. Lt. Col. Herbert F. Batchelor took over as regimental commander, and the 505th soon secured the crossings of the Volturno at Cancello ed Arnone for the British tankers.

82D SHIPS OUT TO THE UNITED KINGDOM, AND THE 504TH AND 509TH DIG IN

The Sele River and Avellino missions ended the airborne work of the 82d Airborne Division in the Mediterranean. In October, the theater determined that future airborne missions in Italy were unlikely. Moreover, Allied planning had now turned to the invasion of France scheduled for 1944, and the 82d was among the divisions that Allied planners had destined for those operations. Ridgway wanted to take the entire division to the United Kingdom, but Clark prevailed upon Eisenhower to leave Tucker's 504th Parachute Infantry and the 509th Parachute Infantry Battalion, now com-

manded by Yarborough since late September, with the Fifth Army.

Clark promptly attached the 504th to Maj. Gen. John Lucas's VI Corps. Lucas just as quickly placed the 504th in the rugged mountain on the right of his line to maintain contact with Montgomery's British Eighth Army that was advancing up the eastern side of the Italian boot. Operating on the 34th Infantry Division's right flank during November, the 504th's tenacious skills in independent, small-unit operations were fully demonstrated in the fighting up to and along the Germans' Gustav Line, a defensive line anchored on Monte Cassino that the Allies called the Winter Line.

In December, the 504th moved to the Venafro sector and the hills overlooking the village of San Pietro Infine down the Liri valley from Cassino. In the hard fighting to take and hold these barren, steep, rocky hills, Tucker's troopers lost 54 killed and 226 wounded.

Stalled along the Winter Line, Clark planned to outflank the German defenses and draw their reserves away with an amphibious landing on January 22 at Anzio (Operation SHINGLE), some 35 miles south of Rome. An important role was initially laid out for the 504th. It would jump eight miles behind the landing beaches at Aprilia and Carroceto to block the main road and rail connection between Rome and the Anzio-Nettuno area to interrupt movement of German reinforcements. Two days before the operation, Clark canceled it, fearing the landing would alert the Germans to the seaborne attack. Instead, the 504th came into

the beachhead "feet wet" after the 3d Infantry Division, landing from the sea rather than from the air.

Both the 504th and 509th played major roles in the tough fighting in the Anzio beachhead. While the 509th secured the harbor of Nettuno, on January 24 the 504th was thrown into the right sector of the beachhead along the Mussolini Canal. The 509th was soon attached to the 3d Infantry Division and fought in the tough defensive battles in and around the town of Carano. Holding the division's left flank, the 509th distinguished itself in the heavy fighting of February and March. Indeed, the battalion received a Distinguished Unit Citation (DUC) for their role in blunting a major German attack at Carano on February 29 and Company C earned another DUC for a bold night attack on March 14. In the fighting at Carano on February 8, Cpl. Paul B. Huff became the first paratrooper to be awarded a Medal of Honor in World War II.

top left
Troopers of the 504th Parachute Infantry come ashore "feet wet" from a Landing Craft Infantry on D-Day at Anzio, Italy, on January 22, 1944. *82d Airborne Division War Memorial Museum.*

bottom left
Preparing for the Anzio landing on January 22, 1944. Aboard the troopship *Winchester Castle*, Lt. Col. William P. Yarborough, center, commander of the 509th Parachute Infantry, with the 509th's pocket patch prominently displayed, and Lt. Col. Roy A. Murray, commander of the 4th Ranger Battalion, study a model of the beach where their troops will join in the amphibious assault. Capt. S. F. Nedigate, the ship's skipper, looks on. *National Archives.*

top left
Anzio 504th Combat
Team wringing out wet
clothes after amphibious
landing January 22, 1944.
*82d Airborne Division War
Memorial Museum.*

top lower left
Pocket patch of the
504th Parachute Infantry
after they adopted their
"Devils in Baggy Pants"
nickname. *U.S. Army.*

top right
Paratroopers of Col.
Reuben H. Tucker's 2d
Battalion, 504th Para-
chute Infantry RCT, cross
the Mussolini Canal on
a footbridge, spearhead-
ing the 504th's attack
on January 26, 1944.
National Archives.

In the first days of February, the 3d Battalion, 504th, was sent to the northern front and attached to the British 1st (Guards) Division in the Carroceto-Aprilia sector. In the same place that the troopers were to have jumped in January, they helped stop the German offensive in difficult hand-to-hand fighting against repeated attacks in the area of Aprilia, one of Mussolini's model farm settlements that the soldiers dubbed the "Factory" because it looked like one. For its gallant stand here from February 8–12, the 3d Battalion received a DUC.

While the 3d Battalion fought in the north, the remainder of the RCT was attached to the 3d Infantry Division in the south, fighting over the Mussolini Canal and up to the Cisterna River. Besieged and under constant German artillery fire, the 504th then went over to the defensive, a role not well suited to the troopers' aggressive, attacking temperament. On March 24, the 504th was finally withdrawn from the Anzio beachhead and shipped to Naples in preparation for movement to rejoin the rest of the 82d in the British Isles. Its stay at Anzio had been expensive—the regiment had lost 120 killed, 410 wounded, and 60 missing.

The 504th's long months in hard combat with the Fifth Army had taken a great toll. Ridgway had gone personally to Marshall to obtain the regiment's release. When it finally arrived in England on April 22, Ridgway later comment-ed "They were so badly battered, so riddled with casualties from their battles in Italy, that they could not be made ready for combat in

time to jump with us." The 509th was pulled out at the same time as the 504th, but with only 125 men left. While the 504th headed to England, the 509th was assigned to the planned invasion of southern France.

Indeed, units of the 82d Airborne Division spent a total of 142 days in combat in Italy from September 1943 through March 1944 during which it suffered 327 dead, 1,929 wounded, and 71 missing.

"THE DEVILS IN BAGGY PANTS"

The 504th Parachute Infantry RCT emerged from Italy with a special badge of distinc-tion—the Germans gave them their honored designation, "The Devils in Baggy Pants," which was symbolically incorporated into their unit pocket patch and today's distinctive unit insignia. The German units opposing the 504th quickly learned of the troopers' fear-some combat prowess. During the fighting at Anzio, a regimental intelligence officer looking through the belongings of a dead German of-ficer found a diary including this entry:

American parachutists—devils in baggy pants—are less than 100 meters from my outpost line. I can't sleep at night. They pop up from nowhere and we never know when or how they will strike next. Seems like the black-hearted devils are everywhere.

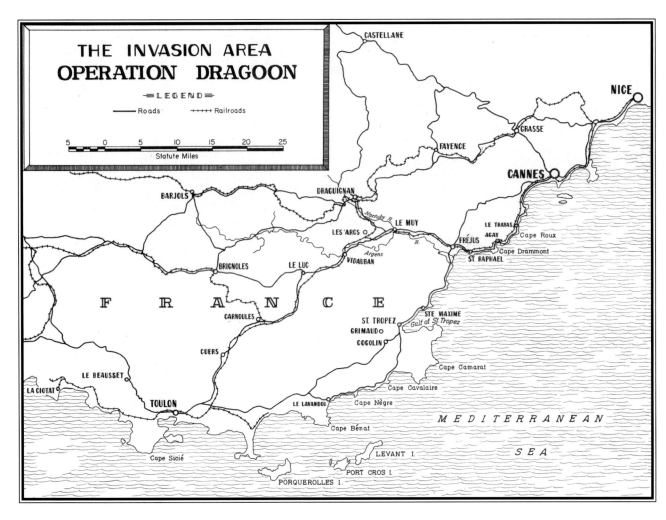

THE INVASION AREA
OPERATION DRAGOON

═LEGEND═

—— Roads   ┼┼┼┼ Railroads

A NEW MISSION: THE INVASION OF SOUTHERN FRANCE

As operations dragged on in Italy, the Allies planned a two-pronged invasion of the continent for 1944—Operation OVERLORD that would strike Normandy from across the British Channel in June and two months later the off-again, on-again Operation ANVIL (later renamed DRAGOON) that would hit southern France.

Scheduled for August 15, Operation ANVIL was targeted along the Mediterranean Riviera coast between Toulon and Cannes. The initial planning for the invasion fell under Clark but later came under Lt. Gen. Jacob L. Devers, North African Theater of Operations, U.S. Army, and deputy commander of AFHQ, and Lt. Gen. Alexander M. Patch, commanding the Seventh U.S. Army.

From the outset, Allied planners wanted airborne support for the landings but were uncertain of what forces might be available. Eventually, the Anglo-American 1st Airborne Task Force was put together under Maj. Gen.

Robert T. Frederick, former commander of the American-Canadian 1st Special Service Force. With the invasion of France already staged, in July Eisenhower was able to lend additional experienced troop carrier and glider pilots who had participated in Operation OVERLORD.

The paratroopers and glider forces of the 1st Airborne Task Force included the British 2d Independent Parachute Brigade and the American 517th Parachute Infantry along with the 509th and 551st Parachute Infantry Battalions, the 550th Glider Infantry Battalion, and 460th and 463d Parachute Field Artillery Battalions. They were to land in the area of Le Muy and Le Luc in the Argens River valley to block German attempts to counter the invasion forces of VI Corps and to secure LZs for the glider-borne infantry units that were to follow.

Fog over the drop areas and poor navigation resulted in the inaccurate delivery of American pathfinder teams, although the British teams of the 2d Independent Parachute Brigade landed on target. The leading elements of the 509th and 463d Parachute Field Artillery Battalions landed close to the designated DZ but

The Mediterranean coast of France from Toulon to Cannes was the objective of Operation DRAGOON, August 15, 1944.
U.S. Air Force.

top right
Troopers of 517th
Parachute Infantry in
Operation DRAGOON,
southern France,
August 1944. *XVIII
Airborne Corps Historian
from National Archives.*

center right
American paratroopers
standing and hooked up
to jump over southern
France in the airborne
assault of Operation
DRAGOON. August 15,
1944. *U.S. Air Force.*

bottom right
American airborne team
in southern France.
Heavily armed, this
dirt-covered American
airborne infantry team
heads for a command
post immediately after
landing in southern
France on D-Day.
August 15, 1944.
Library of Congress.

those trailing went astray by miles. None of the 517th Parachute Infantry landed on their DZs. Although less than 40 percent of the paratroopers in the predawn lifts landed in their assigned DZs, 60 percent of the troopers actually reached their assembly areas at Le Muy. Fortunately, few German troops were in or near the landing areas and resistance was light.

Some problems occurred with the first glider echelons due to weather and visibility, which forced the C-47s towing the 2d Independent Parachute Brigade's gliders with artillery and antitank guns to turn back. They returned later that afternoon to complete their missions. Subsequent glider echelons bringing in artillery and vehicles were able to land close to their LZs beginning at 0930, with the 550th Glider Infantry arriving at 1830. The 551st Parachute Infantry jumped into the 517th's DZ shortly after 1800.

While generally successful and assuring a constant flow of troops, equipment, and supplies into the airhead, glider operations suffered some losses from German antiglider obstacles but more from bad landings on either overcrowded or poorly located emergency LZs. The glider forces suffered more than 200 serious injuries and deaths due to crashes upon landing, including 16 glider pilots killed and 37 injured. After the operation, only 50 of the 400 gliders could be used again.

Casualties were an overall 2.5 percent of the 9,099 airborne troops who arrived in southern France on August 15. By that evening 90 percent of the troops and equipment were ready for operations. Like Sicily, the scattering of the paratroopers produced the unintended result of confusing the Germans, cutting their communications, disrupting command and control, and thus slowing their reaction to both the airborne and seaborne attacks. One unplanned benefit of this wide dispersion was that wherever the troopers landed they destroyed German wire communications. Soon the headquarters of the German LXII Corps at Draguignan, seven miles northwest of Le Muy, was isolated and unable to exercise command and control of the divisions defending the beach landing areas.

An aggressive Frederick quickly pushed his paratroopers out in all directions once they had assembled and gathered their supplies and equipment. The 551st had already headed northwest toward Draguignan where, together with the French Forces of the Interior, it captured part of the LXII Corps headquarters and the local German military governor, Maj. Gen. Ludwig Bieringer. In two days of heavy fighting the 1st Airborne Task Force had completed its initial mission and linked up with the 36th and 45th Infantry Divisions.

The 1st Airborne Task Force remained in action as the Seventh Army moved north up the Rhone River valley to link up with the Allied forces that had broken out of the Normandy beachhead in late July and August. Finally, late in November, Frederick's task force was dissolved. The American airborne units were transferred to Lt. Gen. Omar Bradley's 12th Army Group and would soon see more significant combat.

bottom left
Troopers of 517th Parachute Infantry, 1st Airborne Task Force, in Operation DRAGOON, southern France, in a roadside ditch after landing at La Motte, France, on August 15, 1944. *National Archives.*

CPL. PAUL B. HUFF:
FIRST PARATROOPER TO RECEIVE A MEDAL OF HONOR IN WORLD WAR II

Rank and organization: Corporal, U.S. Army, 509th Parachute Infantry Battalion. Place and date: Near Carano, Italy, 8 February 1944. Entered service at: Cleveland, Tenn. Birth: Cleveland, Tenn. G.O. No. 41, 26 May 1944.

Citation: For conspicuous gallantry and intrepidity at risk of life above and beyond the call of duty, in action on 8 February 1944, near Carano, Italy. Cpl. Huff volunteered to lead a 6-man patrol with the mission of determining the location and strength of an enemy unit which was delivering fire on the exposed right flank of his company. The terrain over which he had to travel consisted of exposed, rolling ground, affording the enemy excellent visibility. As the patrol advanced, its members were subjected to small arms and machinegun fire and a concentration of mortar fire, shells bursting within 5 to 10 yards of them and bullets striking the ground at their feet. Moving ahead of his patrol, Cpl. Huff drew fire from 3 enemy machineguns and a 20mm. weapon. Realizing the danger confronting his patrol, he advanced alone under deadly fire through a minefield and arrived at a point within 75 yards of the nearest machinegun position. Under direct fire from the rear machinegun, he crawled the remaining 75 yards to the closest emplacement, killed the crew with his submachine gun and destroyed the gun. During this act he fired from a kneeling position which drew fire from other positions, enabling him to estimate correctly the strength and location of the enemy. Still under concentrated fire, he returned to his patrol and led his men to safety. As a result of the information he gained, a patrol in strength sent out that afternoon, one group under the leadership of Cpl. Huff, succeeded in routing an enemy company of 125 men, killing 27 Germans and capturing 21 others, with a loss of only 3 patrol members. Cpl. Huff's intrepid leadership and daring combat skill reflect the finest traditions of the American infantryman.

A HARD AND BLOODY TESTING

From Operation TORCH in November 1942 through Operation DRAGOON in August 1944, the Allied operations in the Mediterranean were a long, hard, and bloody testing ground for the American concepts of airborne organization and warfare. Many highly trained and experienced men had been lost so that commanders and staffs could learn how to employ airborne forces in combat.

Problems with troop carriers were being solved slowly, as were myriad technical issues in the airborne units, especially as to how much and what kinds of supplies were needed to sustain them in isolated ground actions. Staffs had also learned to plan troop carrier operations and coordinate the air and naval support of them.

Some sound principles had emerged from some very negative experiences. Paratroopers had to be used in mass at the point of decisive effort and not in isolated, widely scattered groups for purely localized, tactical missions. The role of higher theater and army headquarters was clearly shown—to coordinate the use of airborne forces with ground, air, and naval forces to achieve the most effective operational and strategic employment. A great trial of what had been learned was in the offing in the peaceful French province of Normandy.

Chapter 4

Honing the Airborne Force: D-Day to MARKET-GARDEN, 1943–44

OPERATION OVERLORD: THE ALLIED INVASION OF FRANCE

GATHERING THE EAGLES

In November 1943, the Chief of Staff, Supreme Allied Commander (COSSAC), the agency planning the cross-Channel invasion of France in the spring of 1944 (code name Operation OVERLORD), asked the Mediterranean theater for a senior American airborne advisor. Brig. Gen. James M. Gavin, the assistant division commander of the 82d Airborne Division, was sent and was soon shaping the airborne component of the largest land, sea, and air invasion ever staged.

When Gavin arrived in London, he found Maj. Gen. William C. Lee's 101st Airborne Division, with Col. Robert F. Sink's attached 506th Parachute Infantry, already settled in the United Kingdom. Minus the 504th Regimental Combat Team (RCT), the 82d was on its way from Italy to Northern Ireland to refit and train. The 2d Airborne Infantry Brigade, with the 507th and 508th Parachute Infantry, was due from the United States in January as was Col. Howard R. Johnson's 501st Parachute Infantry. If the 504th returned in time, Gavin could plan on two airborne divisions, with three parachute regiments and three glider infantry regiments and supporting units, plus three additional separate parachute infantry regiments. Of the units, only the 504th, the 505th Parachute Infantry, and the 325th Glider Infantry had any combat experience; the rest were untested.

One problem that Gavin helped resolve was the lack of strength that had existed within the airborne division since 1942. Brig. Gen. Matthew B. Ridgway had pushed the War Department for an enlarged, more potent division after Sicily and Italy, but so far had achieved little. With the additional parachute infantry regiments in England, Gen. Dwight D. Eisenhower agreed to attach the 507th (temporarily in place of the 504th) and 508th to the 82d, and the 501st to the 101st. At the same time, the 101st Airborne's 401st Glider Infantry was split, with its 2d Battalion going to the 82d's 325th and the 1st Battalion to the 101st's 327th Glider Infantry. In giving each division a three-battalion glider infantry regiment, these changes meant that each airborne division now had four infantry regiments.

Early in February 1944, the airborne force faced a serious loss when Lee suffered a heart attack. This event incapacitated one of the key leaders who had shaped the development of the airborne force since its birth. By March 4, it was determined that Lee's medical condition would not permit his return to command, and he was ordered home. In his place, Brig. Gen. Maxwell D. Taylor, the 82d's Division Artillery Commander, was selected to head the 101st Airborne Division and promoted to major general.

The pace of preparation and training also picked up in February, March, and April. The 82d relocated in February from Northern Ireland to England to train with the 52d Troop Carrier Wing that would carry it to France on D-Day. The 101st in southwestern England teamed with the 50th and 53d Troop Carrier Wings. Ridgway also changed commanders of the 505th Parachute Infantry, bringing in then Lt. Col. (later Col.) William E. Ekman in late March. Training jumps, constant physical conditioning, and practice exercises kept the paratroopers' skills honed and worked out the kinks in the ground plans and coordination with the troop carrier units. Moreover, it was now clear that the 504th Parachute Infantry would not participate in the invasion. This deprived the 82d of a seasoned combat regiment for the biggest airborne operation to date.

INITIAL AIRBORNE PLANNING

From the onset, British and American airborne units were included in the invasion. Based on these estimates, the number of troop carrier units, aircraft, and gliders was determined. Information regarding any problems encountered in airborne operations in the Mediterranean was quickly fed into the planning process in London.

As in the Mediterranean, the initial assault landings needed to be carried out under the cover of darkness to evade the German air and ground defenses. While gliders were considered critical because of their carrying capacity, the British experience at Sicily showed that they were risky to use at night. Thus, the paratroopers would make the initial night assault.

The main problems in previous night drops were faulty navigation and poor formation flying, which required rigorous training to correct. After Sicily, the 82d Airborne Division had developed pathfinder teams to guide the C-47s to the drop zones (DZs) and had used them in the Salerno drops of September 1943. Specially trained pathfinder air crews would fly C-47s, outfitted with more precise navigational and airborne radar systems borrowed from the bomber offensive, to drop the pathfinder teams. Using new techniques for ground marking and an improved Rebecca-Eureka system,

pathfinders would go in ahead of the main force and guide the troop carrier serials to their DZs and landing zones (LZs).

The C-47s would use their standard V of Vs formation in which each serial of 36 to 45 aircraft from a troop carrier group would usually carry about one battalion to a specific DZ. In each V, two aircraft were echeloned off the leader, and two trailing Vs were echeloned off the leading trio to form the V of Vs. Nine aircraft from one troop carrier squadron made up a flight that usually carried one company. Each following flight was echeloned higher to provide safety for the jumping paratroopers. The objective was to get as many paratroopers as possible on each designated DZ.

As for gliders, the American Waco CG-4A was still the workhorse, but the British had developed two other gliders that far exceeded the 3,750-pound cargo capacity of the Waco. The plywood Horsa could lift 6,700 pounds, including a 75-mm pack howitzer and a Jeep to tow it. The Horsa had some technical problems, but it had performed fairly well in Sicily and could be towed by a C-47. The Hamilcar glider could carry 17,500 pounds and even the small British Tetrarch tank, but few existed and it required a four-engine bomber as its tow aircraft.

In October 1943, Maj. Gen. Lewis H. Brereton assumed command of the new Ninth U.S. Air Force set up in England to provide tactical air support for the invasion. Under him came the IX Troop Carrier Command, led by Brig. Gen. Paul L. Williams, who had directed the troop carriers in most airborne operations in the Mediterranean. The final air piece came in December when the Allied Expeditionary Air Forces (AEAF) under Royal Air Force Air Marshal Trafford Leigh-Mallory, which controlled tactical air, took over firm operational control of Ninth Air Force. Of the

Glider Assembly, combat art by Olin Dows. Assembly of Waco CG-4 gliders for Operation NEPTUNE. The gliders were shipped to England by ocean transport and assembled for operations. Each crated glider weighed 20,000 pounds. *Army Art Collection, U.S. Army Center of Military History.*

many skeptics of the use of airborne forces in the invasion, Leigh-Mallory might well have been one of the most outspoken.

When Gavin arrived at COSSAC, he found that plans fully incorporated an airborne assault to pave the way for Allied landings on the French Normandy coast between the Vire and Orne rivers. Paratroopers and a small glider-borne force of the 82d and 101st Airborne Divisions would land from Bayeux to Caen where the British 6th Airborne Division would drop. A second lift of gliders would follow.

The Americans would block German reinforcements from the beaches and attack the coastal defenses from the rear. The terrain in the Bayeux-Caen corridor, however, was well-suited for German tanks. Lacking antitank weapons, the lightly armed airborne units would find it hard to defend themselves. Recalling his experience in Sicily, Gavin "took rather a dim view of the entire plan."

IKE AND MONTY CHANGE THE PLANS

Much of the initial planning changed when Eisenhower became Supreme Allied Commander in early December 1943, and the British appointed Lt. Gen. Bernard Law Montgomery to command the

British 21st Army Group with responsibility for planning the ground campaign. Both considered the existing plans too weak and limited. The plans for the landings themselves (now code-named Operation NEPTUNE as part of the overall Operation OVERLORD) soon changed to a larger attack, with three British divisions in the east and three U.S. divisions in the west.

Lt. Gen. Omar N. Bradley, now commander of First U.S. Army, the American ground component for Operations OVERLORD and NEPTUNE, added a third U.S. division farther to the west for an early seizure of the port of Cherbourg. This division would land on beaches at the base of the Cotentin Peninsula, later named Utah Beach. Here some natural obstacles presented significant concerns.

Germans could and did flood the swampy areas immediately behind the beaches to limit egress to four causeways. To the west and south of the landing beaches, the valleys of the Douve, Merderet, and Vire rivers presented potential problems. Just north of Carentan on the Douve, the La Barquette lock controlled the flow of tidal waters back into the Douve and Merderet rivers that ran west and north from the peninsula. Opening the locks could flood large areas of

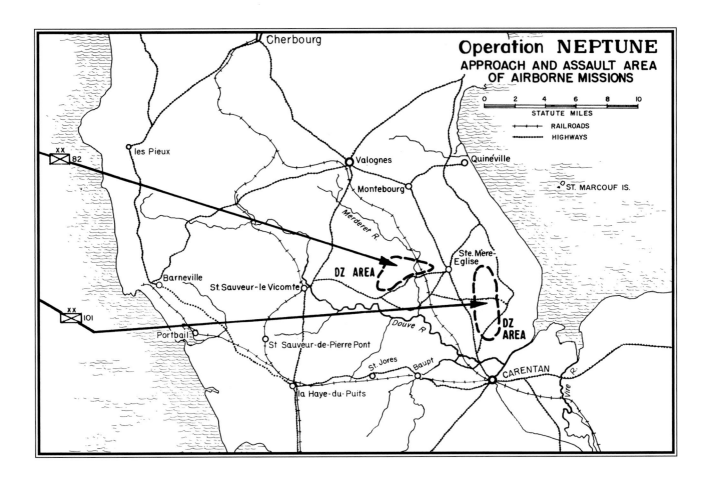

Map courtesy:
U.S. Air Force.

both river valleys and would add another formidable obstacle to any invading force. The Douve and Vire rivers at the base of the peninsula also separated Utah Beach from the beaches to the east. Major highway and rail routes entering the peninsula funneled through the town of Carentan. If the Germans held it, they could block any linkup between the beaches.

Airborne troops offered the solution to these concerns. They could take and hold the causeways and the La Barquette lock, and clear the way across the Douve for the landing force to take Carentan and connect with the V Corps landing on Omaha Beach to the east. The areas behind Utah Beach and on the peninsula generally consisted of small fields with meadows, streams, and hedgerows of tangled undergrowth, trees, and scrubs that offered suitable terrain for airborne landings but restricted grounds for gliders. More importantly, these areas were not good for German armor. The new plan meant at least one American airborne division would take part in Operation NEPTUNE.

In March 1944, Montgomery and Bradley won Supreme Headquarters Allied Expeditionary Forces' (SHAEF's) approval for landing a second U.S. airborne division on the western side of Cotentin Peninsula near St.

Sauveur-le-Vicomte to cut the western access to Cherbourg. This would prevent the garrison's reinforcement while hastening the port's fall and opening as an Allied supply port. Because the landing area was 20 miles from Utah Beach, the division landing there might be cut off for several days until the invasion forces could reach it. Thus, the battle-hardened 82d received this more difficult mission and the 101st Airborne Division was assigned the Utah Beach mission.

Troop carrier aircraft and crews, and the gliders and glider pilots, were major limiting factors in planning for any airborne assault. The Army Air Forces (AAF) solved the troop carrier problem by building up the groups in the United Kingdom from 52 to 64 aircraft each and adding nine more for reserve. By late May 1944, 986 C-47s in 13-1/2 U.S. troop carrier groups were ready for the invasion, along with 1,100 crews.

Gliders were earmarked for a prominent role in the D-Day airborne landings, but their actual tactical employment was a matter of contentious debate for several months. The AAF pushed hard to train and move glider pilots in sufficient numbers to the theater and to ship and assemble enough gliders to

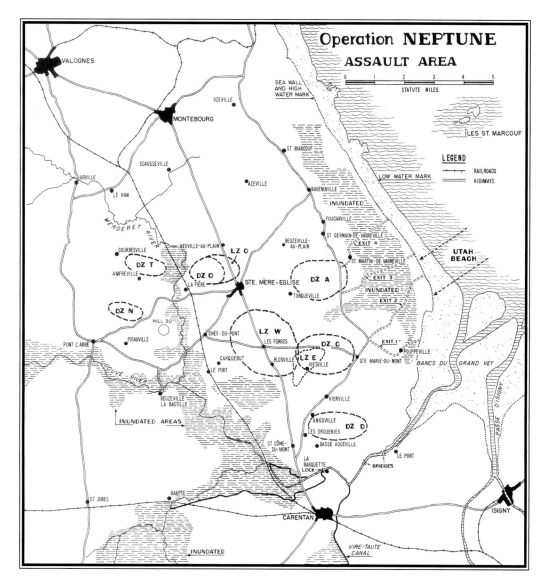

Map courtesy:
U.S. Air Force.

support both the training and operational requirements. By late May, IX Troop Carrier Command had 1,118 Wacos and 301 Horsas ready to go with enough pilots for 951 gliders, which exceeded demands.

During the late spring of 1944, the Germans suddenly stiffened their antiairborne defenses in Cotentin and Normandy. Allied intelligence detected extensive new antilanding obstacles in scattered pockets, along with new German divisions, which presented real threats to the planned airborne landings. Unfortunately, what went undetected was that the Germans had also flooded large areas of the Douve and Merderet river valleys, which would come as a nasty shock to many paratroopers on D-Day.

The minutely crafted plans now had to be changed. On May 27 a new airborne plan shifted the 82d about 10 miles to the east near Ste. Mère Église where it would cover the 101st's right flank. Maj. Gen. J. Lawton Collins, com-

mander of U.S. VII Corps that was landing on Utah Beach, recommended that the 82d should land west of the Merderet River to establish bridgeheads for his Utah Beach landing force. This change was made, but still kept the two airborne divisions' DZs and LZs far enough apart to avoid confusion. Only a limited number of good DZs existed west of the Merderet for an entire division, so two regiments would jump west of the river and one to the east near Ste. Mère Église.

The quiet, little-known Normandy town of Ste. Mère Église was a critical road junction on the main north-south highway in the eastern Cotentin Peninsula. A forceful German reaction was expected here, so the 505th Parachute Infantry, the 82d's and the airborne's most experienced unit, drew this assignment along with the job of seizing the bridges across the Merderet near La Fière and Chef-du-Pont. The 507th would jump to the west of the Merderet around Amfreville

(DZ T) and establish a defensive sector covering La Fière in preparation for moving west, while the 508th would land to the south of it in the Pont L'Abbe-Picauville area (DZ N) to establish a defense to the west of the Chef-du-Pont bridge. Gliders would bring in reinforcements, artillery and antitank guns, ammunition, medical personnel, and supplies in the predawn hours of D-Day morning, with a follow-on wave again toward evening.

For the 101st Airborne Division, the objectives remained the four causeways exiting from Utah Beach and the critical bridges over the Douve and Vire rivers north and east of Caren-tan. With Ste. Mère Église turned over to the 82d, the 1st and 2d Battalions, 501st Parachute Infantry, were now available for use in the criti-cal southern sector at DZ D and with the 3d Battalion to reinforce the 506th in the center (DZ C). The 502d was assigned to DZ A in the north near St. Martin-de-Varreville to take out a coastal battery and to control the northern two beach exits. Landing at DZ C in the center with the southern two exits as their objectives

would be the 506th, less its 3d Battalion. That battalion would join a company of the 326th Airborne Engineer Battalion headed to DZ D to take the bridges in the south and the important La Barquette lock.

These shifts led Leigh-Mallory, commanding the AEAF, to ask Eisenhower to cancel the entire U.S. airborne operation, which he now feared would be an utter disaster. After carefully weighing Leigh-Mallory's concerns, Eisenhower decided to go ahead with the airborne missions. He saw them as essential to success at Utah, and success at Utah was essential to the success of Operations NEPTUNE and OVERLORD. The paratroopers would jump as planned.

OPERATION NEPTUNE

D-DAY, JUNE 6, 1944: THE PATHFINDERS
Following a one-day postponement due to weather, after dark on June 5, 1944, D–1, the first of 20 C-47s of the IX Troop Carrier Command's pathfinder force lifted off with

top left
These heavily loaded men of the 101st are receiving their final instructions prior to boarding their C-47 for the drop over Normandy. A wartime censor tried to white out all distinguish-ing insignia and marking on the aircraft. *National Archives.*

top right
Paratroopers of the 508th Parachute Infantry, 82d Airborne Division, at Saltby, England, chuting up and checking their equipment on June 5, 1944, before boarding C-47s for the flight to Normandy for their combat jump on D-Day. Carrying their parachute, weapons, extra ammunition, grenades, and rations, the men often ended up hauling more than 100 pounds of additional weight and had to be pushed aboard the aircraft. *National Archives.*

bottom
A "stick" (planeload) of paratroopers of the 101st Airborne Division over the English Channel en route to their drop on D-Day. *National Archives.*

Gen. Dwight D. Eisenhower speaks with 1st Lt. Wallace Strobel and members of Company E, 502d Parachute Infantry, 101st Airborne Division, at Greenham Common airfield on the evening of June 5, 1944, before they board their C-47 for the flight to Normandy. *National Archives.*

the pathfinders of the 101st and 82d Airborne Divisions. They formed a small vanguard of a stream of 821 C-47s carrying 13,348 paratroopers and eventually stretching for 300 miles. The largest airborne assault in history was under way as a prelude to the largest amphibious operation ever.

The pathfinder aircraft took the same course that the C-47s carrying the 82d and 101st would soon follow. They carefully skirted the invasion fleet to the west. Over the Channel west of the Cotentin Peninsula, they separated into two streams, with the aircraft carrying the 82d heading in from the northwest while those of the 101st angled farther to the south and then approached from the west. Poor weather over the Channel, heavy clouds over the peninsula, and German antiaircraft fire soon disrupted the formations.

Some of the pathfinder aircraft were thrown off course despite their more sophisticated navigation equipment and radar devices. They dropped the pathfinder teams an hour ahead of the main serials carrying the units targeted for specific DZs, with the 101st in the lead scheduled to jump at 0020 and the 82d at 0121. Capt. Frank L. Lillyman, the 101st's lead pathfinder, stepped out of his C-47 at 0015, landed near St. Germain-de-Varreville, and became the first American paratrooper to set foot on French soil in World War II. Once on the ground, the pathfinders located their DZs as best they could and set up their equipment to guide in the main force. Although the pathfinders were not nearly as effective as hoped, most

of them at least were somewhat close to their designated DZs and carried out part of their difficult assignments.

101ST AIRBORNE DIVISION

Sweeping in low over the Cotentin Peninsula, the troop carriers were greeted with the same heavy clouds and German ground fire that had thrown the pathfinders off course. At H-hour minus 5, approximately 0120-0130, the first of the 101st Airborne Division's 6,750 paratroopers jumped from the leading serials of 432 transports of the 50th and 53d Troop Carrier Wings. As they exited their aircraft, all the paratroopers yelled "Bill Lee!" in honor of their recent commander who jumped with them in spirit only. Less than two years earlier, just days after the 101st's activation, Lee had told his division that it "has no history, but it has a rendezvous with destiny." That rendezvous had now begun.

A large number of paratroopers, perhaps 1,500 or more, jumped well outside of their intended areas and were soon killed, wounded, missing, or captured. However, 70 percent of the lift was dropped in an eight-square-mile area from Ravenoville in the north to Carentan and from the Carentan-Cherbourg railroad line east to Utah Beach. In addition to the many troopers soon missing and lost to the battle, many were injured seriously on landing, including Col. George Van Horn Moseley, Jr., commanding the 502d Parachute Infantry, who suffered a severely broken leg and was soon replaced in command.

Such personnel losses were serious, but they did not affect mission completion nearly as much as the many 101st units that landed nowhere near their DZs or objectives. The 2d Battalion, 502d Parachute Infantry, was intended for DZ A in the north to take out the coastal battery at St. Martin-de-Varreville. Unfortunately, it landed far to the south with 29 sticks nicely clustered on or near DZ C west of Ste. Marie-du-Mont, had difficulty in assembling, and took little part in the D-Day fighting as an organized unit. In such instances, other commanders swiftly took over critical missions when they realized that the assigned unit was not there. Upon landing, Lt. Col. Robert G. Cole, commanding the 502d's 3d Battalion that was to back up the 2d Battalion, realized he and his battalion were near Ste. Mère Église, well off their DZ and planned objective. He collected his troopers and others from the 506th as well as the 82d's 505th and 508th and headed east where he found the St. Martin battery destroyed by bombing and unoccupied. He pushed directly on to take control of the western ends of the northernmost causeways, trapping the fleeing German defenders and linking up with the 4th Infantry Division at about 1300.

The 1st and 2d Battalions of Sink's 506th Parachute Infantry were to occupy the two southern causeways exiting the beach. Twenty-two sticks of the 1st Battalion at least landed in the vicinity of DZ C and Ste. Marie-du-Mont just to the west of the objectives. The 2d Battalion, which was to take the causeways, landed widely dispersed around Ste. Mère Église and along the flooded areas behind the beaches as far north as Ravenoville in the area of the 502d. Although badly scattered, the leaders assembled whoever they found as quickly as possible and moved out for their objectives.

As with Cole in the north, other commanders in the south soon plugged the breach. Lt. Col. Julian Ewell's 3d Battalion, 501st, landed widely scattered but near DZ C as the division reserve. Ewell collected as many men as he could. Taylor, the division commander; Brig. Gen. Anthony C. McAuliffe, the division artillery commander; and other members of the division staff landed close to DZ C, gathered up a small group with more officers than men, and pushed toward Ste. Marie-du-Mont. Taylor later quipped about his officer-heavy team that "Never were so few led by so many." Realizing that his small force could do little to secure what the missing units were to do, Taylor directed Ewell to take Pouppeville and the critical southernmost exit. The 101st and the 4th Infantry divisions linked up there at about noon on D-Day, assuring the survival and success of the 101st's airborne bridgehead.

In the critical southern sector, the 101st had to establish a strong defensive arc to protect the landing beaches from attack. It had to take and hold or destroy critical bridges over the Douve north of Carentan and at Le Port over the Vire River as well as the La Barquette lock. The first day's successes were mixed at best.

Off Normandy Beach, combat art by Gary Sheahan. Tracer rounds from the invasion fleet create multicolored arcs across the predawn sky. *Army Art Collection, U.S. Army Center of Military History.*

Lt. Col. Robert G. Cole's leadership in the confusion on the morning of June 6 secured the two northernmost exits from Utah Beach. Then, on June 10–11, he led his battalion in a charge that finally took the critical causeway and bridges north of Carentan. On September 18, he was killed by a sniper in Holland. Cole was the first member of the 101st Airborne Division to receive a Medal of Honor in World War II. *National Archives.*

Much of the 3d Battalion, 506th, landed in a prepared German defense at DZ D near Angoville-au-Plain and suffered heavily. After landing, Capt. Charles G. Shettle immediately moved out, took the two wooden bridges at Le Port, and established a small bridgehead. Strong German forces soon pushed his little group back across the Vire where he dug in to anchor the 101st's left flank.

Except for Johnson and his stick, the 1st and 2d Battalions, 501st, were dropped too soon and scattered widely, many landing in the swampy areas of the Douve River. Other sticks landed in enemy-held territory well west and south of Carentan. Johnson landed almost on his DZ, scraped together what he could of his two battalions, pushed to the La Barquette lock, and took it in a rush. His men fought hard to hold on to the locks over the next several days against attacks from both the front and rear, where the German 6th Parachute Regiment had infiltrated. The 2d Battalion under Col. Robert Ballard got into a major fight at Les Droueries and St. Côme-du-Mont and failed to carry out its mission of taking and blowing up the road bridges over the Douve and Madeleine rivers. By the close of D-Day, only the 501st's mission of taking the locks had been accomplished.

As in Sicily, the little groups of paratroopers (LGOPs) from both divisions again played an important part in baffling and disorienting the German defenders and cutting their communications. Pre-invasion training had focused on grouping scattered soldiers of different units into effective combat formations rather than immediately taking on any Germans they ran into. Paratroopers were given the "cricket clicker" as a signaling device to recognize each other and speed assembly. While the paratroopers still took on the enemy where they found them, regrouping efforts were much more effective than on Sicily. Widely scattered over the Cotentin Peninsula and to the south, the paratroopers initially confused the local defenders and higher German commanders as to their number and intentions.

Some paratroopers remained isolated well behind German lines for days after they landed, fighting and surviving as best they could. In just trying to assemble and get moving after hitting the ground, many paratroopers and their commanders found themselves disoriented and confused as they confronted the impenetrable hedgerows of the *bocage* country and the extensive flooding. Ably assisted by the Germans, the terrain of Normandy and the flooding seriously affected the speed with which American paratroopers and units coalesced and got into the fight.

The arrival of the 4th Infantry Division allowed Taylor to move elements of the 502d and 506th to the southern sector to reinforce the 501st. Also, as soon as they arrived by sea, Taylor pushed the fresh battalions of the 327th and 401st Glider Infantry to the Carentan front. On

June 8, a concerted attack of the 501st, 506th, and 401st took St. Côme-du-Mont and pushed down the road and causeway toward Carentan.

Now it was the job of Cole's 3d Battalion, 502d, to take the causeway and Bridge Nos. 3 and 4 and clear the rest of the way into Carentan. After two days of hard fighting against stiff German resistance on June 10–11, he did this in a spectacular fashion. Pinned down just across Bridge No. 4 by heavy German fire on June 11, Cole led a desperate bayonet charge across an open field that cracked the enemy defense. For his "cool fearlessness, personal bravery, and outstanding leadership" in this action, Cole received the first Medal of Honor awarded to the 101st Airborne Division. Tragically, Cole would never wear the nation's highest award for bravery because he was killed by a sniper near Best, Holland, on September 18; his award was authorized on October 4.

In general, the 101st fared better than the 82d on its drops, timing, and completing its assigned missions. The 101st cleared the way for the 4th Infantry Division's inland movement after it landed on Utah Beach. That was the 101st's basic mission in the first place, and it was completed. Once relieved by the 4th Infantry Division and reinforced with its seaborne elements, the 101st collected itself and put its full weight into the fight on the southern flank. Taking Carentan on June 12, the 101st linked up with V Corps on June 13 and defeated a Ger-

man counterattack the same day. The 101st's last major action was on June 16–17, after which it was in reserve until relieved on July 10. It then returned to the United Kingdom to rest and refit. During the fighting in June, the division had lost 4,670 men killed, wounded, missing, captured, and injured. The men of the 101st had purchased a large piece of destiny with their blood.

82D AIRBORNE DIVISION

Dense clouds over the peninsula and now-alerted German defenders forced the troop carriers into inaccurate drops for many of the 82d's 6,350 paratroopers who jumped that night. With their missions and DZs located west of the Merderet, the 507th and 508th Parachute Infantry needed on-time and accurate drops. They arrived as scheduled between 0230 and 0300, but their drops were not accurate. Many of their sticks landed east of the Merderet, some as far east as the 101st's drop areas where they quickly enlisted with the Screaming Eagles to fight on. Numerous troopers from both regiments, along with most of their door bundles and automatic weapons, bazookas, radios, and equipment, were lost in the flooded Merderet, which was 1,000 feet wide at places.

Although Ridgway decided just before D-Day to jump with the 505th that morning rather than come in with the seaborne elements, Gavin retained tactical command of all the regiments on the ground as originally planned.

top left
Paratroopers of the 101st Airborne Division posing with a "liberated" Nazi flag, German helmet, and sword in a French village shortly after D-Day.
National Archives.

top right
La Fière Causeway, combat art by Bernard Arnest. Capture of the causeway and bridge over the Merderet River were essential elements of the 82d Airborne's success in Normandy.
Army Art Collection, U.S. Army Center of Military History.

top right
PFC Charles N. DeGlopper, Company C, 325th Glider Infantry, 82d Airborne Division, received the Medal of Honor posthumously for his actions at La Fière bridgehead over the Merderet River on June 9, 1944. *National Archives.*

bottom right
The arrival of the 325th Glider Infantry on June 7, 1944, allowed Brig. Gen. James M. Gavin to attack to take the La Fière and Chef-du-Pont bridges and causeways across the Merderet River and push to the west. Here Col. Harry I. Lewis, the 325th's commander (second from right, bending over), looks at a map with a lieutenant and his troopers at an 81-mm mortar position. *National Archives.*

He landed with the badly intermingled and widely scattered 507th and 508th regiments in the swamps northeast of Amfreville and west of the Merderet. Col. Roy E. Lindquist, commander of the 508th, landed in the same general area as Gavin. Both of them collected as many men and as much equipment as possible before splashing across the swamps to the prominent railroad embankment cutting through the flooded area. They and many other paratroopers followed the rail line south over the river toward the fighting already in progress around La Fière and Chef-du-Pont, key objectives for the 82d.

Unlike the rest of the division, Ekman's 505th Parachute Infantry landed pretty much on its DZ near Ste. Mère Église. Lt. Col. Edward Krause's 3d Battalion, 505th, quickly made Ste. Mère Église the first French town to be liberated. He was soon joined by Ridgway, Ekman, and the 2d Battalion of Lt. Col. Benjamin H. Vandervoort, who had badly fractured his ankle on landing. But just as quickly, they came under strong German attacks from the north and south. 1st Lt. Turner B. Turnbull's 3d Platoon, Company D, with 42 men, was sent up the road to Neuville-au-Plain to hold a German attack from Montebourg in the north while the rest of the men defended against a more dangerous attack from the south. Turnbull's platoon held for eight hours against a vastly superior German force, but emerged from the fight with only 16 men. The time they bought allowed Ekman to repulse the southern attack.

The widely scattered drops, especially of the 507th and 508th, left pockets of paratroopers isolated on the western side of the flooded Merderet River. Col. George V. Millett, Jr., commander of the 507th Parachute Infantry, was supposed to land at DZ N near Picauville but ended up surrounded at Amfreville near

DZ T in the north. Lt. Col. Robert J. Timmes, commanding the 507th's 2d Battalion, had another group to the east of Millett that was pinned against the river. The Germans captured Millett as he tried to break out on June 8, but Timmes held out until relieved by the 325th Glider Infantry on June 9.

Lt. Col. Thomas J. B. Shanley, commanding 2d Battalion, 508th, landed around DZ N and collected one of the larger groups to the west of the river near Picauville. He quickly gave up any thought of trying to push to the bridge at Pont L'Abbe and destroy it due to the strong German defenses in the area. He pulled back to Hill 30, the regiment's assembly area overlooking Chef-du-Pont, and organized an all-around defense. Although under heavy enemy pressure and shelling, he and his men held on until the 90th Infantry Division relieved them on June 10 after La Fière was finally taken.

Elements of all three regiments were soon involved in long, tough, seesaw fights along the Merderet River line for the bridges at La Fière and Chef-du-Pont. Gavin set up his headquarters at Chef-du-Pont but moved back and forth between the two bridges directing the fight. The 82d was especially hard-pressed because it faced German armored vehicles. The first glider lift was to bring in the antitank batteries of the 80th Airborne Antiaircraft Artillery Battalion, but some of the badly needed 57-mm antitank guns were lost or heavily damaged on landing.

With the 325th Glider Infantry's arrival on the Merderet, Gavin could plan a new attack on the La Fière bridge and causeway. Using the 325th and battalions of the 507th and 508th, Gavin finally gained the west bank of the Merderet on June 9, freeing Timmes's group and pushing the Germans back to the west. During the fighting in the La Fière bridgehead, the platoon of PFC Charles N. DeGlopper, Company C, 1st Battalion, 325th Glider Infantry, was cut off and came under heavy German attack. An automatic rifleman, DeGlopper moved into an exposed position on the road to cover his platoon with more accurate fire. He was soon wounded multiple times but continued firing, on bended knees, until killed. The heavy toll that he exacted on the Germans helped his unit escape. For his gallant sacrifice, DeGlopper became the first paratrooper of the 82d Airborne Division to receive a Medal of Honor in World War II.

Like the 101st, the 82d Airborne Division was soon reinforced with its ground echelon. An advanced element was a special armored task force under Col. Edson Raff, formerly of the 509th Parachute Infantry Battalion, and a renowned fighter. Within days, Ridgway gave Raff command of Millett's 507th Parachute Infantry. In the critical days of June, the paratroopers could not be spared as VII Corps built up its strength and cut the Cotentin Peninsula in half. The 82d drove west, crossed the Douve River, and liberated the town of St. Sauveur-le-Vicomte on June 16, routing the German defenders. Ironically, St. Sauveur-le-Vicomte had been one of the 82d's original objectives.

Only on July 8, after 33 days in combat without relief, was the division pulled out of the line. The 82d paid a high price in those 33 days. On D-Day alone it had suffered 182 killed, 1,068 wounded, and 501 missing and presumed dead or captured. Later wartime accounting put the totals for the 33 days at 1,142 killed or died of wounds, 3,927 wounded (1,554 of whom returned to duty), 1,206 injured (only 502 returned to duty), and 661 missing and prisoners of war (POWs)—6,936 officers and men.

GLIDERS AT NORMANDY
Gliders played a crucial role in the airborne landings, with six missions and 525 gliders scheduled to fly on D-Day and D+1. The C-47s towing the gliders came in from the east over Utah Beach, tracking along the exit routes of the parachute missions and returning the same way after their gliders were released. Each division had two glider missions on D-Day to provide reinforcements as well as artillery, antitank guns, ammunition, equipment, and supplies. In the predawn missions that landed about 0400, 52 Wacos each were intended for the 82d and 101st, but some became lost en route and others fell to enemy ground fire.

Even when the LZs were marked, many glider pilots failed to locate them and landed where they could, frequently crashing in the small meadows and into the high trees and hedgerows surrounding them. Brig. Gen. Don F. Pratt, the 101st's Assistant Division Commander, was killed when his Waco crashed into a hedgerow after landing at LZ E, two miles west of Ste. Marie-du-Mont. Despite the problems, the gliders brought in men, supplies, and ammunition along with a number of Jeeps and 57-mm antitank guns.

D-Day's evening missions featured the larger Horsa gliders and Wacos. The 101st's mission carried elements of the 327th Glider Infantry in

top left

At an air base in England on June 7, 1944, men of the 325th Glider Infantry sit in their Waco CG-4A awaiting takeoff to reinforce the paratroopers of the 82d Airborne Division who landed on D-Day. *National Archives.*

top right

C-47s release their gliders above the hedgerow country of Normandy. A number of gliders are already on the ground below from previous missions. *National Archives.*

32 Horsas. Two missions of 76 and 100 gliders went to the hard-pressed 82d, including 140 Horsas. These missions brought in the 319th and 320th Glider Field Artillery Battalions with more than 1,100 men as well as 37 guns, 123 vehicles, ammunition, and supplies. German ground fire was much heavier now, while some enemy troops even held part of LZ W and others had it under heavy fire. Enemy fire killed and wounded many on board during the descent and landing. Often with wounded or dead pilots, many gliders crashed on landing, killing and injuring occupants and damaging cargo.

Two additional glider missions were flown for the beleaguered 82d on the morning of D+1. The first mission landed 100 gliders (18 Horsas and 82 Wacos) with 1,300 men, 57 artillery pieces, and 164 vehicles. In the second mission, 30 Horsas and 70 Wacos carried elements of the 325th and 401st Glider Infantry with 2,200 men, 20 guns, 75 vehicles, equipment, and supplies to the 82d. Again, ground fire and many crashes due to conditions on the landing fields caused losses of gliders and their cargos. However, the gliders provided critical reinforcements.

In general, the glider missions had gone better than expected. The glider units had proven they could bring in men, artillery, vehicles, and supplies with acceptable losses, under enemy fire, and in bad weather and night conditions. Terrain and weather caused much of the trouble and damage encountered in the Normandy

glider operations. The heavier Horsas had fared far worse than the lighter Wacos, which stood up pretty well in the crashes. The Horsas, which often broke up on crashing, largely accounted for the landing casualties, with an estimated 186 on D-Day and 154 on D+1 versus 123 Wacos in all six lifts (excluding glider pilots). Out of a total of more than 3,900 troops carried, some 463 were killed, wounded, or injured. In the end, 97 percent of the American gliders themselves were written off as too heavily damaged or simply nonrecoverable. Despite the terrible conditions and fierce German fire, the glider pilots had done an outstanding job, but 57 of the 1,032 who were dispatched were listed as dead, wounded, or missing afterward.

NEW ORGANIZATIONS, NEW MISSIONS

By mid-July 1944, both airborne divisions had returned to their bases in England to rest and refit. Reinforcements came in from the Airborne Center at Camp Mackall to replace those who had been lost in Normandy. Rebuilding the exhausted units was a difficult task, but both divisions worked hard to return to full combat-ready status as soon as possible. After Operation NEPTUNE, Col. Reuben H. Tucker's 504th Parachute Infantry returned to the 82d refreshed and ready for action. Maj. Gen. William Miley's 17th Airborne Division was due to land in England in August, bringing the American airborne force to three full divisions. Now commanded by Raff, the 507th was reassigned from the 82d to the incoming 17th to give it two parachute infantry regiments. As

82d Airborne Division paratroopers get a last-minute inspection by their jumpmaster before boarding a C-47 of the 36th Troop Carrier Squadron, 316th Troop Carrier Group, 52d Troop Carrier Wing at Cottesmore airfield, England, for the Allied airborne invasion of Holland, Operation MARKET, September 17, 1944. *XVIII Airborne Corps Historian from National Archives.*

the summer wore on, new airborne missions were already on the planning boards, along with significant changes in airborne organization and tactics.

FIRST ALLIED AIRBORNE ARMY

In June, Eisenhower approved a British proposal that predated the invasion to establish a unified command for Allied airborne forces. This included the IX Troop Carrier Command, which in the past was under Eisenhower's command because it belonged to the AAF. Lt. Gen. Lewis H. Brereton, commander of Ninth U.S. Air Force, was named commander of the new, as yet unnamed, organization on July 16 and British Lt. Gen. F. A. M. Browning became his deputy commander on August 4. It was not until August 16 that the new command was officially designated as the First Allied Airborne Army (FAAA) that would report directly to Eisenhower and SHAEF. For the first time in the war, all elements of the Allied airborne force—U.S., British, French, and Polish paratroopers and U.S. and British troop carriers—were under a single command.

Brereton was an experienced flyer and commander. His responsibility was now to plan future airborne operations with SHAEF and the Allied army groups, train the airborne and troop carrier forces, and control any operations until airborne and ground forces linked up.

Command of the different Allied contingents comprising FAAA was exercised through the British 1 Airborne Corps under Browning and the new U.S. XVIII Airborne Corps established

on August 25, 1944, under Ridgway. Despite Leigh-Mallory's protests, SHAEF moved the IX Troop Carrier Command under Maj. Gen. Paul L. Williams, who was now back from Operation DRAGOON, from AEAF and also gave Brereton some control of the Royal Air Force's troop carrier groups.

The new XVIII Airborne Corps for the first time unified American airborne divisions under a single commander and staff, but did not include the AAF's IX Troop Carrier Command. With Ridgway's move to the corps, Gavin was promoted to command of the 82d Airborne Division and to major general in October. At 37 years old, Gavin became the youngest division commander in the U.S. Army in World War II and the youngest since the Civil War. He had earned his promotion the hard way in Sicily, Italy, and Normandy.

After Normandy, Gen. George Marshall and Gen. Henry H. Arnold, commanding general of the AAF, in Washington had urged Eisenhower to use the new airborne weapon in his hands with daring and imagination. In July Eisenhower challenged SHAEF and new airborne command planners to be bold in planning future operations for the Allied airborne divisions that now constituted his strategic reserve. Over the summer, 17 potential airborne operations were proposed but none was ever executed. Several factors caused this. The Allied ground operations, after the breakout from the Normandy lodgment in July and August, had driven far and fast, rendering some of the operations unnecessary. Although both the 82d

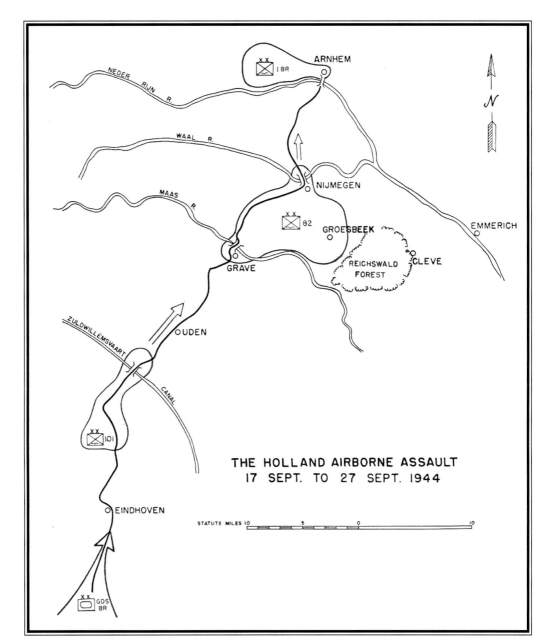

A sketch map of the drop zones and area for Operation MARKET, September 17, 1944. *XVIII Airborne Corps Historian.*

and 101st Airborne Divisions were still recuperating from Normandy, by August they were approaching operational readiness. The 17th Airborne Division was not considered ready or listed as available for operational use without additional training after it arrived in England. Moreover, Operation ANVIL (DRAGOON) in southern France siphoned away troop carrier and glider assets until the end of August. Then, as the Allied ground armies stretched their supply lines, the FAAA's troop carriers were heavily relied on to ferry gasoline, ammunition, food, and troops to the forward units. Nonetheless, Eisenhower and SHAEF were anxious to use the airborne weapon again soon.

INTO HOLLAND: OPERATION MARKET-GARDEN

PLANNING
In early September, FAAA began working on a new mission in response to Field Marshal Montgomery's ambitious plan to seize the bridge across the Neder Rijn (Lower Rhine) River at Arnhem, Holland, using the British 1st Airborne Division and the Polish Parachute Brigade. Operation COMET was ready to go on September 8, but Montgomery postponed it due to operational concerns and stiffening German resistance. A review of the airborne plans showed Operation COMET to be a risky proposition—the Nijmegen-Arnhem area was more than 50 miles behind German lines with seven easily defended rivers or canals separating the paratroopers from friendly ground forces.

In a September 10 meeting in Brussels with Montgomery, Eisenhower approved an expanded Operation COMET. FAAA would place an airborne carpet on the road to Arnhem for the British 30 Corps, British Second Army, to drive north along one road from Eindhoven to Nijmegen to Arnhem and on to the Zuider Zee in the ground phase, Operation GARDEN. Code-named MARKET, the airborne phase called for the British 1st Airborne Division and Polish Parachute Brigade to take Arnhem and the bridge over the Neder Rijn; the 82d Airborne Division to take and hold the bridges in the Nijmegen-Grave area; and the 101st to seize areas along the road and waterways from the south of Grave to Eindhoven. The 101st would thus be closest to the approaching British ground force. With three full airborne divisions plus the Polish Brigade, MARKET now became the largest airborne operation in history, exceeding Normandy.

Montgomery set September 17 as the date for what now became Operation MARKET-GARDEN—a sophisticated, complex, and inherently risky air and ground operation. If successful, Operation MARKET-GARDEN could cut off the Germans in western Holland, make an end run around the German Westwall (Siegfried Line), and put Montgomery's 21st Army Group in position to strike deep into the North Ger-

man Plain and take the Ruhr industrial area. Montgomery reasoned that this could end the war. Eisenhower agreed; it was the daring plan he had been seeking.

Brereton and his commanders had seven days for the detailed planning. He decided that Browning would command the mission despite the much larger American contribution, and the 82d and 101st would come under him. Ridgway did not much like this, but he and his XVIII Airborne Corps headquarters were relegated to the role of observers and coordinating supplies for the two American divisions. Browning would command from an advanced command post with Gavin and the 82d Airborne Division.

TACTICAL CHANGES

Brereton also decided a major change in tactics—the mission would be flown during the day. The overwhelming Allied air superiority over the front was a driving factor allowing this change. However, this decision was also based on an analysis of the time of the month for D-Day (no moon), the lack of coverage by long-range navigational aids, and intelligence estimates on potential German fighter opposition and antiaircraft defenses in the landing areas. Airborne operations in southern France had been recently completed successfully during daylight.

At Cottesmore airfield, England, Brig. Gen. James M. Gavin, commander of the 82d Airborne Division, checks his equipment before boarding his C-47 for the airborne invasion of Holland on September 17, 1944. *National Archives.*

Paratroopers of 82d
Airborne Division check
their equipment prior to
loading onto C-47s
at Cottesmore airfield,
England, on
September 17, 1944.
National Archives.

Before any final decision was made to go,
Brereton and the airborne divisions needed
current and accurate photographic intelligence
on the terrain, German dispositions in the
landing areas, and what ground and air defenses might be expected. In addition, the commitment of plentiful close air support, fighter
escort, and preliminary attacks was required
to suppress the air defenses, reduce enemy
ground forces, and intercept any Luftwaffe
fighters trying to reach the slow and vulnerable
C-47s and gliders.

Once the airborne landing forces were on the
ground deep inside German-held territory, air
resupply missions that exceeded anything ever
attempted before would be required to provide
ammunition, food, weapons, and other supplies. Parachute resupply was first needed on
D+1, with American divisions requiring 264
tons per day. However, this day all available
C-47s were needed for continued landings of
the three divisions. So, U.S. Eighth Air Force
B-24s would fly the parachute resupply mission on September 18, after which IX Troop
Carrier Command would take over.

The commanders of the airborne divisions
wanted to fly in as much of their divisions as
possible on the first day while the weather
held and the initial surprise had the Germans
reeling with their defenses down. However, the
troop carrier commanders objected that their
crews could not fly more than a single lift a
day because their bases were two-and-one-half
hours' flying time from the DZs. After returning, there was insufficient time to prepare and
fly another mission. Brereton sided with the

troop carriers and decided to stretch delivery of
the divisions over three to four days.

The decision to go with daylight missions
meant many tactics could be changed. Flying in daylight allowed the C-47s to tighten
their formations to get more paratroopers and
gliders on the ground sooner. Timing between
the lead C-47s in the serials was cut to four
minutes, and the time between each nine-
aircraft flight to 20 seconds. A new technique
was introduced to mass serials in three parallel
columns about one-and-one-half miles apart
rather than using a single column. This would
get more aircraft over the DZs faster, reduce
vulnerability to ground fire, and produce better
concentrations of paratroopers on the ground
and ready to fight. Drops would still be from
400–500 feet.

In addition, a northern and a southern route
were laid out for the troop carriers due to the
location of the DZs in relation to the basing of
the divisions and wings in England. The groups
of the 50th and 52d Troop Carrier Wings supporting the 82d Airborne Division and those of
the 53d supporting the 101st were experienced,
having flown in Operation NEPTUNE or more
recently in DRAGOON. The 53d Troop Carrier
Wing would use the southern route to Eindhoven, while the 50th and 52d flew to Nijmegen
along the northern route.

Williams's IX Troop Carrier Command now
had 1,274 C-47s and 1,284 crews available. As
for gliders, 2,160 Wacos stood ready by September 16, and 90 percent of them were scheduled for use. The 2,060 glider pilots available
would be sufficient because no co-pilots would

fly on missions during Operation MARKET. After their sad experiences in Normandy, the Americans had no use for the 104 Horsas they had. Unfortunately, the AAF still refused to provide the C-47s with self-sealing fuel tanks and armor protection for the cargo area, even for the critical pathfinders.

OBJECTIVES

Because the destruction of any of the key bridges on the single road to Arnhem spelled trouble for the entire operation, Gavin and the 82d Airborne Division chose to focus on taking the Groesbeek heights first. The 300-foot-high ridge at Groesbeek, two miles southwest of Nijmegen, was critical to the 82d's success in taking and holding its other objectives. Close to the German border and just north of the Reichswald Forest that could hide large enemy forces, these heights were the only high ground for miles and the region's dominant terrain feature. Then, he would take the bridge over the Maas at Grave and at least one of the four bridges over the Maas-Waal Canal between Grave and Nijmegen, and only lastly the bridge over the Waal at Nijmegen. Tucker's 504th had the job of taking the important Grave bridge by attacking it from both ends. Gavin calculated that without the heights and the crossings of Maas, the Nijmegen bridge meant little.

Gavin tried to land as close as possible to his objectives but that was not possible for the Nijmegen bridge. He planned an arc of DZs and LZs three to four miles southeast of Nijmegen on the south side of the Groesbeek heights. This would allow his troopers to take the ridge and set up a defensive perimeter to prevent Germans from attacking and occupying the glider LZs as in Normandy. Learning from their experiences in Normandy, Gavin also decided to drop his 376th Parachute Field Artillery and its 75-mm pack howitzers for immediate fire support rather than bring them

in on gliders. In addition, he had the troopers carry as many antitank mines as possible on the first day. The intricate network of rivers, canals, and roads in the 82d's landing area provided distinctive landmarks for pilots.

The 101st's objectives were a number of towns as well as rail and road bridges over rivers and canals strung out over 15 miles from Eindhoven to Veghel, which would make the division vulnerable to any concerted German flank attacks. Taylor decided to concentrate his landings between St. Oedenrode and Zon, north of the Zonsche Forest and more in the middle of his assigned area. From there he would move north and south except for part of the 501st that jumped north and south of the Veghel bridge to take it on the first day.

OPERATION MARKET: THE AIRBORNE PHASE

The weather was clear along both routes from England and over Holland. Some German ground fire was reported, but the thousands of Allied tactical and strategic aircraft that had preceded and now supported them had silenced most opposition. Pathfinders who had worked together at Normandy were used to mark the DZs for both the 82d and 101st Airborne Divisions. They were on target at 1247 for DZ O for the 82d. The 101st lost one pathfinder aircraft to ground fire, but the others marked DZ A also at 1247 at Veghel and DZs B and C north of the Zonsche Forest at 1254.

German airborne pioneer Gen. Kurt Student, now commanding the First Parachute Army in Holland, was in his command post at Vught when he heard the C-47s overhead and the antiaircraft guns. What he saw was "the endless stream of enemy transport and cargo planes, as far as the eye could see . . . ." Operation MARKET was well under way.

Long lines of C-47s of the IX Troop Carrier Command loaded with paratroopers and equipment for Operation MARKET airborne assault on Holland, September 17, 1944. *National Archives.*

Parachutes open overhead as waves of American paratroopers "hit the silk" from C-47s over Holland during the opening phase of the First Allied Airborne Army's Operation MARKET on September 17, 1944. *National Archives.*

Both the 82d and 101st Airborne Divisions had their best drops ever to open the airborne phase of Operation MARKET. For the 82d, 481 troop carriers dropped 7,229 paratroopers of the 504th, 505th, and 508th Parachute Infantry on or close to their designated DZs. They were also well grouped, so they could head immediately for their objectives. This time they had artillery support because the 376th Parachute Field Artillery's 12 guns were set up and firing within an hour of landing. Gavin's overloaded troopers also carried antitank mines, 2,000 in all. On the first glider lift, the 80th Airborne Antiaircraft Artillery Battalion brought in eight 57-mm antitank guns to handle German armor.

The 101st's first serial of 424 C-47s that dropped 6,713 paratroopers of the 501st, 502d, and 506th was over their DZ at 1307, and the rest followed on schedule. While some drops were off target, they were generally accurate, compact, and quickly done—better than any ever before. All troops were on the ground in 90 minutes so they were able to assemble and get to missions swiftly.

By nightfall on D-Day, Tucker's 504th had taken the Grave bridge as well as the bridge over the Maas-Waal Canal at Molenhook, the only one over the canal to be taken undamaged. The 505th had the Groesbeek heights and soon the town of Groesbeek with its delighted Dutch citizens. Lindquist's 508th was widely spread out executing its varying and difficult missions. He had to hold DZ T for the mass glider landing on D+1, take and hold the high ground from Wyler to Nijmegen, take bridges over the canal at Hatert and Honinghutie, and try to take the Nijmegen bridge. German pressure on the sector from Beek to Wyler to Groesbeek grew more intense each day and seriously tested the 508th and the 82d. The 1st Battalion's attempt to seize the bridge failed the first night, and it was finally taken after a long struggle on D+3 with help from the 505th and Guards Armoured Division.

In the 101st's Eindhoven sector, Johnson's 501st had the railroad and road bridges at Veghel taken intact on D-Day. The 502d took the St. Oedenrode bridge intact the same day but had a back-and-forth struggle for the bridge at Best. The 506th took Zon, but the bridge there had

been blown days earlier. Eindhoven was cleared at 1300 on D+1, 45 minutes after the 101st linked up with the British Guards Armoured Division. By evening on September 18, the Guards were through St. Oedenrode and on the way to Veghel, which they left at 0645 on D+2 headed north to the 82d's area. For the 101st the airborne phase of Operation MARKET was over once the Guards Armoured Division went through, but it was not pulled out and replaced with British ground forces. Heavy German counterattacks beginning on D+5 held the 101st in place, and the heaviest fighting the division encountered actually came after its airborne mission was completed.

For the 82d, the situation was more difficult, being farther up the road. The 508th had a major fight on its hands to clear LZ T and DZ T between Groesbeek and Wyler and defeat a German counterattack from the north just before the glider mission arrived on D+1. The Guards Armoured Division's advanced elements contacted the 82d's southernmost

roadblock below Grave at 0830 on D+2, soon followed by the main body. They then moved north to assist in taking the Nijmegen bridge on September 20.

Each division had glider missions on D-Day, but the larger missions were scheduled for September 18–20. On D+1, 429 of 450 gliders for the 101st landed at Zon with 2,605 men, 151 Jeeps, and 244 tons of cargo, while 424 landed at LZ T with 1,650 men, 54 artillery pieces, 177 Jeeps, and 211 tons of cargo. The same day, the B-24s dropped 241 tons of supplies to the 101st, only 50 percent of which was recovered. The 82d received 247 tons, with 70 percent recovered. On D+2, the 101st received another glider mission, but the 82d's carrying the 325th Glider Infantry was postponed to D+3 due to bad weather over England and the Channel. Continuing bad weather had trumped Brereton's gamble to stretch out the arrival of the airborne units over four days rather than get them all in on the first day. The resulting slow buildup hampered both divisions' operations.

top left
CG-4A gliders from September 17's initial missions lay strewn about Dutch fields below as a U.S. Eighth Air Force B-24 flies an aerial resupply mission on the second day of Operation MARKET. *National Archives.*

bottom left
Not all landings earned style points. This First Allied Airborne Army paratrooper hit the ground headfirst during initial landing operations in Holland. Photo released on September 24, 1944. *National Archives.*

Nijmegen, Holland, and its crucial bridge after seizure by the 82d Airborne Division. This panoramic view of Nijmegen and the bridge over the Waal (Rhine) River seen in the background shows the damage that German and Allied bombing and shelling had done to the Dutch city.
September 28, 1944.
National Archives.

The airborne phase was basically over for both American airborne divisions on D+3, September 20. However, German attacks intensified over the first three days on the narrow and vulnerable salient held by the Americans to allow the British to drive north toward the British 1st Airborne Division trapped in Arnhem. The German 6th Parachute Regiment, the 101st's old foe from Carentan, presented a serious threat at Mook where the 505th held them. The heavy fighting now had both American airborne divisions tied down in ground combat as British divisions were slow to arrive.

When the British 1st Airborne Division withdrew across the Neder Rijn from Arnhem on D+8, September 25, the airborne phase of Operation MARKET ended. In that time, the IX Troop Carrier Command had flown for the British and Americans 1,848 paratrooper drop missions, lost 40 C-47s, and had 321 damaged. They had delivered 13,941 American paratroopers on D-Day, and a total of 20,011 troops and 1,256 tons of cargo by parachute over the eight days. Glider missions in support of the 82d and 101st Airborne Divisions numbered 1,899, and 1,618 gliders landed. They brought in 9,469 men, along with artillery, Jeeps, trailers, and cargo.

The British failure at Arnhem has overshadowed the very real successes that were achieved. The American airborne operations in Operation MARKET were daring and effective, demonstrating what a ready and well-trained airborne force, supported by courageous troop carriers and strong air forces with air superiority, could accomplish in a brazen daylight operation under short notice. Clearly, mass airborne operations in daylight were not only feasible but also highly effective. The ground phase was another matter altogether.

It was originally intended to withdraw the 82d and 101st as soon as the British Second Army took over their sectors. That had occurred on D+3. However, the serious tactical situation in protecting the narrow supply line jutting up through Nijmegen to Arnhem was tenuous. The British divisions that were to replace the 82d and 101st were badly needed elsewhere, meaning neither division was released at the end of the airborne phase of Operation MARKET.

The divisions stayed on to fight side-by-side with the British soldiers. The road was under constant heavy pressure from both flanks as the Germans tried frantically to cut the road and the 30 Corps's lifeline. Attacks and

Lt. Gen. Sir Miles Dempsey, left, commanding general of the British Second Army and in overall command of ground operations, discusses planned operations with Brig. Gen. James M. Gavin, right, commander of the 82d Airborne Division, at Nijmegen, Holland, on September 28, 1944. *National Archives.*

shelling were incessant. Thus, the GIs and Tommies soon called the 20-mile section of highway from Eindhoven to Veghel "Hell's Highway" because of the constant battering they and the road took. The 101st was especially tested during its time on "Hell's Highway" in late September when the Germans cut the road for several days north of Veghel. Early in October the 101st moved north to "The Island," what the Allied soldiers called the area between the rivers Waal and Neder Rijn from Nijmegen north to Arnhem. It was here that Taylor was wounded and Johnson, commander of the 501st, died of wounds from German artillery fire on October 8.

Heroism was commonplace among the paratroopers. Two more soldiers distinguished themselves by their selfless courage and would receive posthumous Medals of Honor. PFC Joe E. Mann, a lead scout with the 502d Parachute Infantry, 101st Airborne Division, at Best, Holland, on September 18 attacked and destroyed a German gun position. After being wounded and taken to cover, he sacrificed his life by falling on a German grenade to save other wounded soldiers. Pvt. John R. Towle, a bazooka man with the 504th Parachute Infantry, 82d Airborne Division, at Oosterhout, Holland, on September 21 dueled with superior German armor and infantry to hold a strong attack that threatened his unit before enemy mortar fire fatally wounded him.

Losses by September 25 when the airborne phase ended were stiff for the two divisions, but they would continue to mount until the divisions were pulled out of the line. From September 17 through November 11, the 82d later reported 3,878 casualties (excluding sick)—658 killed, 2,617 wounded (1,796 never returned to duty), 523 battle injuries (327 did not return), and 80 missing. The 101st lost 2,111 men killed, wounded, and missing in the airborne phase, and 1,912 through November 25 when it left the frontlines. Operation MARKET-GARDEN cost the American airborne divisions a total of 7,901 paratroopers—3,878 of the 82d and 4,023 of the 101st.

In his book *On to Berlin*, Gavin summarized what the airborne divisions had achieved through Operation MARKET:

> What had been a dream in 1941 had now become a reality. We had the First Allied Airborne Army. Solutions to our problems, from that of individual training to the massing of thousands of transports, gliders, and fighter-bombers, had been found. Equipment, weapons, and standardized operating procedures had all been developed. Now we could move and strike an enemy with an army by air, not only against Germany but later against Japan.

The Normandy American Cemetery and Memorial overlooking Omaha Beach and its companion cemeteries in Europe attest to the human cost of combat. The cemetery contains the graves of 9,387 U.S. military dead, most of whom lost their lives in the 1944 D-Day landings and ensuing operations. There are 1,557 names inscribed on the Walls of the Missing. The Netherlands American Cemetery near Margraten contains the graves of 8,301 of our military dead and names of 1,722 missing service members lost during the 1944 campaigns. *Photo by Robert Uth, Courtesy American Battle Monuments Commission.*

REST AND RECUPERATION

The FAAA had decided that neither U.S. airborne division would return to England, but would be forward-based in France along with elements of the IX Troop Carrier Command. Accordingly, the 82d was trucked to Suippes and Sissone, France, where it settled in for some well-deserved rest and relaxation. The 101st went to Mourmelon-la-Grand near Reims, France, to begin recuperating and rebuilding its badly depleted combat units. The airborne units that had served under the 1st Airborne Task Force in southern France, including the 517th Parachute Infantry, the 509th and 551st Parachute Infantry Battalions, and the 550th Glider Infantry Battalion, soon arrived from the Seventh U.S. Army. For the time being, the 17th Airborne Division remained training at Camp Chiseldon in England. Eisenhower now had his veteran American airborne units concentrated on the continent, but they needed time to recuperate after months of hard fighting. Adolf Hitler, however, had other plans.

Chapter 5

Finishing Off Hitler: From the Bulge to Berlin to Bragg, 1944–46

THE BATTLE OF THE BULGE: PLUGGING THE GAP

Adolf Hitler was a gambler. On September 16, 1944, he concocted an armored uppercut to take Antwerp, split the British and Americans, and perhaps force a separate peace in the west. To succeed, he needed two things: bad weather to ground the Allied air forces and enough seized Allied gasoline to fuel his armored vehicles. For the attack, he chose familiar ground from his 1940 offensive—the Ardennes forests of Belgium and Luxembourg.

Maj. Gen. Troy H. Middleton's VIII Corps held most of the quiet Ardennes sector along a heavily forested 88-mile front. Lt. Gen. Omar Bradley, 12th Army Group commander, considered it "a combined training ground and rest area." Two battle-weary veteran divisions and two fresh divisions were in the line. One of the newly arrived divisions, the 106th Infantry Division, held the northern part of the sector. The other green division, the 9th Armored Division, was parceled out among the other divisions except for Combat Command B, which was with the neighboring V Corps to the north. To the 106th's south covering most of Luxembourg were the experienced, but badly battered, 28th and 4th Infantry Divisions, both still recovering from recent heavy losses in the Hürtgen Forest.

Hitler's gamble seemed to be paying off when a period of bad winter weather descended over Western Europe in mid-December and shut down Allied air operations. At 0530 on December 16, 1944, the German Fifth and Sixth Panzer Armies opened their offensives and smashed into the V and VIII Corps, hitting the 106th Infantry Division straight on, ripping the front open, and flooding west. On the southern flank of V Corps to the north, the 99th and 2d Infantry Divisions stubbornly held critical positions along the north shoulder of the breakthrough. This seriously disrupted the Germans' precise timetable to reach and cross the Meuse River. In the south, the 28th Infantry Division stood and fought on the main routes that the German Fifth Panzer Army needed for its push to take the vital road hub of Bastogne, Belgium, and drive on to the west.

Supreme Headquarters Allied Expeditionary Forces (SHAEF) soon realized the gravity of the situation. They had only two experienced divisions in theater reserve that could be thrown in to hold the flanks and then plug the widening gap in the Allied lines—the 82d and 101st Airborne Divisions. On December 17, SHAEF released Maj. Gen. Matthew B. Ridgway's XVIII Airborne Corps and its two divisions to Bradley's 12th Army Group and ordered them into immediate action.

Glider pilot's view of two Waco CG-4A gliders of the aerial armada lifting the 17th Airborne Division to Wesel, Germany, in Operation VARSITY, March 24, 1945. *XVIII Airborne Corps Historian from National Archives.*

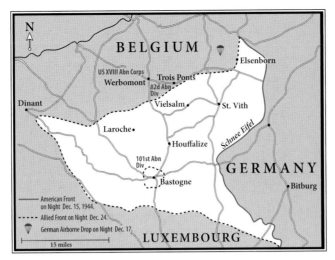

The area of Belgium and Luxembourg where the "Bulge" developed in mid-December 1944. *Map by Paprika Creative.*

On the evening of December 17, when Ridgway learned of the attack, he was in England at the corps's main headquarters located with Maj. Gen. William Miley's 17th Airborne Division. Maj. Gen. Maxwell Taylor, commander of the 101st Airborne Division and next senior officer, was in the United States resolving issues with the War Department on organization of airborne divisions. Thus, Maj. Gen. James Gavin, commanding the 82d Airborne Division, was the acting corps commander on the scene. Ridgway and his headquarters departed England on the morning of December 18 and arrived safely at Reims about noon.

After some initial confusion as to where the divisions were actually headed, First U.S. Army headquarters finally issued orders to Gavin, and then Ridgway upon his return, which split the corps. Gavin's 82d was sent to the north shoulder to fill a dangerous gap that was developing between the 30th Infantry Division in the north and 7th Armored Division fighting to hold the critical road junction of St. Vith. A powerful armored force of the Sixth Panzer Army's I SS Panzer Corps was driving toward Liège and the Meuse River and headed for this void. The 82d's mission was to plug that gap. The 101st would go to Bastogne to deny control of the vital road network to the Fifth Panzer Army for as long as possible. To Ridgway's regret, in this operation he would not have both of his battle-hardened divisions fighting together under his command.

During the night of December 17–18, a cobbled-together force of about 1,000 German paratroopers dropped on the high ground at Baraque Michel. The troopers were widely scattered and had little effect on the success of the offensive. This was the last German airborne drop attempted in World War II.

By the morning of December 18, Gavin had his troopers on trucks headed to Werbomont, Belgium, loaded with a four-day supply of ammunition and food. Both Ridgway and Gavin made their separate ways to Bastogne to meet with Middleton and his staff at VIII Corps and with Brig. Gen. Anthony C. McAuliffe. McAuliffe, the 101st's artillery commander, was acting commander and already onsite with the advanced elements of the division. Gavin told McAuliffe to prepare for an all-around defense and then to stay put until he received further orders. Airborne commanders and units were trained to fight surrounded and deep in enemy territory, so such orders did not bother McAuliffe and the 101st. Once the 101st was assigned to VIII Corps, Middleton provided more detailed guidance, not Ridgway. Gavin then drove north along the Amblève and Salm rivers, passing between elements of the Nazi spearheads, to his new headquarters at Werbomont. Ridgway also reached Werbomont where he located the XVIII Airborne Corps command post for the fight ahead.

THE 82D HOLDS IN THE NORTH

Trucks loaded with the men and equipment of the 82d arrived at Werbomont continuously through December 18 and into the following morning. As the units arrived, Gavin quickly directed them to their assigned defensive positions: the 504th east toward Rahier, Habiemont, Cheneux, and Trois Ponts to link with the 30th Infantry Division to the north; the 505th to cover from Trois Ponts southward along the Salm River to Grand-Halleux and toward Vielsalm; and the 508th to protect the southern flank from Vielsalm through Salm-château and to the west toward Lierneux while maintaining contact with the forces at St. Vith. The 325th Glider Infantry soon took over part of the area from the 508th to tie in with the 3d Armored Division to the west.

Paratroopers of Lt. Col. Julian J. Ewell's 501st Parachute Infantry, 101st Airborne Division, head out of Bastogne on the morning of December 19 to reinforce armored roadblocks east of the city at Longvilly. The leading soldiers are equipped with the ineffective 2.36-inch bazooka antiarmor weapon. *XVIII Airborne Corps Historian from National Archives.*

The 82d confronted one of the most powerful German panzer armies ever assembled on the western front. Facing the heavy Panther and King Tiger tanks of the SS panzer divisions, the lightly armed 82d had its ineffectual bazookas and 57-mm antitank guns, some tank and tank destroyer support, captured German Panzerfaust antitank weapons, and a lot of guts.

Small pockets of American engineers, infantry, tankers, and others courageously stood their ground. They frustrated the efforts of the Sixth Panzer Army's advanced Kampfgruppe (battle group) under Obersturmbannführer (Lt. Col.) Joachim Peiper of the 1st SS Panzer Regiment, 1st SS Panzer Division. Peiper's mission was not only to drive directly to Liège and over the Meuse River but also to find major American fuel dumps for himself and the following forces. These soldiers bought time for the 82d to arrive and deploy, and forced Peiper to use up his fuel while denying him the fuel he desperately needed. They also gained time for the 30th Infantry Division to arrive and entrap Peiper's column around La Gleize, Belgium, where it soon ran out of fuel.

Early on the morning of December 20, Gavin met Col. Reuben Tucker, commander of the 504th, at Rahier. There he learned that a strong German armored column of Kampfgruppe Peiper had curled up into the town of Cheneux, just to the east and overlooking the Amblève River.

Although badly outgunned and without tank support, Tucker decided to attack. Lt. Col. Willard E. Harrison's 1st Battalion drew the mission with the 3d Battalion in support. Tucker armed them with some deadly German Panzerfausts, rocket-propelled antitank weapons, from a truckload he had captured in Holland and had kept for just such an occasion. He concluded that with the Panzerfausts, his paratroop infantry would be an even match for the Germans and their armored vehicles.

Harrison attacked that day with his Companies B and C. The fight continued into and through the night and through the next day as the 3d Battalion enveloped Cheneux from the south. In a nasty battle that cost the 504th 23 killed and 202 wounded, the 1st and 3d Battalions finally took the town. After the fighting, Company B had no officers and 18 men, and Company C had three officers and 38 men fit for duty. The 504th captured so much German heavy equipment that the troopers began calling themselves the "504th Parachute Armored Regiment."

Farther to the east, the 505th Parachute Infantry joined a group of Army engineers holding the pivotal town of Trois Ponts and its bridges over the Amblève and Salm rivers to the west of Malmédy. Lt. Col. Benjamin Vandervoort pushed his 2d Battalion to the east of the town, confident that his paratroopers and the engineers already there could hold the approaches.

Maj. Gen. J. Lawton Collins, left, commander of U.S. VII Corps; Field Marshal Bernard L. Montgomery, commander of 21st Army Group; and Maj. Gen. Matthew B. Ridgway, commander of XVIII Airborne Corps, confer at Collins's headquarters on December 26, 1944. *XVIII Airborne Corps Historian.*

On December 20, Kampfgruppe Hansen of the 1st SS Panzer Division, trying to free Peiper at La Gleize, hit Vandervoort's positions. Vandervoort soon realized he was up against something he could not stop. Uttering his classic command, "Let's get the hell out of here!" Vandervoort pulled his men back across the rivers. With the engineers, they then frustrated further German attempts to get across the rivers or to relieve Peiper, who eventually escaped on foot during the night of December 24–25 after abandoning his vehicles.

Gen. Dwight D. Eisenhower shuffled the frontline commands on December 20. He split the "bulge" that now protruded far to the west into Allied lines toward the Meuse River. Field Marshal Bernard L. Montgomery, with the 21st Army Group, took the north shoulder and Bradley, commanding 12th Army Group, took the south. First U.S. Army and XVIII Airborne Corps now came under Montgomery's overall command. Once Ridgway and his corps headquarters were in place at Werbomont, the divisions in this sector came under him.

On December 22–23, another German threat emerged in the south as the II SS Panzer Corps appeared. The 2d SS Panzer Division hit the 325th at the Baraque de Fraiture crossroads and Manhay. The 9th SS Panzer Division struck the 505th and 508th from the east and south. Facing a difficult situation, on December 24–25, Ridgway and Gavin withdrew to a

more defensible line running from Manhay northeast to Trois Ponts.

The nondivisional parachute infantry units, the 517th Parachute Infantry and the 509th and 551st Parachute Infantry Battalions, were also thrown into battle where needed along the thinly stretched front. Elements of the 517th and 509th were temporarily attached to the 3d Armored Division in hard fighting to hold the towns of Soy and Hotton after December 22. The 509th had only 55 men fit for duty out of an original strength of 745 when it was pulled from the line. The 551st, attached to the 30th Infantry Division and then the 82d after December 26, suffered similarly heavy losses through mid-January.

The 82d Airborne Division's quick reaction and tenacious fighting blunted the German drive to the Meuse River and forced them to the west, where Maj. Gen. J. Lawton Collins's VII Corps and British forces took them on. These battles gave Eisenhower the time he needed to shift more Allied divisions from other sectors into the line to contain the German offensive. The tipping point had already come as the weather had cleared, and Allied aircraft could now go after the German columns and supply lines. Moreover, the forward German mechanized columns were also now running out of fuel. Stalled in the north, the German high command began shifting forces back to the fight at Bastogne and in the south in hopes of clearing another way to the west.

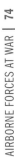

Brig. Gen. Anthony C. McAuliffe, division artillery commander and acting commander of the 101st Airborne Division, in Bastogne on January 5, 1945. *National Archives.*

BASTOGNE AND THE 101ST AIRBORNE DIVISION

As the 82d moved to Werbomont on December 18, troopers of the 101st began boarding the first of 380 trucks and trailers that would carry them from Mourmelon to the Belgian crossroads city of Bastogne, 100 miles to the east, where destiny awaited. The trucks drove as fast as they could during the day and through that night.

Meanwhile, at Bastogne, McAuliffe and his G-3, Lt. Col. Harry W. O. Kinnard, found Middleton's headquarters faced with a disintegrating front and demoralized troops streaming in from the east. Elements of the 9th and 10th Armored Divisions had arrived and had already moved into blocking positions on the roads to the east and north. Before Middleton and his staff left the city for Neufchâteau, he told McAuliffe he had to hold Bastogne.

Lt. Col. Julian J. Ewell, who had taken over the 501st Parachute Infantry after Col. Howard R. Johnson's death in Holland and had coincidentally spent two days in Bastogne on rest leave afterward, led the first unit into Bastogne on the night of December 18. McAuliffe immediately ordered him east at 0600 the next day. Ewell's mission was to reinforce Combat Command R, 9th Armored Division, and Team Cherry, 10th Armored Division, which were at Longvilly blocking the road from St. Vith

and Clervaux. Before reaching Longvilly, he encountered advancing reconnaissance and armored units of the Fifth Panzer Army's XLVIII Panzer Corps. They were probing toward Bastogne after moving around, encircling, and destroying the roadblock at Longvilly. The 501st's ensuing fights at Neffe, Bizory, Mont, and Wardin on December 19–21 bought valuable time and space for the defense of the city. They were only the beginning of eight days of unrelenting fighting, courage, and misery.

By the evening of December 19, all of the 101st's other combat units had closed into Bastogne and pushed out as far as possible to establish a defensive perimeter—the 327th Glider Infantry in the south and west, 502d Parachute Infantry in the northwest blocking the road to Bertogne, and the 506th Parachute Infantry in the northeast at Noville and Foy on the road from Houffalize. The 101st's divisional artillery and the tanks, tank destroyers, and guns of other units now assembled under McAuliffe covered all major roads leading into the city.

On December 20, McAuliffe went to Neufchâteau to see Middleton at VIII Corps. When told that the Germans were probably sending a fourth division against him, McAuliffe remarked, "I think we can take care of them." Middleton wanted the 101st to hang on for at least 48 hours, longer if possible, to give the Allies time to reinforce the frontline corps. As McAuliffe left, Middleton said, "Now, don't get yourself surrounded." McAuliffe took that as a joke to relieve the tension. He left Neufchâteau to hasten back to Bastogne. Soon after his departure, German forces cut the road between Neufchâteau and Bastogne. McAuliffe, the 101st, and Bastogne were now surrounded.

BASTOGNE

When Bradley took over the fighting on the Bulge's south shoulder on December 20, the VIII Corps and the 101st passed to control of Lt. Gen. George S. Patton's Third U.S. Army. Patton already was moving his III Corps into position to relieve Bastogne from the south. However, the defenders of Bastogne were under intense and constant pressure from German infantry, artillery, and tank attacks around the perimeter. The situation looked bleak at best.

At 1130 on December 22, four German emissaries approached the 327th Glider Infantry's lines carrying a large white flag and a demand for the defenders to surrender or die. When McAuliffe was shown the German note containing the surrender demand, he chuckled and said, "Aw, nuts!" He thought that he was winning and the Germans were giving up. When pressed to write a response to the Germans, McAuliffe finally adopted Kinnard's idea just to say "Nuts!" Col. Joseph H. Harper, commander of the 327th Glider Infantry, delivered the response to the Germans, who at first did not understand. When pressed by the Germans on what the reply meant, Harper made it unmistakably clear:

"If you don't understand what 'Nuts' means, in plain English it is the same as 'Go to Hell.' And I will tell you something else—if you continue to attack we will kill every goddamn German that tries to break into this city."

Hard days of fighting followed as the Fifth Panzer Army redoubled its efforts to crush the defenders. German artillery pounded them, and the normally invisible Luftwaffe bombed them nightly after December 22. American tanks and tank destroyers bounced from threatened sector to threatened sector in the south and west and northwest to prevent German penetrations or to counterattack those that made headway. The attackers made such little progress that the Fifth Panzer Army now had to return some of its armored units to the east to finish the job, and, in so doing, depleted its own offensive force.

Food, ammunition, and medical supplies were running low in Bastogne, so the 101st sent a request for aerial resupply to VIII Corps on December 22. The skies were clearing, and the paratroopers' old buddies of the IX Troop Carrier Command flew to the scene with parachute supply drops the following day. The lead C-47s dropped their pathfinders shortly after 0930, and 90 minutes later 16 C-47s made the first drops. By late that afternoon, 260 C-47s had dropped 1,446 bundles with 144 tons of supplies, 95 percent of which was recovered.

top left
Pamphlet for Bastogne, combat art by Olin Dows. The piece combines elements of the Bastogne saga: winter weather, aerial resupply, and a determined American soldier. *Army Art Collection, U.S. Army Center of Military History.*

top right
Soldiers of Company F, 2d Battalion, 325th Glider Infantry, 82d Airborne Division advance toward Baraque de Fraiture crossroads. After a hard fight against the 2d SS Panzer Division on December 23, only 44 of the company's 116 men returned from the encounter. *National Archives.*

top right
Soldiers watch as the IX Troop Carrier Command's C-47s drop supplies to the 101st encircled at Bastogne, December 26, 1944. *National Archives.*

bottom right
On December 29, 1944, troopers of the 101st Airborne Division move out of Bastogne to counter continued German attacks around the perimeter of the city. *XVIII Airborne Corps Historian from National Archives.*

Through December 27, a total of 927 C-47 resupply sorties were flown and 61 CG-4A gliders landed. German ground fire shot down 19 C-47s and 17 Wacos during these supply missions. The troop carrier and glider pilots braved that fire to get through to keep the men fed and fighting.

Patton's relief effort jumped off on December 22 only 12 to 15 miles south of Bastogne. Protecting the Fifth Panzer Army's southern flank, the German Seventh Army pushed forward to bulk up the defenders south of Bastogne and gave the III Corps a tougher fight than estimated. The U.S. XII Corps then joined in to the east of III Corps. In a phone call with Middleton on Christmas Day, McAuliffe told him, "The finest Christmas present the 101st could get would be a relief tomorrow." Late on the afternoon of December 26, McAuliffe's Christmas present arrived as the 4th Armored Division's leading elements broke the German ring and lifted the siege of Bastogne.

The last German effort to take Bastogne failed on January 2, but much hard fighting remained. Through January 6, 1945, the 101st casualties were significant—29 officers and 312 men killed, 103 officers and 1,588 men wounded, and 34 officers and 482 men missing. The cost had been high, but the 101st had won a hard-earned victory that helped stop the Ger-

man offensive. Bastogne will forever honor its stand and sacrifice. Today the 327th Airborne Infantry, which traces its history and lineage to the 327th Glider Infantry, has as its official U.S. Army special designation, or nickname, the "Bastogne Bulldogs." The Screaming Eagles gave themselves another designation, although it was never official: "The Battling Bastards of Bastogne."

There was little time to reflect on this victory. Bastogne was just the beginning of a long and hard campaign. The "bulge" created in the American lines now had to be destroyed, and a war still remained to be finished against a tough and able foe.

ERADICATING THE BULGE

Both the 82d and 101st Airborne Divisions had played central roles in stopping the German Ardennes offensive in difficult and costly fighting after December 18. Now came the even harder and more costly phase of eradicating the German bulge during a cold and severe winter. Ridgway's XVIII Airborne Corps on the north shoulder played a major role in these operations with the 1st, 30th, 75th, and 84th Infantry Divisions; the 3d, 7th, and 9th Armored Divisions; and Gavin's 82d Airborne Division, which now included the 551st Parachute Infantry Battalion and the 517th Parachute Infantry.

For the coming offensive operations, XVIII Airborne Corps came under First U.S. Army and occupied the frontal sector between V and VII Corps on the north shoulder of the protruding bulge. The Allied offensive began with VII Corps on January 3 in snow and winter weather over difficult terrain against a stubborn enemy. Operations went well, and soon the First and Third U.S. Armies met at Houffalize on January 16, cutting off the bulge to the west.

The XVIII Airborne Corps now carried the offensive burden and pushed east to the original frontlines held when the German offensive began. More problems often came from the

rugged terrain and snow, ice, and cold than from the enemy. The corps carried on eastward through the Siegfried Line in heavy and costly fighting.

For example, in two months of combat the 82d lost 4,759 men—670 dead, 3,109 wounded (2,073 never returned to duty), 973 battle injuries (609 never returned), and seven missing. In fighting a determined foe under terrible weather conditions in most difficult terrain, Ridgway and his XVIII Airborne Corps had earned a reputation as tough, resourceful, and aggressive.

During these operations three more Medals of Honor were awarded to paratroopers. PFC Melvin E. Biddle, Company B, 517th Parachute Infantry, with utter disregard for his own safety on December 23–24 at Soy, Belgium, helped break the German hold on the key town of Hotton. On January 4, 1945, at Flamierge,

top left
A 75-mm pack howitzer of the 82d Airborne Division in action in Belgium, January 1945. *XVIII Airborne Corps Historian from National Archives.*

top right
Maj. Gen. Matthew B. Ridgway, XVIII Airborne Corps commander, left, and Maj. Gen. James M. Gavin, commander of the 82d Airborne Division, converse before an awards ceremony somewhere in Belgium on January 20, 1945. The hand grenades on Ridgway's battle dress harness became his personal trademark. *XVIII Airborne Corps Historian.*

Paratroopers of the 3d Battalion, 504th Parachute Infantry, 82d Airborne Division, and a Sherman tank of the attached Company G, 740th Tank Battalion, push through the heavy snow and thick pine forests of the Ardennes toward their objective in the vicinity of Herresbach, Belgium, in late January 1945. *National Archives.*

Belgium, Staff Sgt. Isador Jachman, Company B, 513th Parachute Infantry, 17th Airborne Division, a German émigré born in Berlin, was fatally wounded when he exposed himself to enemy fire to attack two German tanks with a bazooka and drive them away from his company. 1st Sgt. Leonard A. Funk, Company C, 508th Parachute Infantry, 82d Airborne Division, on January 29 at Holzheim, Belgium, took over headquarters company, formed it into an assault unit, and killed and recaptured a large number of German prisoners of war (POWs) who, having been freed by an enemy patrol, threatened the entire company.

Meanwhile, the 101st continued to fight under VIII Corps as Third Army pushed the Germans back from Bastogne and linked up with First Army at Houffalize. On January 20, it was transferred to the XV Corps, Seventh U.S. Army, in Alsace to bolster it against the German offensive in that area. However, the division saw little action. When operations were completed in February, the division moved back to Mourmelon to rest and refit, back with the XVIII Airborne Corps.

After a short attachment to the XVIII Airborne Corps, the 17th Airborne Division had been sent to the VIII Corps in the Bastogne area where it fought through early February to push the Germans back to their starting line of December 16. It was then pulled back into SHAEF Reserve under First Allied Airborne Army to reorganize and then prepare for an airborne assault over the Rhine River.

OPERATION VARSITY: JUMPING THE RHINE RIVER

On March 1, 1945, the War Department made the change in airborne divisional structure that Ridgway had advocated. The separate 517th Parachute Infantry and 509th and 551st Parachute Infantry Battalions were disbanded, and their men transferred to the airborne divisions to fill out the enlarged parachute and glider infantry regiments. The 88th (13th Airborne Division), 193d (17th Airborne Division), and 401st Glider Infantry (101st) also were disbanded and their assets likewise transferred. The 517th Parachute Infantry was now assigned to the 13th, the 507th to the 17th, and the 506th to the 101st.

top left
President Harry S. Truman presented the Medal of Honor to 1st Sgt. Leonard A. Funk, Company C, 508th Parachute Infantry, then attached to the 82d Airborne Division, for his heroic actions on January 29, 1945, near Holzheim, Belgium. *National Archives.*

top right
Infantrymen of Company B, 325th Glider Infantry, 82d Airborne Division, slog through snow-covered terrain near Herresbach, Belgium. January 28, 1945. *National Archives.*

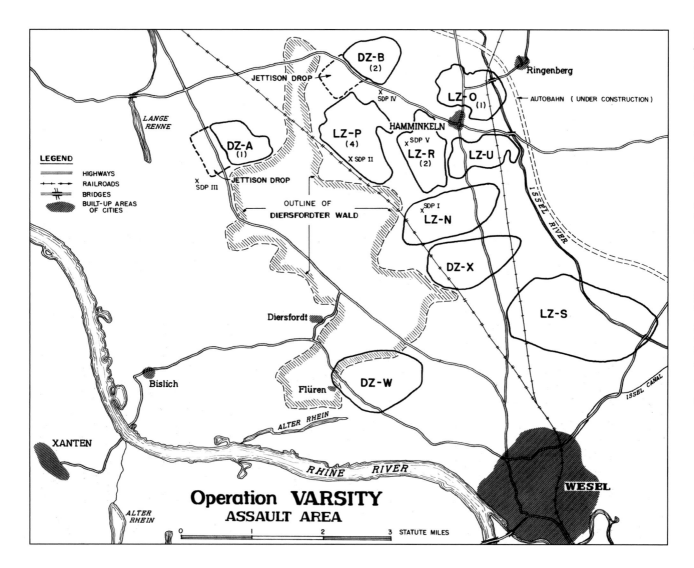

Operation VARSITY
ASSAULT AREA

Map of Operation VARSITY's designated drop and landing zones for the March 24, 1945, air assault. *U.S. Air Force.*

In the fall of 1944, Bradley had first considered employing airborne assaults across the Rhine River to facilitate a major crossing. However, the strategic situation from November 1944 through January 1945 negated any thought of a crossing operation. After the threat of the German Ardennes offensive receded, SHAEF returned to examining how and where to cross the Rhine when the time came. The main effort was assigned to the British Second Army of 21st Army Group, in the sector near Wesel, Germany. First Allied Airborne Army had planned the operation earlier, and was ready to execute.

The XVIII Airborne Corps would command the operation. Its 82d and 101st Airborne Divisions were still engaged in active combat operations in early February 1945 and would need rest and refitting before another airborne operation. Hence, they were reserved for airborne operations planned for later. The 17th Airborne Division and British 6th Parachute Division were available, along with the newly arrived 13th Airborne Division under Maj. Gen. Elbridge Chapman, Jr. However, it was scratched because only enough aircraft were on hand to lift two divisions.

Eight of the landing areas for Operation VARSITY were east of the Diersfordter Wald and two were west, several miles north of Wesel on the Rhine River. The drop zones (DZs) and landing zones (LZs) were clustered in a highly concentrated area less than six miles long and five miles wide. All landings were to be compressed into just a little more than two-and-one-half hours. Lt. Gen. Lewis Brereton, First Allied Airborne Army's commander, had learned from Operation MARKET that all the airborne forces had to be delivered in one lift.

Since Normandy, the German command had been wary of Allied airborne operations that might strike deep into the German rear areas. To guard against this threat, it kept a number of divisions tied up in reserve and spread out in western Germany. The Germans had also

top left
IX Troop Carrier Command flew the new C-46 Curtiss Commando in Operation VARSITY. Its fuel tanks were not self-sealing, making it more vulnerable to antiaircraft fire than the C-47. *U.S. Air Force.*

bottom left
On the night of March 23–24, 1945, glider infantrymen of the 194th Glider Infantry, 17th Airborne Division, make final checks before loading into their Waco CG-4A glider for the aerial assault at Wesel in Operation VARSITY. First aid bandage packages on their helmets are ready for quick use. *National Archives.*

worked hard to airborne-proof many of the suitable LZs and DZs east of the Rhine with ground obstacles and antiaircraft defenses. The Wesel area was one such defense zone.

Daylight was chosen for the operation to take advantage of Allied air superiority. Unlike Normandy and Holland, this time the ground operation would begin the night before, followed by the airborne assault. The paratroopers would also go deeper and well in front of the ground forces to facilitate their advance. Using a lesson learned in Holland, they would jump directly onto the German artillery and antiaircraft positions to neutralize them.

By late February, IX Troop Carrier Command had 1,264 C-47s, 117 C-46s, and 1,922 CG-4A Waco gliders to support the British and American airborne divisions.

The 17th Airborne Division was concentrated and training at Châlons-sur-Marne, France. IX Troop Carrier Command's units were based conveniently for parachute and glider training with the airborne divisions. Coordinated airborne-troop carrier training began on February 28.

A IX Troop Carrier Command C-47 tows a CG-4A aloft as other single-tow flights form up in the sky above before heading east to release the gliders near Wesel, Germany, in Operation VARSITY, March 24, 1945. *XVIII Airborne Corps Historian from National Archives.*

Montgomery set March 24 as the crossing date. Assisted by artillery on the west bank, Allied bombers and fighter-bombers worked over the German defenses in crossing and landing areas well before the first troops began crossing the river that night. By the morning of March 24, the British assault forces had a bridgehead on the eastern shore. The first troop carrier serials arrived before 1000. Col. Edson Raff, commander of the 507th Parachute Infantry, 17th Airborne Division, was the first man out of the lead C-47 piloted by Col. Joel Crouch, who had flown the lead pathfinders in airborne operations in Italy, Normandy, southern France, and Holland. Raff had made the first combat jump in Algeria on November 8, 1942; now he led the final paratroop assault of the European war.

The troop carrier squadrons suffered heavy losses to German ground fire, but pushed on to drop their troopers before going down. Troop carrier losses totaled 38 C-47s and 20 C-46s destroyed or missing. The paratroop and glider landings were largely on or close to the designated DZs and LZs. The British and American paratroopers and glider infantrymen soon overcame tough German resistance. By landing behind the German defenses along the river and on top of the gun positions and rearward defense lines, the airborne assaulters were immediately caught in difficult fighting but also smothered the German defenses that may have held up the crossing force.

top left
Men of the 17th Airborne Division quickly take cover behind vehicles as German defenders fire on them in the assault landing area during Operation VARSITY, March 24, 1945. *National Archives.*

bottom left
Glider infantry moving out from CG-4A gliders of the 17th Airborne Division that have landed east of the Rhine River in Operation VARSITY on March 24, 1945. *XVIII Airborne Corps Historian from National Archives.*

top right
The 17th Airborne Division captured more than 3,100 German prisoners on March 24, 1945, the first day of Operation VARSITY. *XVIII Airborne Corps Historian from National Archives.*

All objectives were taken by the afternoon of D-Day, including an important bridgehead across the Issel River to the east. Ridgway came across from the west bank and assumed command. British 6th Guards Armoured Brigade was attached to the corps and with the 513th Parachute Infantry drove east toward Münster, with 6th and 17th Airborne Divisions following. On March 29, the U.S. 2d Armored Division passed through the 17th Airborne Division and linked up with the 3d Armored Division, First U.S. Army, near Paderborn, creating the Ruhr pocket and encircling two armies and more than 300,000 German troops.

Operation VARSITY resulted in the largest number of Medal of Honor recipients in one airborne operation in World War II. PFC Stuart S. Stryker, Company E, 513th Parachute Infantry, and PFC George J. Peters, Company G, 507th Parachute Infantry, both received posthumous awards for their actions on March 24. T./Sgt. Clinton M. Hedrick, Company I, 194th Glider Infantry, received his award for his heroism and self-sacrifice at Lembeck Castle on March 27–28. In 2002, the Army named its new family of wheeled combat fighting vehicles "Stryker" in honor of Stuart Stryker and Spec.

Robert Stryker, 1st Infantry Division, a posthumous Medal of Honor recipient in Vietnam.

FINISHING OFF HITLER

No sooner had Ridgway's corps headquarters returned to Épernay than the 12th Army Group ordered it to First Army to reduce the Ruhr pocket it had just helped to create. On April 1, the corps, with the 8th and 78th Infantry Divisions, assumed responsibility for the western sector between the Rhine River and III Corps. Later adding the 86th and 97th Infantry Divisions and 13th Armored Division, it smashed German resistance, which quickly crumbled. When the Ruhr pocket ceased to exist on April 18, the corps had destroyed two German armies, three corps, and 14 divisions and taken 160,000 prisoners.

While the XVIII Airborne Corps was busy crushing the Germans in the Ruhr pocket, the 82d and 101st Airborne Divisions were assigned to Fifteenth Army's XXII Corps to guard the western shore of the Rhine River from Bonn to north of Düsseldorf against any attempted breakout. Then the 82d headed north to rejoin the XVIII Airborne Corps while the 101st was assigned to the Seventh Army in

top left
Duisburg, Germany, April 1945. Troopers of the 17th Airborne Division raise the American flag over the liberated city in the Ruhr region. *XVIII Airborne Corps Historian from National Archives.*

bottom left
Liberated by the 82d Airborne Division, these former prisoners of the Wöbbelin concentration camp await transport to a hospital for medical attention, May 4, 1945. *National Archives.*

Bavaria to clean up Hitler's reputed "National Redoubt" in the Alps. The 101st spent some days bagging Nazi leaders in the area, rounding up wandering German soldiers, accepting surrenders, and enjoying some much-deserved rest and relaxation. Appropriately, the Screaming Eagles ended the war at Berchtesgaden perched atop Hitler's mountaintop retreat, the Eagle's Nest (Adlerhorst).

Ridgway expected a brief respite after the Ruhr pocket. Instead, SHAEF assigned the XVIII Airborne Corps to the Ninth U.S. Army and moved it 250 miles north to where it teamed with the British Second Army to cross the Elbe River on April 28 and drive to the Baltic Sea. Here the 82d Airborne Division rejoined the corps in time for the 505th Parachute Infantry to make an assault crossing of the Elbe River with four companies at Bleckede on April 30. When the 504th joined them that night, together they rapidly expanded the bridgehead against feeble resistance. The British 6th Airborne Division was once again with the corps and in action. It established the first contact with the Soviets at Wismar on the Baltic Sea on May 2. Next day, the 8th Infantry Division met Soviet troops south of Schwerin and the 82d contacted them east of Ludwigslust.

At Ludwigslust on May 2, Gavin and the 82d had the unique privilege of receiving the surrender of the entire German Twenty-First Army of some 150,000 soldiers. Shortly thereafter, they also witnessed the horror of Nazi Germany when they found the Wöbbelin concentration camp outside the city. Gavin made the city leaders dig graves and bury the dead inmates in front of the city's palace, and all citizens had to visit the camp and attend the burial service for the victims.

Paratroopers of Company I, 505th Parachute Infantry, 82d Airborne Division, made their final combat assault across the Elbe River on April 30, 1945, aboard armored tracked landing vehicles operated by the British Second Army. *National Archives.*

The XVIII Airborne Corps had captured 360,000 prisoners. The once vaunted German Army was finished, and Nazi Germany was about to be no more. The war in Europe ended on May 8.

OCCUPATION AND INACTIVATIONS

With the end of the war, the 82d and 101st Airborne Divisions settled into a routine of training and military occupation duties. The men who had spent the most time overseas and had distinguished themselves in combat were designated "high-point men." They were to return to the States the soonest but also were often the key officers and noncommissioned officers in the companies and battalions. Meanwhile, the 101st performed military occupation duties in the Alpine regions of Bavaria and Austria. In August it moved to France in preparation for return to the United States.

The 82d was chosen for occupation duty in Berlin following the Potsdam Conference. When it arrived in the former capital of Nazi Germany in late July 1945, it found a city largely demolished by bombing and the Soviet assault of April and only slowly beginning to revive under occupation by the United States, Great Britain, France, and the Soviet Union. The troopers quickly secured the American sector of the city, reestablished law and order,

and forcefully ended the criminal depredations of armed, roving bands of Red Army soldiers. As senior U.S. Army commander, Gavin was also the first American member of the Berlin Kommandatura that jointly governed the city. On November 19, the 82d Airborne Division was replaced by the 78th Infantry Division and departed for France to ready for shipment to the United States. In their short months of occupation duty, Gavin and the 82d laid the firm foundations of friendship and cooperation with the British and French forces and with the people of Berlin upon which future American policies in the city successfully rested until U.S. forces left Berlin in September 1994.

Gavin learned during the time in Berlin that the 82d would join many other wartime units on the inactive rolls of the Army. As an Organized Reserve division, it was not part of the Regular Army and would cease to exist with the postwar demobilization. The 101st Airborne Division was chosen to be the sole airborne division in the postwar army. However, Lt. Col. Barney Oldfield, a former press agent for Warner Brothers and member of the 505th Parachute Infantry back in 1942, directed a concerted publicity campaign to retain the 82d. The War Department reversed itself in November and decided to inactivate the 101st and retain the 82d. Hence, the division that had become two on August 15, 1942, became one again on November 30, 1945.

Maj. Gen. James M. Gavin led the U.S. Army's 82d Airborne Division through the Washington Arch as the vanguard of the victory parade up Fifth Avenue in New York City on January 12, 1946. *Library of Congress.*

The end of the war in the Pacific and demobilization resulted in the rapid dismembering of the U.S. Army's airborne force that had served in Europe, the mightiest in history. Ridgway and the XVIII Airborne Corps returned to the United States on July 11 on their way to the Pacific. The 17th Airborne Division was also ordered to the Pacific via the United States, where it arrived on September 15, after the war ended, and was inactivated the next day. The XVIII Airborne Corps lasted another month before it was inactivated on October 15. The 13th Airborne Division, which had not seen combat, returned on August 23, 1945, and was inactivated on February 25, 1946.

On January 3, 1946, the ocean liner *Queen Mary* docked in New York with the men of the 82d Airborne Division, many of them until recently proud members of the 17th and 101st Airborne Divisions. On January 12, Gavin led the division up Fifth Avenue in the Victory Parade. After receiving the thanks of the city, the division headed for its new permanent station at Fort Bragg, North Carolina.

Chapter 6

Airborne Forces in the Pacific, 1942–45

A DIFFERENT KIND OF WAR

The war against Imperial Japan in the Pacific and Far East took place in three distinct but interconnected theaters. Each received limited resources because the Allies chose to defeat Germany first. The three theater commanders began with the mission to halt the Japanese advance, and then try to push them back. Each fought in a different way. Central Pacific island-hopping fell under the U.S. Navy's direction, while the British took charge of China-Burma-India (CBI). Army forces played supporting roles in both. Only Gen. Douglas MacArthur's Southwest Pacific Area (SWPA) remained primarily an Army show.

MacArthur gathered his forces in Australia and nearby Papuan-New Guinea with the ultimate objective of liberating the Philippines and Netherlands East Indies. Only in his theater would any substantial airborne assault operations take place. These airborne operations never exceeded a regiment in size nor approached the size or significance of those staged in the Mediterranean or European theaters. But here and in the CBI the different challenges led to different kinds of operations where new tactics and techniques pointed the way to the future.

THE SOUTHWEST PACIFIC AREA THEATER

MacArthur's Australian base sat in isolation. Reinforcements had to come 6,000 miles from the United States along a threatened line of communications. SWPA's vast area spread Allied forces even thinner, and it took longer to move men and equipment within the theater. Brisbane, Australia, lay more than 1,100 miles from New Guinea and 3,600 miles from Manila. Ground troops had to cope with primitive conditions, disease, and terrain that ranged from mountains to jungles to widely scattered islands.

Basic facilities required to sustain modern military operations had to be built from scratch. Men, equipment, supplies, and materials needed for that work could move into position only by sea or air. Thus, control of the air and seas became MacArthur's first priority.

MacArthur and his chief airman, Lt. Gen. George C. Kenney, devised a new strategy to deal with the theater's daunting physical environment. Rather than a traditional advance, SWPA would leapfrog via air and sea to isolate and bypass many of the Japanese strongholds. Ground forces would move in a succession of bounds, always within range of covering air forces. Each push would secure an area for new airfields and bases. Airborne troops had a role to play, but one limited by available transport planes. Strategic and operational necessity put priority on moving men, equipment, and supplies rather than dropping paratroopers.

The 503d Parachute Infantry made the first combat jump in the Pacific on September 5, 1943, at Nadzab in New Guinea. *National Archives.*

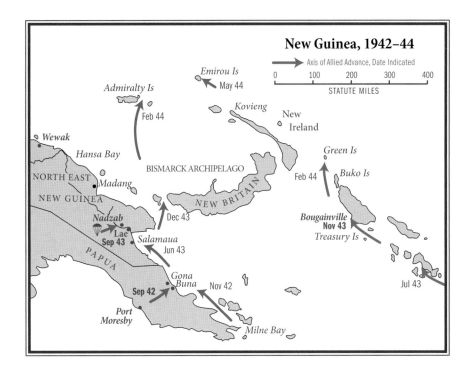

New Guinea, 1942–44

→ Axis of Allied Advance, Date Indicated

0   100   200   300   400
STATUTE MILES

The 503d Parachute Infantry arrived in Australia on December 2, 1942, as the first airborne unit sent to SWPA. It left Fort Bragg with only two battalions (the other had already gone to England) plus Company A from the 504th. Its convoy went first to Panama where it took onboard the former 501st Parachute Infantry Battalion as its new 2d Battalion, and the 504th company became the new Company D. By the time it came ashore, MacArthur and Kenney had established a pattern for much of their later airborne and air-mobility operations. In September Kenney pressed available civilian and military aircraft into flying part of the 32d Infantry Division from Brisbane to Port Moresby in Papua to reinforce defending Australians. Over the next two months he ferried more than 15,000 Allied troops over the Owen Stanley Range to primitive airstrips. With the help of these men, SWPA carried out offensive operations against Buna and Gona and drove the Japanese out of the Papua portion of New Guinea.

Kenney's transport units flew men and supplies into the forward bases and flew out the sick and wounded. The C-47 crews also worked out basic airdrop techniques. They learned to drop supplies from low levels without parachutes because those were scarce items in the theater. Movement, reinforcement, and resupply of combat forces in the jungles by air became standard operating procedure in SWPA. MacArthur and Kenney still had to cope with their low priority for resources which limited the number of available C-47s.

NADZAB: THE FIRST AMERICAN AIRBORNE OPERATION IN THE PACIFIC

Several proposals to use the 503d Parachute Infantry to strike Japanese rear areas came during the regiment's first months in theater—in fact such planning had started before it landed. Early targets considered included the major base areas at Lae and Hollandia. Neither won approval because of shortages or a concern that enemy fighters and bombers would inflict unacceptable losses.

By August of 1943 conditions finally improved enough for the 503d's first operation. MacArthur's offensive westward along the north shore of New Guinea had progressed to the point where a major operation was now feasible against the Japanese stronghold and airfields at Lae. The target sat on the coast of the Huon Bay at the mouth of the Markham River valley. Australian Army Lt. Gen. Thomas Blamey, who commanded the Allied New Guinea Force, developed a complex plan to capture it. Blamey's coordinated amphibious, airborne, and ground operation would be the first of its kind conducted in any Pacific theater.

The assault intended both to destroy the Japanese garrison and secure the area for the construction of Allied airfields. It had three major components. The 9th Australian Division's amphibious landing at Bulu Plantation would lead the attack along the coast from the east. A day later, with the Japanese defenders now distracted, the 503d Parachute Infantry would jump on the abandoned civilian airstrip

The Nadzab objective for the parachute assault was about 20 miles up the Markham River from Lae. *Map by Paprika Creative.*

at Nadzab, some 20 miles inland along the
Markham River, and quickly secure it. A force
of Australian and American combat engineers
would come down the Watut River and overland from Marilinan and Tsili Tsili, 30 miles
away, and prepare the strip for the arrival of
American aviation engineers and their equipment on September 6. They would expand the
field for the transports to fly in the 7th Australian Division from Marilinan and Port Moresby. The 7th would advance down the valley and
attack from the rear in coordination with the
9th's advance westward.

The airborne part of the plan followed existing
doctrine—a daylight airfield seizure for follow-
on air-landing forces. The full regiment would
jump at once from C-47s using three battalion
drop zones (DZs). The 1st Battalion's task was
to take and secure the airfield proper; the other
two to protect the flanks. 2d Battalion jumped
to the north and 3d to the east to secure the
village of Gabmatzung. Gliders (27 along with
62 pilots reached Australia between February
and April) had been a part of the plan to lift
Australians and equipment, but were not actually used. Weather conditions and problems assembling enough aircraft delayed the offensive
until September.

Blamey's troops came ashore on September 4. Next morning Col. Kenneth H. Kinsler's
503d loaded into 54th Troop Carrier Wing
(TCW) aircraft at fields around Port Moresby.
A detachment of volunteer Australian gunners
with two 25-pound howitzers accompanied
them, despite never having had jump training.
At 0825 the lead C-47 went wheels up, and all
were in the air within 15 minutes and starting
out on a 200-mile trip. In all, 302 planes from
eight different airfields participated in the
operation, counting escorting fighters, ground
attack aircraft, and three B-17s with their fighters. MacArthur and Kenney rode in the B-17s
as observers. After crossing the Owen Stanley
Range the transports descended to jump height
of 400–500 feet. Red Light went on at 1009
and Green Light at 1020. In less than five
minutes some 1,700 men went out the door of
more than 80 C-47s, with Lt. Col. John J. Tolson, III, commanding 3d Battalion as jumper
one of stick one. There were no refusals; the
only man not to jump did so because he had
passed out from the heat.

The drop went well, but it did not quite achieve
the precision intended. 3d Battalion had gone
first but landed wide. Many troopers landed
in 12-foot-high, razor-sharp kunai grass and

tangled vines. The other battalions achieved tighter landing with 95 percent hitting the DZ. Fortunately no Japanese were in the area so the regiment rapidly assembled and moved out to accomplish all assigned tasks. The artillerymen didn't make their maiden jump from their five C-47s until the afternoon. Five B-17 heavy bombers dropped 15 tons of supplies instead of explosives thanks to SWPA's ingenuity.

While the 1st Battalion prepared the airfield, the 2d and 3d Battalions moved to defensive positions to east and north in case of a Japanese attack. In late afternoon the Australian engineer column moving down the Watut River arrived and promptly went to work. By first light on September 6, C-47 transports began arriving. They carried a detachment from the 871st Airborne Engineer Battalion to continue improvements and the first of the 7th (Australian) Division being airlifted from Port Moresby. The theater's first major tactical airlift of combat forces turned out to be a major success. On September 10, Australians relieved the regiment of its defensive responsibilities although the 3d Battalion continued to carry out offensive patrols for six more days.

Lae fell to the Allies on September 16. The next day transports began flying the 503d back to Port Moresby. Thereafter the regiment began airborne training to be ready for the next mission. Losses had been light with only 36 jump injuries (three fatal) and just eight paratroopers killed and 12 wounded in action. To MacArthur and his generals Nadzab showed that airborne troops belonged on the SWPA battlefield as part of combined operations. It also highlighted the feasibility of conducting air assault operations that combined paratroopers with ground forces flown into an airhead, and the value of aerial resupply.

The 503d's success had important but unintended consequences. Problems experienced during Operation HUSKY (see Chapter 3) cast serious doubt on the future of the Army's airborne forces. For many in the fledgling airborne community the success at Nadzab in September 1943 came as welcome proof of what airborne troops could accomplish. Maj. Gen. Joseph Swing, then heading the Swing Board but soon to arrive in the Pacific in command of the 11th Airborne Division, used Nadzab as an example of the kind of airborne operations that he envisioned. In addition, Kenney enthusiastically wrote to Gen. Henry "Hap" Arnold, Army Air Forces (AAF) commander, that "the operation was a magnificent spectacle," which did not hurt the airborne cause. In its own way, the 503d at Nadzab helped to save the airborne force. It also profoundly influenced the thinking of future senior leaders such as Tolson.

NOEMFOOR ISLAND
After Nadzab SWPA learned the same lesson that the airborne experienced in Europe—planning for operations had a hard time keeping up with the changing situation. Finally, in June 1944 SWPA formed Cyclone Task Force around the 158th Regimental Combat Team (RCT). The 503d remained in General Headquarters Reserve but on call as reinforcements.

Cyclone's task supported MacArthur's capture of Wakde and Biak islands off the northwest coast of New Guinea. Fierce Japanese resistance encountered on Biak threatened the timetable for the conclusion of the campaign. Intelligence concluded that reinforcements were infiltrating from Noemfoor Island, 80 miles farther west. Therefore MacArthur ordered its capture by Lt. Gen. Walter C. Krueger's Sixth Army as Operation TABLE TENNIS.

right
Paratroopers from the 503d landing at Kamiri Strip, Noemfoor Island, as a B-17 keeps watch overhead.
Library of Congress.

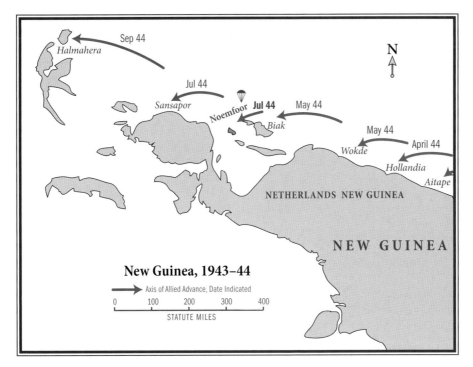

New Guinea, 1943–44

Axis of Allied Advance, Date Indicated

0   100   200   300   400
STATUTE MILES

COL. GEORGE M. "THE WARDEN" JONES

Col. George M. "The Warden" Jones earned a strange distinction at Noemfoor: he became the only airborne officer in the war to carry out a bombing and strafing attack on an enemy naval vessel. One morning as the ground combat was nearing its end, he climbed into a two-seat artillery observation plane with his Thompson submachine gun and a bag of hand grenades. After turning back due to low fuel, he and the pilot spotted about a dozen Japanese fleeing the island in a small native boat. As the pilot made several passes like a dive-bomber Jones leaned out, fired, and threw his grenades. He only hit one man, but the rest were captured later.

Noemfoor is only 14 miles long and 11 miles wide with several large hills and thick jungle on the south side. But it does have a belt of coral reef around the edges and several beaches. The Japanese used slave labor to start building three airfields late in 1943. Only two, Kamiri on the flatter north coast and Number on the southwest, could be considered even partially usable. Kamiri, with two runways and a nearby beach, became the primary objective. It was also the most heavily defended of the airfields.

Cyclone's amphibious assault on July 2, 1944, employed more than 13,000 men. The 158th RCT quickly overran the airfield and drove the Japanese back into the jungle. Engineer equipment followed and work immediately began to extend the airfield. About three hours after the first wave came ashore, Brig. Gen. Edwin Patrick's intelligence staff told him that prisoners reported a much stronger enemy garrison than the Americans expected. Although this later proved to be wrong, he radioed Krueger to request more troops for his task force. Patrick specifically wanted paratroops. The 503d at Hollandia received Krueger's orders to jump in as reinforcements on D+1.

By 0630 on July 3 Col. George M. Jones, now the regimental commander, had his 1st Battalion lifting off from Cyclops airdrome. He rode as jumpmaster in the first of 41 C-47s from 54th TCW. The transport aircraft shortage meant that only a single battalion could be flown on each lift. The DZ at Kamiri was a long (1,500 feet), relatively narrow (only 250 feet)

Noemfoor Island fit nicely into the leapfrogging events of the 1944 New Guinea campaign. *Map by Paprika Creative.*

Coast Guardsmen converse with paratroopers injured during the combat jumps on Noemfoor Island, New Guinea, by 503d Parachute Infantry, July 3 and 4, 1944.
U.S. Coast Guard photo.

clearing next to a runway. Thus the plan called for the planes to fly two abreast instead of the normal three. That morning Patrick realized that equipment, supplies, and damaged aircraft still lined the field, but his warning to narrow the drop to single file did not reach Jones before Green Light went on at 1000.

Although the 503d knew that it was not jumping into hostile terrain, they had many more problems here than at Nadzab. The two lead C-47s approached at only 175 feet, not the planned 400, although succeeding aircraft were closer to the proper altitude. High winds blew men about. And the DZ turned out to be much harder and more cluttered than anyone expected. Some chutes barely opened before the men hit the ground. Losses were high even though no enemy fire took place. Hard landings caused 10 percent jump injuries in the 20 minutes it took for all 739 paratroopers to reach the ground. This total did not include Jones who refused medical attention for what he feared was a concussion. Half of the men in his stick (nine of 19) had critical injuries.

The 3d Battalion's turn came on D+2. Using the aircraft from the previous day it approached at 400 feet and in a single column. These 658 paratroopers began going out the door at 0955, five minutes ahead of plan. They knew of the problems encountered on the ground the day before and made every effort to correct them. Most of the men did avoid the obstacles and land in sand. Enough still struck hard coral to cause 56 more jump casualties. This was enough to change the original concept of operations. The remaining 2d Battalion came ashore in landing craft on July 11.

The 503d paid a heavy price for its second combat jump. It lost 128 men—nearly nine percent. Fifty-nine injuries were serious fractures of the type that ended careers in the airborne. Losses among the leaders included one of the two battalion commanders and three of the six rifle company commanders.

Once on the ground Patrick assigned Jones a sector of the line, and it joined in the difficult task of mopping up; that is, breaking down into squads and platoons to find and eliminate snipers and pockets of Japanese who refused to surrender and fought to the death. On July 23 a platoon was surprised and got pinned down. Sgt. Ray E. Eubanks took his squad and moved to their rescue. Eubanks kept going even after being wounded and led from the front. Before being killed himself, he clubbed four of the enemy to death with his ruined rifle. Eubanks received a posthumous Medal of Honor for this action. It was only the first for the 503d.

The regiment remained in action until August 28 when it withdrew to a base camp back at Kamiri. Sixth Army officially declared the campaign completed three days later. Ground combat cost 38 men killed in action and 72 wounded. More than 400 had serious illnesses. But now the 462d Parachute Field Artillery Battalion and Company A of the 161st Parachute Engineer Battalion arrived to join the infantry and create the 503d RCT. In mid-November they left Noemfoor and moved to Mindoro in the Philippines to prepare to join in the liberation of Leyte.

LEYTE

Only one of the five airborne divisions served in the Pacific. The 11th Airborne Division under Gen. Swing had the normal configuration but without the modifications that took place in Europe. It contained the usual artillery, engineer, and support elements, but only three infantry regiments. Swing, however, believed in cross-training, making the 511th Parachute Infantry and 187th and 188th Glider Infantry more flexible than most of their counterparts. It arrived at Oro Bay, New Guinea, in late May 1944. From then until October Swing put his men through intensive training in both airborne and amphibious operations, and jungle fighting. During that entire period it formed an important part of MacArthur's strategic reserve.

The division's baptism in combat came on Leyte between November 18 and December 27. SWPA called the 11th forward from New Guinea to reinforce Sixth Army, and upon landing it went into action as part of the force used to clear the southern end of the island. It had the mission of driving west into the mountains to link with other troops converging on Ormoc from the north and south. But it did not enter action on November 18 in the airborne manner; it went ashore across the beach at Bito on the island's east coast.

Four days later XXIV Corps ordered Swing to relieve the 7th Infantry Division and begin clearing its assigned sector while at the same time protecting the corps's rear. The 11th assembled the force chosen for the offensive mission at Burauen. On November 25 it entered the mountains and began an attack up the central valley. The operation took place in miserable conditions where terrain and weather caused even more trouble than the Japanese—mud, jungle, steep slopes, and frequent rains. At best only a single battalion could attack. Flanking maneuvers were impossible. The 511th Parachute Infantry led off with the 3d Battalion reaching the high ground at Mahonag on December 6.

Along the way companies were sometimes cut off and needed aerial resupply from the division's small spotter planes such as the L-4 and L-5. The terrain eliminated normal artillery support because the 75-mm pack howitzers could not be moved as usual. One option overcame that problem. The small table-top plateau at Manarawat provided a potential DZ even though steep cliffs surrounded it on three sides. On December 3–4 a single C-47 made 13 separate sorties from San Pablo airfield to drop the men and howitzers of Battery A, 457th Parachute Field Artillery. The men jumped from a height of only 300 feet with the battalion commander acting as jumpmaster. A platoon from Company B of the 187th also jumped into Manarawat to guard a portable surgical hospital set up to evacuate casualties using spotter planes capable of landing on the tiny spot used as the DZ.

Members of Company E, 2d Battalion, 503d Parachute Infantry, approach the military headquarters building in San Jose, Mindoro, Philippines, December 15, 1944. *National Archives.*

When the advance resumed Company G of the 511th made first contact with the 32d Infantry Division on December 15. But it had been separated from the main body for four days. Finally, on December 20, the 187th passed through the 511th and took up the drive. Two days later it reached the 32d. During the mountain combat Pvt. Elmer E. Fryar of Company E, 511th Parachute Infantry, attempted a one-man battle against an enemy platoon, recovered several wounded, and finally took a sniper's bullet intended to kill his platoon leader. The posthumous Medal of Honor awarded to Fryar was the division's first. Once the mopping up ended, Swing took his men back into reserve. Training in the Dulag area restored its airborne proficiency.

JAPANESE PARATROOPS

As the 11th fought its way through the mountains one of the war's strangest airborne incidents took place in its rear area.

Japan's small airborne force made only several minor jumps in early 1942 as they overran the East Indies, with little success, but the campaign won control of vital raw materials. Now Imperial General Headquarters knew that American control of Leyte and its airfields would choke their war industries by cutting off the route to the Indies. To defend Japan itself, they had to destroy the airstrips.

Tokyo ordered the 3d and 4th Airborne Raiding Regiments in Luzon to carry out the mission. They allocated 39 transports, each carrying 15 jumpers, with supporting fighters and bombers. Plans targeted San Pablo, Buri, Bayug near Burauen, and two other airfields.

The jumpers would land in three waves and link up with other troops infiltrating through American lines.

One hundred and fifty infiltrators hit Buri airfield, striking early in the morning of December 6. It had been intended to occur in tandem with the airborne attack but the infiltrators did not know that bad weather had delayed the jump by a day. They failed to break through the support troops stationed at the field. A counterattack by 1st Battalion, 187th Glider Infantry chased the survivors off. Unfortunately the 187th came from San Pablo, which took most of its defenders away before the paratroops struck.

The Japanese lost 18 transports to antiaircraft fire but still dropped about 350 men at dusk on December 6. Most of them reached the ground near the San Pablo airstrip and attacked there. Others headed toward Buri. The paratroopers who struck San Pablo encountered a detachment of the 127th Airborne Engineer Battalion, division artillery's headquarters battery, some support troops, and AAF ground personnel. These defenders held their own until the 674th Parachute Field Artillery Battalion, acting as infantry, arrived. Together they drove away the enemy.

The situation at Buri was different. During the night the men stationed there had withdrawn. When the Japanese arrived in the morning of December 7 they occupied the field unopposed. Although their attacks were poorly coordinated, enemy paratroopers used abandoned weapons and ammunition to resist.

The 11th took four days to secure the airfield completely. The Japanese gamble accomplished nothing and had no effect on the capture of Leyte.

TAGAYTAY RIDGE

The 11th Airborne Division's second assault landing came as part of Lt. Gen. Robert Eichelberger's Eighth Army. SWPA wound up committing two armies and the equivalent of 15 divisions to the capture of Luzon, making this the largest Army action anywhere in the Pacific during World War II. Planners looked at the idea of inserting the 11th into the central plains as part of Sixth Army's main effort. Largely because of the usual shortage of planes, that option was dropped.

At the end of January 1945, Krueger's invasion forces neared Manila from the north, and now MacArthur needed to put in Eichelberger to the south. A secondary part of his landings brought in the 11th at Nasugbu 55 miles south of Manila and almost astride Route 17. Control of that highway cut the capital off from reinforcements and sealed the Japanese garrison's fate. Accordingly the division boarded landing craft and headed to the objective. Attrition from earlier fighting left it with only about 8,200 men, including the 2,000 in the 511th and 1,500 in each of the glider regiments.

At 0830 on January 31, 1945, Swing's soldiers once again arrived on landing craft. Lt. Col. Ernest LaFlamme's 1st Battalion, 188th Glider Infantry led the way, taking advantage of his knowledge of the area. After graduation from West Point in 1937 he had served in the Philippines. By noon the rest of the division was established on shore except for Col. Orin D. Haugen's 511th Parachute Infantry. The 511th formed the main element of a task force held back on Mindoro so that it could jump on Tagaytay Ridge. That critical terrain lay only 20 miles east of Nasugbu along the highway. Haugen's assignment looked like a mini-version of Operation MARKET (see Chapter 4). Although

EQUIPMENT

Paratroopers in the Pacific carried the same basic items as their counterparts in Europe. This photograph taken during training in Australia shows an assistant light machine gunner's equipment laid out for inspection. His personal weapon is the M-1 Garand rifle with one 8-round clip of ammunition at the ready and 200 more rounds of ammunition also in clips. His share of the crew-served .30-caliber machine gun is the tripod and one 136-round belt of ammunition. The final item is a watch compass.

lack of transports required three lifts, the airborne operation would open an inland path for the advancing ground troops.

As soon as the division's base started to function on D-Day, Swing retained only the 1st Battalion of the 187th to defend it and sent the other, plus both battalions of Col. Robert H. Soule's 188th, toward the ridge. It was clear that the Japanese did not intend to hold in place and in fact withdrew inland. On the morning of February 1 Soule found the enemy dug in between two small mountains to defend Aga Pass. Hard fighting all day long failed to break through, causing Swing to postpone the jump a full day. Despite continued resistance the Americans made better progress on February 2, coming within two miles of the ridge when they halted for the night. The 511th's pathfinder platoon then infiltrated forward to mark the DZ.

Back on Mindoro the 915 men of the first wave boarded 48 C-47s from the 317th Troop Carrier Group. By standard airborne practice, Haugen sat as jumper one of stick one. Right on schedule at 0815 the lead 18 aircraft came in and put 345 men down with pinpoint accuracy. One of these, Lt. Hobart B. Wade, held the distinction of being an original member of the Test Platoon. Unfortunately the rest of the planes about six miles behind misinterpreted two bundles that fell by accident and put their 570 jumpers out prematurely. That drop pattern was also perfect, but five miles from the DZ and in thick jungle. This group didn't make it to the assembly area until afternoon.

The 51 C-47s forming the second wave arrived around noon. Pathfinders marked the DZ and at 1210 once again the men leaped into the air at the wrong place. Jumpmasters saw the used parachutes littering the ground from the earlier mistake. In a classic example of missed communications between paratroopers and airmen, the crew chiefs trying to stop the premature exit were ignored.

Fortunately the landings were a surprise, and jump injuries were light (including a third wave which came in on the morning of February 4): only about 50 and few of them serious. Soule had finally broken through the pass. At 1300 the two forces linked up. 511th patrols reached the eastern end where Highway 17 turned north and started downhill toward Manila. By nightfall Haugen reported to Swing that the entire ridge was clear.

Swing now shifted away from the pre-landing concept. Instead of wiping out a few remaining pockets and blocking any enemy troops from crossing the ridge on their way to Manila, he decided to maintain offensive momentum. All available vehicles moved up to support Haugen and sent the 511th racing up the highway to Manila in the afternoon, with the 188th under orders to follow when possible. Trucks for this operation were as scarce as the C-47s had been, allowing only a single battalion to move at one time.

The suddenness and speed of the drive caught the Japanese detachments assigned to block Route 17 by surprise. At Las Piñas 2d Battalion took the bridge in a quick firefight before it could be blown. The tired paratroopers halted there to hold that part of the road open. Now 1st Battalion, coming north on a second truck shuttle from Tagaytay Ridge, passed through and at 1800 continued the race toward Manila. The advance encountered more and more fire as it pushed north toward Nichols Field. Unknown to the Americans, this had been turned into the most heavily defended place in all of the Philippines.

When the 511th reached the Parañaque River two miles beyond Las Piñas, it came to a halt. The bridge there was too damaged to be rushed, and forces on the north bank were too strong to tackle without supporting heavy weapons. Regimental casualties during the day had only been eight men killed and 19 wounded; those of the entire division since landing less than 200 (not counting the jump injuries). Nichols lay a mile and a half beyond and the Manila city limits were just four miles away. But in its own way on February 4 Parañaque became the 11th Airborne Division's "bridge too far."

On February 5 Swing and his soldiers started a new kind of war—slow, costly urban combat. They had to punch through the Genko Line with its barbed wire entanglements, concrete bunkers, and even 5-inch guns taken off warships. One frustrated company commander being pounded by those weapons radioed division headquarters to "Tell Admiral Halsey to stop looking for the Jap Fleet. It's dug in here on Nichols Field." After getting past the airfield the division had to repeat the process at Fort McKinley.

The hard fighting dragged on until the city surrendered on February 21. Victory came at a high price for the airborne. About two-thirds of the 900 killed, wounded, or missing came from the two glider regiments. The 511th lost Haugen mortally wounded on Libertad Avenue on February 11, and PFC First Class Manuel Perez, Jr., near Fort McKinley. Perez was a scout with Company A. He captured one of the largest bunkers single-handed using grenades, his rifle and one he took from an enemy he had killed, and finally a bayonet. His Medal of Honor came through long after Perez died conducting another one-man charge a week after the original action.

Paratroopers of 503d Parachute Infantry hooked up and ready to shuffle to the door for the jump on Corregidor. *National Archives.*

CORREGIDOR

The other airborne asset in SWPA also saw action in the fighting to liberate Manila and its bay. After Noemfoor the 503d RCT had been able to rebuild its strength and carry out intense training on Mindoro. Frequently men made multiple practice jumps in a month. Everyone in the team assumed that they would be dropping on Nichols Field, but MacArthur decided that using them to carry out one of the three main operations around the bay made more sense. Given the subsequent discovery of Japanese strength at Nichols, this was a fortunate change.

On February 5, he approved an operations plan drawn up by Sixth Army to retake Corregidor Island (nicknamed "the Rock") in a classic coup de main—a much larger and more sophisticated version of the German capture of Eben Emael in 1940. Jones would command Rock Force to accomplish the task. His RCT would jump directly onto the heavily fortified island while a battalion landing team (BLT) built around the 3d Battalion, 34th Infantry, simultaneously came in from Bataan on landing craft. Tolson had moved on after Nadzab to become one of the best airborne planners of the war, but came back for this jump as Jones's deputy.

It took a week to work out the details. Krueger directed that the drop take place on the high ground ("Topside") to achieve maximum surprise. The paratroopers would then fight their way down to link up with the force coming ashore "Bottomside" and fighting upwards. Corregidor stretched three and a half miles long, with its widest part being only a mile and a half; the highest peak stood 550 feet above sea level. Intelligence believed that the defenders numbered about 600. Unfortunately the actual garrison amounted to 5,000, most of them Japanese Imperial Marines. Nearly all of their attention, however, was directed toward repelling an attack from the sea.

Only two DZs were at all feasible, both quite small. One, a former golf course, measured about 1,000 feet by 550 feet. The other, a former parade ground, was only 975 feet long but 750 feet wide. Both were at the extreme safety limit and exposed to disaster if adverse winds caught the men in the air. Officially the plans estimated jump injuries at 20 percent of the force. Privately, Jones feared that fully half would be hurt, although they would jump from 600 feet. Aerial congestion further complicated matters. Postage-stamp DZs required the transports to fly single file and to circle for repeated passes because only six to eight

Jumpers descend toward the parade ground DZ in the "Topside" of Corregidor. *National Archives.*

men could safely go out the door on each pass. H-Hour would be 0830 on February 16 with the 58 C-47s coming from the 317th Troop Carrier Group. The 503d employed two waves on D-Day leaving one battalion in reserve to follow on D+1. Each battalion team included a platoon of engineers, a reinforced battery of field artillery, and a proportion of headquarters and support personnel.

Takeoff from Hill Field and San Juan Field and the flight to Luzon went smoothly. At 0833, just three minutes behind schedule, Lt. Col. John Erickson went out the door. The rest of his 3d Battalion followed along with a reinforced battery from the 462d Parachute Field Artillery Battalion, engineers, and part of the combat team headquarters including Jones. The full drop onto the two DZs took one-and-one-half hours by which time all of the initial objectives were secure. Twenty-mile-per-hour winds caused some problems, and the landing left the battalion somewhat scrambled. Because the assault turned out to be even more of a surprise than the planners had dared to hope, and because the men reacted swiftly, no real harm came of it. In fact, as icing on the cake, a grenade thrown by one of the paratroopers killed the island commander in the opening minutes effectively eliminating Japanese command and control.

The BLT crossing from Miraviles Point had ringside seats to watch the 503d perform its mission. They reached the designated beach without incident and began landing about 1030 where Corregidor's "tail" joined its "head." The first four sets of boats discharged two tanks along with the infantrymen. Malinta Hill, the key terrain, fell to the BLT hands with minor losses. Japanese opposition really began only as the last of the landing craft approached, but the heavy fire didn't produce casualties.

At 1240 Tolson and the second wave flew overhead in 51 C-47s. This put the 2d Battalion team, including the entire Service Company, onto both the golf course and the parade ground. Its jump pattern was better, but still not perfect. And because surprise was no longer a factor, they came under more ground fire. Once on the ground the 2d Battalion took over responsibility for the perimeter, and 3d Battalion pushed out to start clearing Topside. By the end of the day about 2,050 men had jumped onto the island at a cost of 280 casualties (13.7 percent). Most were jump injuries because the fighting turned out to be easier than expected.

Just after daylight on February 17, 40 B-24 heavy bombers dropped supplies and ammunition. Japanese small arms fire hit 16 aircraft, but also revealed positions for the paratroopers to attack. The plan called for the last of the RCT, the 1st Battalion force, to jump at 0830 on February 17. Jones decided to have it land on Bataan and use the previous day's land-

Notice the parachutes of the individual sticks on the ground and in the air during the drop on Corregidor, February 16, 1945. *National Archives.*

ing craft rather than suffer needless injuries. Because supply bundles had already been loaded, the C-47s still flew over Corregidor and dropped them on schedule.

The new arrivals came ashore that afternoon expecting to find most of the resistance over. Instead they walked into a much more intense battle than D-Day's. The large garrison's determination to hold out to the last man occupied Rock Force for the next 10 days. Combat frequently took place at such close range that the 462d's 75-mm pack howitzers had to be used in direct fire mode. One man was killed by a sword. On the morning of February 19 Pvt. Lloyd G. McCarter of Company F culminated a string of exceptional deeds by playing a critical role in breaking up a large banzai charge. He went through three weapons in a short period, discarding them as they overheated. Finally, when the pile of dead in front of his foxhole became too high, he had to climb out in order to keep shooting. A chest wound finally dropped him, and even then he argued with the medic trying to pull him to safety until he passed out from a loss of blood. McCarter received the only Medal of Honor given for the capture of Corregidor.

Losses mounted as a result of action and exhaustion. At 1100 on February 26 the regiment took its heaviest blow when several hundred Japanese committed suicide by blowing up Monkey Point Tunnel. The massive explosion tossed a tank 50 yards through the air and left 54 paratroopers dead and another 145 wounded. It left 1st Battalion combat ineffective. Company A, the hardest hit, had come ashore on February 17 with six officers and 126 enlisted men; by February 26, it was down to two officers and only 42 men. By the end of the day the last of the island fell, and Rock Force began mopping up.

MacArthur landed on March 2 with a group of dignitaries and arrived at the parade ground about 1100 to find an honor guard from the RCT and the 3d Battalion, 34th Infantry, in formation. Col. Jones welcomed him with the words, "Sir, I present you the Fortress Corregidor," and the American flag was ceremonially raised. Six days later the 503d left for Mindoro. Not counting the BLT's casualties, Jones had lost a total of 169 dead and 615 wounded or injured.

LOS BAÑOS AND BEYOND

The 11th Airborne Division ended its role in the liberation of Manila and pulled back to the Laguna de Bay with only about 7,000 combat effectives left. Even as Swing attempted to clear a sector of the previously bypassed Cavite-Ternante area in February, he received a warning to be prepared to conduct a special mission. The chance of harm coming to more than 2,000 civilians being held in Internment Camp No. 2 at Los Baños became an important issue for senior American commanders. The execution order arrived on February 17, setting February 23 as D-Day. In only a week the tired staff put together an operation that stands as a classic airborne raid.

Camp No. 2 lay about 50 miles southwest of Manila and near the shore of Laguna de Bay. Confirmed intelligence identified 0700 as the critical time to strike. Not only were all the prisoners lined up and counted at that time, but nearly all of the 80 guards conducted a half-hour of physical training which left only a skeleton force watching the camp. Using this information the plan provided for five separate but interrelated actions. The raid itself would first insert a small reconnaissance element and then use a jump close to the camp to overpower the guards. The internees would be extracted and then cared for in a secure location. A diver-

sion had to draw away any possible reinforcements. With no time for rehearsal, the planners kept things flexible and prevented the complex operation from becoming complicated.

Swing put Soule in overall command and allocated troops to perform the various tasks. Three parts of the 511th Parachute Infantry received the job of making the rescue: Lt. George Skau's reconnaissance platoon to infiltrate; Company B under Lt. John M. Ringler to make the jump; and the rest of Maj. Henry Burgess's 1st Battalion for the extraction. The latter force included a company of engineers and two 75-mm assault guns, all carried by the 672d Amphibious Tractor Battalion. Isolating the battlefield fell to the 1st Battalion, 188th Glider Infantry, two of the division's artillery battalions, and a company of tank destroyers. On February 20 and 21 these units learned of the mission and pulled back from the front lines. They had only a day or two to prepare.

Skau's 31 men infiltrated without difficulty just after dark on February 21 and made contact with about 300 guerrillas operating in the Los Baños area. During the night of February 22, the combined force used the cover of darkness to get into position around the camp and situate pathfinders to mark the DZ. The airborne force got into position on the same night. Ringler moved his 155 paratroopers to Nichols Field and joined the nine C-47s from the 65th Troop Carrier Squadron in Leyte. Bulldozers hastily cleared the runway to let them land. The paratroopers slept beneath the wings of their transports. The other mission components assembled at their respective jumping-off points and began the round of meetings and briefings that came to be known to later generations as troop-leading procedures.

The actual assault went like clockwork, being completed in a matter of minutes. The planes

The joy of these internees liberated from Los Baños gave rise to the 11th Airborne Division's nickname "The Angels." *National Archives.*

lifted off at 0640 and took only 20 minutes to reach the release point—barely long enough to complete pre-jump checks. Ringler led his team out the door at a height of 800 feet exactly at 0700. Two minutes earlier the pathfinders used white phosphorous grenades to mark the small DZ. While the paratroopers floated down, Skau and the guerrillas hit the guards beginning with a bazooka round blowing up the pillbox at the main gate as soon as the first parachute opened. Just as intelligence had reported there were only a few Japanese conducting the morning roll call, and before any harm could come to the civilians all had been eliminated. Company B's landing had been nearly perfect with no injuries and a tight pattern. They quickly crossed the 800 yards to the camp and eradicated the enemy.

At 0500 Burgess's force boarded the 59 amphibious tractors (amtracs) allocated for the evacuation. The convoy moved by water from Mamatid to the camp. By the time they pulled ashore the assault team was trying to get the stunned prisoners organized and moved to the beach, a task more difficult than the combat. All of the women and children and most of the men fit into the amtracs. They were taken back to base, and transported to the New Bilibid prison where doctors, hot food, and other support awaited. The most able-bodied prisoners and the paratroopers faced only light and erratic gunfire while they waited for a second lift. During the entire raid no civilians were hurt, and only one soldier was wounded at the camp. Two men were killed and two others wounded in the 188th's diversion. The 11th Airborne had written the "how-to" textbook for a successful raid.

The main focus of the 11th after Manila concerned the Lipa Corridor, the most important north-south route in southern Luzon with access to the key east-west lines of communications as well. XIV Corps drew the mission of clearing the corridor and the land beyond including the shoreline forming the north side of the Visayan Passages. Its only combat elements were the division and the separate 158th RCT and these were assigned to execute a pincers movement. The latter would go southeast from Nasugbu and hook north. The division sent the 511th and the 187th Glider Infantry into the corridor from the north and northwest to advance along the west coast, and then turn toward the 158th. The 188th had to protect the lines of communications which kept it out of offensive action.

The corps expected to face 10,000 to 17,000 Japanese with only worn-down soldiers equal to about two-thirds that of a standard infantry division. Actual strength of the Fuji Force amounted to about 13,000 men, but no more than 3,000 were trained infantry.

The 187th kicked off the drive on March 7 by moving down from Tagaytay Ridge. A day later it made contact and the hard fight began. On March 11 the 511th passed through and took the lead and quickly slammed into a stronghold on Mt. Bijiang which only fell eight days later to guerrillas after heavy pounding by artillery. Meanwhile the division sideslipped and pushed on toward Santo Tomas and Los Baños. Because it lacked the strength to punch through Fuji Force's main line of resistance it had to hold until March 23 when the 1st Cavalry Division took up the battle.

This did not end the 11th's labors. Krueger moved it to the other end of the corridor to replace the 158th in the southern sector where it faced a new obstacle—Mt. Macolod. Swing was now down to only four infantry battalions, the 187th and one each from the 188th and 511th, which he formed into two task forces. The 187th took until April 21 to capture the mountain. The other worked in concert with the 1st Cavalry Division in clearing the Lipa Corridor and then turned east with the rest of the corps. Due to reduced strength it had only a reconnaissance function, but carried that out aggressively. As more of the division came up, Swing passed to the offensive and on April 30 ended Japanese organized resistance at Mt. Malepunyo. He then concentrated on rebuilding and training the division to restore it to its former capabilities.

The 503d did the same with its last combat coming on the ground. In June it took part in clearing the island of Negros.

The final airborne operation in the Pacific took place on June 23, 1945, near Appari. Sixth Army had begun a drive to clear the Cagayan Valley. Krueger decided that a jump would be needed to seal the north end before the Japanese could retreat to that town. By the time he ordered Swing to execute the operation, ground pursuit had already reached the area. Krueger still felt that he needed an airborne insertion to reinforce his spearhead and on June 21 set the drop for two days later.

Swing therefore created Gypsy Force with slightly more than 1,000 men to carry out a landing at Camalaniugan Airstrip. Its main element consisted of Burgess's 1st Battalion of the 511th reinforced by Companies G and I from the 3d Battalion. The artillery component consisted of a reinforced Battery C, 457th Parachute Field Artillery Battalion. Along with attachments they flew on 54 C-47s and 14 C-46s from the 317th and 422d TCGs. The unique aspect of the operation was the only combat use of gliders in the Pacific. Six CG-7As and one CG-13 would bring in 19 small trucks, six Jeeps, a trailer, and some supplies.

The men boarded the transports at 0430 on June 23 at the airstrip at Lipa. Wheels up came on time at 0600 with the tugs towing the gliders forming the tail of the aerial column. Pathfinders moving with the ground troops had laid out the DZ the day before and coordinated with the Rangers and a large guerrilla force holding the area. At 0900 fighters laid down a protective smoke screen and the transports made their run. The C-47s in the lead were supposed to drop the paratroopers from 700 feet but came in a bit high. This caused the following C-46s to move up to 1,100 feet to avoid hitting the men. Despite the height, all 937 jumpers landed accurately, and all seven gliders came in safely. A 25-mile-per-hour wind and numerous ruts caused jump injuries of seven percent, but within an hour Burgess had finished assembling and set off to link up with the 37th Infantry Division. By July 2 they had returned to Lipa.

The liberation of the Philippines is symbolized by Gen. MacArthur's flag-raising on Corregidor, March 2, 1945. The 503d Parachute Infantry is in formation on the left. *National Archives.*

The 11th Airborne Division conducted its own jump school at Lipa airstrip in the Philippines. *National Archives.*

In August, after the two atomic bombs had been dropped on Hiroshima and Nagasaki, the 11th Airborne Division moved to Okinawa and prepared to occupy Japan. First elements of the division landed at Atsugi airfield near Tokyo on August 30, 1945, to begin occupation duty.

CHINA-BURMA-INDIA THEATER

None of the Army's airborne units served in CBI, yet it played an important role in the evolution of tactics and procedures for future operations. AAF personnel worked with quartermaster units to refine early British experiments and SWPA techniques into a sophisticated aerial resupply organization. A small detail assembled on March 4, 1943, and conducted its first supply drop two days later. On March 23, after more men were added, the organization became permanent and sent out detachments to work at various airfields. By the end of the year a full battalion had been committed to the mission working closely with two full troop carrier squadrons.

The ground unit conducted the entire process from warehousing the ammunition, supplies, food, and other items to packaging them, loading the transports, and finally putting them out the door. Since that last step required brute force including men lying on their backs and pushing with legs, the process became know as "kicking out." In time the growing organization worked out a production line to assemble a variety of standardized packs which would be placed into containers or strapped bundles containing a mix of items. Because mules rather than vehicles served as the primary form of ground transportation in tactical operations, they also developed standard loads of animal rations.

The biggest problem came in finding enough parachutes and rigging. The large American G-1 aerial delivery parachute with its 24-foot canopy worked best but was the hardest to obtain and recycle. Smaller 18-foot British parachutes made in India were more available but could only support 150-pound bundles. The last expedient involved free dropping, requiring experimentation to determine proper altitudes and which items in which configurations could survive.

The real impetus for these innovations was British. During the Allied retreat from Burma in early 1942, Col. Orde C. Wingate began considering a way to carry out hit-and-run operations behind the Japanese lines as an economy of force measure. He knew that they could infiltrate on foot but would need to be supplied by air to survive. In February 1943 Wingate, now a brigadier, tested the long-range penetration groups he had created in an earlier raid. They moved overland, avoiding contact, and created havoc before coming back out, but suffered heavy casualties. Along the way they gained the name Chindits, a reference to a mythical Burmese animal.

In August 1943, Lt. Cols. Philip G. Cochran and John R. Alison had begun assembling a

Col. Philip Cochran, commander, 1st Air Commando Group. *National Archives.*

composite AAF team tailored for use in remote areas. Cochran and Alison started out with 13 C-47s, 100 CG-4A Waco gliders and 25 more training gliders, some light liaison planes and other aircraft suitable for evacuating casualties, and a section of P-51 fighters as organic air cover. In October they deployed to CBI as the 5318th Provisional Unit (Air) but kept on growing much as the quartermaster force did. Adding a dozen B-25 medium bombers gave the group the ability to perform close air support. On March 29, 1944, the unit was designated as the 1st Air Commando Group led by now Col. Cochran. At its peak the group operated 25 C-46s and C-47s, 225 gliders, 100 small liaison planes, the 12 B-25s, and 30 fighters. Washington even sent Cochran five Sikorsky YR-4 helicopters which he used for combat search and rescue work.

Wingate, Cochran, and Alison became a team. In early 1944 they created a concept of using the Chindits (now the size of a full division) and air commandos that made a dramatic improvement in the tactics used earlier. Instead of walking the Chindits, along with engineers, would land by glider. The engineers would promptly construct an airstrip, by which C-47s and British transports would land additional troops. Supplies would be delivered by air and casualties flown out of the airhead. This was a more sophisticated version of the Nadzab operation using gliders instead of paratroopers and without the linkup with an amphibious landing.

The first use of the idea came on March 5 when the theater commander sent Wingate into action in Operation THURSDAY via Cochran's aircraft. They planned to use two landing zones (LZs), but last-minute reconnaissance showed what were believed to be antilanding obstacles on the one called Picadilly. Therefore, all forces

were inserted 100 miles behind the lines at LZ Broadway. The first wave consisted of 26 C-47s, each towing two gliders, 37 of which landed on the LZ. Capt. Bill Taylor piloted the first glider with British Lt. Col. Mike Scott's infantrymen on board.

More gliders followed, including one bringing in a bulldozer for the engineers. By the end of the day the British controlled the immediate area, and the airstrip was open for business. Thirty men were killed and 33 more injured in the landing, but a total of 539 men, three mules, and almost 15 tons of supplies arrived safely. The airflow continued through D+6 by which time it had delivered 9,052 men, 1,183 mules, 175 ponies, and more than a half-million pounds of supplies. While Broadway operated Cochran developed a method to retrieve gliders by having the tugs fly low overhead and "snatch" them. A second phase of the operation created Aberdeen LZ in the same way.

Wingate's death on March 24 in a B-25 crash effectively brought an end to his campaign, and by the end of June the last of the men had worked their way back to India. They had accomplished their mission to disrupt Japanese offensive efforts but at the cost of 4,000 casualties. Upon return the theater broke up the Chindits, but not the 1st Air Commando Group. It kept trying new things and perfecting old techniques. Two more air commando groups formed along the same lines: the 2d arrived in CBI in November 1944 while the 3d went to SWPA and began flying on Leyte in January 7, 1945. By the end of the war all three

Crewmen and gliders of the 1st Air Commando Group at Landing Zone Broadway after the night assault, March 3, 1944. *National Archives.*

had evolved into conventional units to meet changing circumstances and were inactivated upon returning to the United States.

The other concentration of American forces in CBI served farther north under Lt. Gen. Joseph W. "Vinegar Joe" Stillwell to keep supply lines open to the Chinese. Stillwell did have a ground combat element, the 5307th Composite Unit (Provisional) commanded by Brig. Gen. Frank A. Merrill and popularly known as Merrill's Marauders. It worked with British and Chinese units to drive the Japanese out of Burma by capturing the airfield at Myitkyina.

Like Wingate's original Chindits, Merrill's men walked to their target and relied on supplies coming by air. More to the point, the unit had been deliberately given an organic airdrop capability with a full set of American parachutes, containers, and packing items handled by 250 to 300 members of the rear echelon who also provided the door kickers. The Marauders routinely conducted their supply drops from 200 feet, but dipped to 150 when clothes and bags of grain could fall without using parachutes.

One remaining American organization in the CBI also relied on aerial insertion and supply and had internal airdrop capabilities. Detachment 101 of the Office of Strategic Services (OSS) had been formed in 1942 as an intelligence-gathering unit and to help downed Allied airmen return to friendly lines. It grew into a partisan force of more than 10,000 Kachin tribesmen and Americans completely supported by air.

Although no regular American airborne units served in Burma (one battalion of British Gurkha paratroopers did jump on May 2, 1945, near Rangoon), the supply of the various allied long-range penetration forces and guerrillas made CBI an important testing ground. Aircraft, packers, and kickers turned out to be the only way to overcome the logistical problems caused by the difficult terrain and the lack of good roads and navigable waterways. The organic airdrop capability used here became a key piece of later contingency operations.

Chapter 7
Postwar and Korea, 1945–53

TO TOKYO

War in the Pacific came to a sudden end when the United States dropped atomic bombs on Hiroshima (August 6, 1945) and Nagasaki (August 9). Gen. Douglas MacArthur and Adm. Chester Nimitz were assembling the huge force to carry out the invasion of Japan, a campaign that they expected to require the hardest fighting and heaviest casualties yet. As part of those preparations the 11th Airborne Division had reopened its parachute school at Lipa, and Maj. Gen. Joseph Swing informally started cross-training his two glider infantry regiments.

Japan's leaders offered unconditional surrender and on August 15 President Harry S. Truman declared V-J Day (Victory against Japan). MacArthur immediately had to switch over from combat to carrying out an unopposed landing to start the occupation. The newly appointed supreme Pacific commander landed at Atsugi airdrome near Yokohama on August 30, 1945.

Occupation needed more than just a general. Bringing in the troops required his staff to take immediate action without the benefit of normal planning. For the airborne such hasty planning came easier than it did for other types of units. Because of the 11th Airborne Division's unique mobility, it became the spearhead. At 0430 on August 11 the alert order reached Lipa. The next day the 54th Troop Carrier Wing (TCW) started flying it out to a forward staging area on Okinawa. To move the men and equipment it used 99 B-24s, 346 C-46s, and 151 C-47s.

The final leg of the journey began at 0100 on August 30 when Swing and his key staff members took off. They landed five hours later at Atsugi and had the command post in operation by 0730. By the time the last of the division closed in on September 12, it and the 54th

TCW had set two new records. Going 1,600 miles made it the longest air movement of the war. Transporting 11,708 men, more than 600 jeeps and trailers, and 640 tons of supplies and equipment made it the largest airlift. The air armada included every large C-54 Skymaster passenger aircraft in the world (165). When the Japanese delegation went out to the battleship USS *Missouri* (BB-63) on September 2 to sign the formal surrender, it sailed from docks guarded by the 11th Airborne Division.

OCCUPATION AND HOME

Peace brought rapid demobilization. In the Pacific the newly formed Far East Command (FEC) kept six divisions, cut down in size to peacetime levels, to carry out the occupation of the heart of the former Japanese Empire. Two went to the newly independent Korean peninsu-

C-119 FLYING BOXCAR

The Fairchild C-119 Flying Boxcar entered service in 1949 and immediately increased the combat power of an airborne operation. Its allowable cargo load eventually surpassed 20,000 pounds. The C-119 could carry a 3/4-ton truck plus 105-mm howitzer, or a 2-1/2 ton truck, easily loaded and unloaded from the wide-open clamshell doors at rear.

Paratroopers of the 187th Airborne Infantry don parachutes and Mae West life preservers before boarding a 483d Troop Carrier Wing U.S. Air Force C-119 Flying Boxcar en route from southern Japan to Korea in 1952, during the Korean War. *National Archives.*

la. The 11th Airborne and three other divisions took charge of the Japanese home islands.

After about a year spread out in detachments, FEC realized that it would not have to deal with unrest and began bringing units back together. The 511th Parachute Infantry established its base near Hachinohe and named it Camp Orin D. Haugen after its wartime commander. Now the division resumed serious parachute training.

When the Americans left Korea during the winter of 1948–49 it freed up the airborne to sail back to the United States. The 11th set up at Camp (later Fort) Campbell, Kentucky, with only two of its infantry regiments. The 188th Glider Infantry was inactivated leaving the 511th and the 187th, both of which were renamed as airborne infantry regiments and served on full jump status. The 503d Airborne Infantry did not join the division until March 12, 1951, when it was activated to replace the 187th.

KOREAN WAR

In 1945 the Allies restored the independence of Korea, but split the peninsula into two occupation zones. The Soviet Union took charge in the north and the western Allies in the south. When occupation ended these zones formed two distinct countries, each with armed forces trained during the occupation. North Korea

established its capital in P'yongyang and South Korea used Seoul. The two cities lay south and north, respectively, of the 38th Parallel, the east-west line dividing the peninsula.

On June 25, 1950, the North Korea Peoples Army (NKPA) suddenly attacked its unprepared neighbor and started to overrun the entire peninsula. The United States reacted by committing troops and working diplomatically to gain the support of the United Nations (UN). MacArthur sent a task force composed of his best-trained troops from Japan. However, the token force—Task Force Smith, named for Lt. Col. Charles B. Smith, commanding officer, 1st Battalion, 21st Infantry, 24th Infantry Division—was simply overwhelmed.

Trying to assemble a true army to meet the North Korean threat revealed how deeply the postwar demobilization had cut. Understrength units, old equipment, and shortages in weapons all took time to correct and move into action. Meanwhile MacArthur became the commanding general of all UN forces committed, not only FEC.

As the UN troops were being driven back toward the southern port of Pusan, MacArthur requested immediate reinforcements from the United States. Based on his experience with the airborne during World War II and with the advantage of secure airfields in nearby Japan—a

Trainees from the 11th Airborne Division's jump school earning their wings in Japan in 1947. *National Archives.*

luxury enjoyed by Eisenhower but not by the Pacific—he wanted to have the ability to carry out parachute assaults. In July he specifically asked for a regimental combat team (RCT) from the 82d Airborne Division at Fort Bragg and almost immediately increased the request to the full division. Army Chief of Staff Gen. J. Lawton Collins refused to send any of the 82d, preferring to retain it for other contingencies.

Instead of the "All-Americans," MacArthur got an RCT from the 11th Airborne Division at Fort Campbell. The 187th Airborne Infantry under Col. Frank S. Bowen formed the basis of the team that gave the Korean theater its airborne capability. The 674th Airborne Field Artillery Battalion, Company A of the 127th Airborne Engineer Battalion, and Battery A of the 88th Airborne Antiaircraft Artillery Battalion joined on August 27 to create the combat team. Augmentation personnel included military police and parachute maintenance, medical, and quartermaster personnel. When it deployed, the combat team also included the 11th Airborne Division's pathfinders but soon afterwards organized its own pathfinder team. Total strength consisted of 222 officers, 11 warrant officers, and 4,177 enlisted men.

FIRST MISSION

Bowen assembled his regiment in Theater 3 at Fort Campbell on August 1, 1950, and informed them that they were on alert to go to Korea. Deployment took trains and ships to cross the Pacific and reach port in Japan, trucks to move onward to Ashiya Air Base, and almost immediate airlift by the 314th and 21st TCWs to Korea. The advance party of the combat team landed at Kimpo airfield ten miles west of Seoul on September 22. Their arrival came only one week after the Inchon amphibious landing.

Four days later the full force had assembled. Full, that is, except for a rear detachment including the parachute riggers who set up their base on Kyushu. Although MacArthur tried to use it in several different attacks, the success of the ground advance eliminated the various objectives. Instead the RCT airlanded and became part of the general reserve. He also sent it into immediate action, ordering it to clear the adjacent Kimpo peninsula. On September 27 the first serious combat came when trucks carrying Company L were ambushed by about 400 North Koreans. Three men were killed before the convoy disengaged. Lt. William E. Weber received a Silver Star for this fight.

SUKCH'ON AND SUNCH'ON

MacArthur's forces drove north across the 38th Parallel and took P'yongyang. As the North Koreans retreated from the capital, he decided to use the 187th RCT in a drop behind enemy lines 30 miles north of the capital. Control of

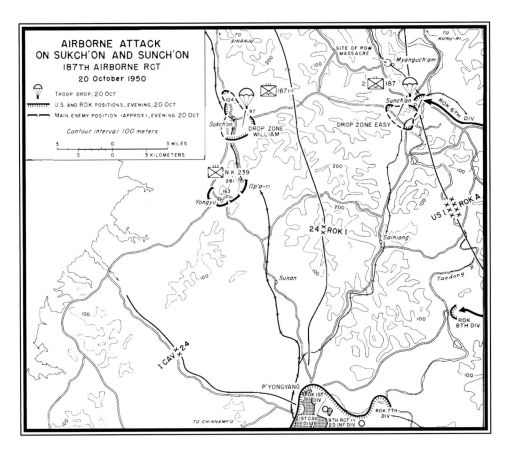

The map label text:

AIRBORNE ATTACK
ON SUKCH'ON AND SUNCH'ON
187TH AIRBORNE RCT
20 October 1950

Troop drop, 20 Oct

U.S. and ROK positions, evening, 20 Oct

Main enemy position (approx), evening 20 Oct

Contour interval 100 meters

Airborne attack on Sukch'on and Sunch'on, October 20, 1950. *U.S. Army Center of Military History.*

this key terrain would cut two important roads and a railroad being used by the enemy which was one of the basic airborne operations. In addition MacArthur hoped to rescue a party of prisoners whom intelligence believed were being moved north—reminiscent of the use of paratroopers at Los Baños.

Bowen worked out a plan to use two drop zones (DZs). The western one, DZ William near the village of Sukch'on, would receive the main body. DZ Easy near Sunch'on would take a task force built around the 2d Battalion. The RCT would attack at dawn in an airborne assault that marked three significant combat "firsts": employment of the C-119 Flying Boxcar transport aircraft, use of a parachute recovery team with the drop instead of coming in later, and conducting a heavy drop of vehicles and supplies. Once on the ground Bowen's men had to hold out for only one day before advancing ground units reached them.

But the North Koreans retreated so fast that the drop had to be moved up one day to October 20. The paratroopers mustered at 0230, ate breakfast, and went out to the aircraft in heavy rain. At 0400 they were issued parachutes but bad weather kept delaying the start. Finally at 1030, as the weather started to clear, they buckled on the main and reserve parachutes and boarded the aircraft. The Air Force assembled

74 C-119s from the 314th Troop Carrier Group (TCG) and 40 C-47s from the 21st TCG, both based in Japan. At noon the lead plane lifted off, carrying Bowen, Lt. Col. Harry F. Lambert from the 674th Airborne Field Artillery Battalion, 13 pathfinders, and a small staff. Two hours later, at 1400, Green Light came on and the commanding officer went out the door first—continuing an important airborne tradition of leading from the front.

The jump on William went very smoothly, with the transports coming over in two separate waves to avoid congestion on the DZ. Lt. Col. Arthur (Harry) Wilson's 1st Battalion went in the first pass and Lt. Col. Delbert E. Munson's 3d Battalion in the second. A total of 1,470 jumpers included all but one battery of the 674th. One man died as the result of enemy fire and only 25 jump injuries were incurred. The 2d Battalion's occupation of DZ Easy also went smoothly, and Lt. Col. William J. Boyle had only 20 men injured in the drop.

In each case the pilots found the precise release point for the DZs. The C-119's design also contributed to a much better landing pattern than those in World War II. Dual side doors allowed the paratroopers to form two sticks, each of 21 men, which exited the transport simultaneously.

top left
Paratroopers board a C-119 transport for the Sukch'on-Sunch'on operation, October 20, 1950. *U.S. Army Center of Military History.*

top right
Seven C-119s release troops over Sunch'on. The C-54 in the background was the Air Force's command and control plane. *U.S. Army Center of Military History.*

Once the men had cleared the DZs the cargo planes carried out the heavy drop. Because the C-119 had a wide rear clamshell door and could be fitted out with rollers on the floor, it became possible to push large items out using platforms and special oversized parachutes. This was the first time the procedure was used in combat and it turned out to be quicker and safer than using gliders. Among other items, the infantrymen received a dozen 105-mm howitzers, four 90-mm antitank guns, light trucks, jeeps, and even a mobile radio transmitter. Supplies and equipment delivered in the operation amounted to 584 tons including ammunition, rations, and water.

Ground action began as soon as the men assembled. The 3d Battalion pushed south to set up the roadblocks. By 1630 it had brushed aside light opposition and secured all of its objectives without suffering any losses. 1st Battalion went north, cleared the village of Sukch'on, and set up additional roadblocks on high ground, also with only minimal enemy contact. At Sunch'on the 2d Battalion accomplished its tasks, once again encountering little resistance. Sadly, North Korean forces had massacred the nearby prisoners of war (POWs). Only 15, all of them wounded, were rescued.

On D+1 patrols from the two DZs made contact and the RCT pushed out from its airhead. The heaviest action came on October 21 when 3d Battalion columns set out toward P'yongyang to find the British 27th Commonwealth Brigade leading the ground advance. Both units became involved in heavy fighting that led to the battalion being awarded a Presidential Unit Citation. In the biggest action Company I ran into a battalion-sized ambush at Opa-ri at 1300. The NKPA overran two of the platoons before the company could break contact at 1530. PFC Richard G. Wilson, a medic, repeatedly exposed himself to fire while treating the wounded, helped them to safety during the withdrawal, and then went back to recover one more soldier. He gave his life trying to protect that man. His posthumous Medal of Honor was the regiment's first.

MacArthur had observed from the air, just as he witnessed the 503d jump into Nadzab. He was treated to a textbook drop that compared favorably to any carried out in World War II, particularly since it had been planned on short notice. Unfortunately, the intelligence experts had failed to estimate the speed of the North Koreans and therefore relatively few were caught in the trap. By the time the 187th RCT withdrew to P'yongyang it had accounted for almost 4,000 prisoners. Victory at Sukch'on-Sunch'on cost it 49 killed, 80 wounded, and 56 jump injuries.

BACK INTO RESERVE

On October 23 the unit came out of the line and passed into Eighth Army's reserve. After shifting farther south in stages it went into blocking positions at Inchon on January 4, 1951. A week later the 187th took up duties guarding the main supply route of X Corps. Finally on February 27 it closed in at K-2 Taegu airfield and began intensive parachute training again to resume full assault capability.

Brig. Gen. Bowen had been promoted after Sukch'on-Sunch'on. Now he brought his men back to Japan where they settled in at Camps Chickamauga and Wood on Kyushu Island. These became the RCT's home between repeated combat deployments in Korea and the place where it reconstituted and restored parachute qualification. Air Force and team planners also developed procedures to spread out the area used in a heavy drop in order to minimize damage.

MUNSAN-NI

Lt. Gen. Matthew B. Ridgway had assumed command of all ground troops in the war in December 1950, while the 187th RCT trained in Japan. After halting an offensive by the NKPA and their Chinese Communist allies he counterattacked to drive the enemy from Seoul. Operation COURAGEOUS exploited that success by pushing them back across the 38th Parallel. As part of that advance he ordered Operation TOMAHAWK to cut off the retreating Chinese and North Korean troops with an airborne assault (Operation HAWK) a relatively short distance beyond the front line.

Bowen had his 187th RCT for the jump. Once again he would conduct a traditional blocking mission and only needed to hold out at Munsan-ni for 24 hours until ground troops arrived. Because of his personal experience as a paratrooper, Ridgway insisted on good weather as a condition for the attack. He set March 19 as D-Day. Again the objective and date had to be changed because the target was overrun, the same condition faced during the breakout from Normandy.

Ridgway shifted Bowen's objective to Munsan-ni and added two airborne Ranger companies to his task force—the 2d composed of African-Americans and the 4th. Munsan-ni sat on the road just south of the Imjin River where it would seal off the enemy's crossing. Adjusting to the new situation took some time and Ridgway did not approve the modifications until March 22 with the next day as D-Day. Fortunately the Air Force had already flown 75 C-119s and 54 C-46s from the 315th Air Division into K-2 airfield outside of Taegu on March 21.

top left
Equipment rigged for heavy drop awaits loading aboard C-119s. Notice the 187th Regimental Combat Team markings on several of the vehicles. *U.S. Army Center of Military History.*

top right
Cargo platforms on the rollers mounted in a C-119. *U.S. Army Center of Military History.*

bottom left
Brig. Gen. Frank S. Bowen Jr., left, commanding general of the 187th Airborne Regimental Combat Team, aboard a U.S. Air Force C-119 before takeoff from Taegu, South Korea, for a training jump on March 7, 1951. Sixteen days later he led the 187th on the combat jump at Munsan-ni. *National Archives.*

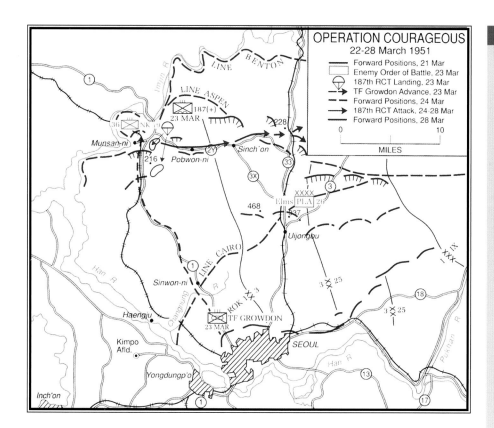

OPERATION COURAGEOUS
22-28 March 1951

Forward Positions, 21 Mar
Enemy Order of Battle, 23 Mar
187th RCT Landing, 23 Mar
TF Growdon Advance, 23 Mar
Forward Positions, 24 Mar
187th RCT Attack, 24-28 Mar
Forward Positions, 28 Mar

0   10

MILES

Operation
COURAGEOUS,
March 22–28, 1951.
*U.S. Army Center of
Military History.*

"RAKKASANS"

To the locals on Kyushu Island the sight of paratroopers floating to the ground during practice jumps seemed strange. They were not familiar with airborne operations and could only think of the canopies as large umbrellas. Therefore the jumpers from the 187th Airborne Infantry were "umbrella men," or "rakkasans." The word became the regiment's official nickname.

Bowen had chosen two drop zones, North and South. The larger one, where most of the force would land, was a mile northeast of the town. The smaller one was four miles to the southeast. The planes would fly in six waves. Four waves were for personnel and bundles, and two waves for the heavy drop of howitzers, Jeeps, and other large items using 48 of the C-119s. Bowen wanted to put the maximum power on the ground in the minimum amount of time. He also arranged for three days' potential aerial resupply.

Meanwhile, the U.S. Army's I Corps created an armored spearhead that would race forward 15 miles to bring support to the airhead. Lt. Col. John S. Growdon commanded, using his own 6th Medium Tank Battalion from the 24th Infantry Division and the 2d Battalion of the 7th Infantry from the 3d Infantry Division. According to custom this became Task Force Growdon. It started forward at 0700 which was two hours before the jump.

The 187th RCT went wheels up (took off) in perfect weather at 0730. The first wave consisted of Bowen, his headquarters elements, the 3d Battalion, and the 4th Rangers. They dropped on the larger zone exactly on schedule at 0900 followed by serials three with the 2d Battalion and 2d Ranger Company and four carrying the 674th Airborne Artillery Battalion. Heavy drop

came in at 1000 on serial five. Accuracy once more turned out to be excellent. The enemy put up minimal opposition. Ridgway quickly arrived overhead in an L-4 Cub light plane to assess the jump for himself.

The second serial of the jump was supposed to fly the 1st Battalion into the smaller zone, followed by its heavy equipment on serial six. Through a mix-up caused by the lead plane with the command group having to turn back because of mechanical problems, they all landed on DZ North. Ironically, at 1030 the final C-46 arrived over the correct drop zone with the delayed men and the one stick went out the door. They landed four miles away from the rest of the regiment.

Having the entire force come in on the single zone caused overcrowding, but quick thinking allowed Bowen to sort things out and start the ground phase of his task on schedule. In fact, his biggest problem came from the civilians who raced into the area to try to steal the parachutes.

The 1st Battalion took the town as planned, detaching Company B to retrieve the men on the other zone. By 1700 the assault force held

all of its D-Day objectives. An hour and a half later Growdon arrived. The attack cost 84 jump injuries, half of whom returned to duty almost at once. Fighting on the ground produced only 19 casualties.

On March 28 the 3d Infantry Division took over the 187th's sector and it passed into Eighth Army reserve. Although the jump itself was a resounding success, through no fault of its own TOMAHAWK failed to accomplish Ridgway's objective. The fluid situation led the UN forces to miss the fact that most of the North Koreans had already passed north of the river.

JAPAN AGAIN

By the end of March 1951 the 187th RCT was back in reserve at Taegu. On April 25, it shifted forward to Yongdungpo to become the spearhead for a ground attack. That drive jumped off on May 25. Once again as soon as the combat situation permitted the team withdrew from contact and went by way of Wonju south to the port of Pusan. On June 26 it sailed back to Japan as a theater reserve. The assessment of the Munsan-ni airborne operation concluded that the confusion in finding DZ South could be corrected by having a joint briefing of the ground and air commanders. It also recognized that constant airborne-troop carrier training had been a key element of the success.

RIDGWAY'S REACTION FORCE

In 1952 the 187th Airborne Infantry spent its third tour of duty in Korea, flying into Pusan when the POWs held at Koje-do Island became unruly. It left its artillery contingent behind in Japan. At Pusan the regiment embarked in Landing Ship, Tanks and sailed to Koje-do a few miles offshore. There, UN forces held 150,000 POWs in 17 different compounds.

Overcrowding cost the military police control. Without that control the hard-line Communists

gradually dominated the others. The lid finally blew off on May 7, 1952. More than 11,000 combat troops, including the infantrymen of the 187th, had to be sent to restore order. Once the situation improved the regiment moved to the mainland and northward to Taegu. There the elements left behind in Japan arrived and the combat team reassembled. It became part of Eighth Army's reserve and again carried out a basic airborne mission of compelling the enemy to allocate forces to deal with the threats of airborne landings at multiple likely locations.

Early in August 1952, the team executed Operation SIDESTEP. By this means it became the 7th Infantry Division's tactical reserve. Between August 11 and October 1 it fought in the center of the division's front. When it came out of the front, it went back into reserve at Yonchon.

FINAL TOUR

On October 7, 1952, the 187th RCT came out of the line and moved back to Taegu. Once there the men started another round of intense training to regain complete airborne readiness. The UN Command had begun planning for an attack at Kojo. The paratroopers' mission contemplated for this operation was one that had become standard fare. The 1st Cavalry Division's amphibious assault formed the main effort. The RCT's jump would support that attack by seizing key terrain to block reinforcements or a Communist retreat. Almost immediately headquarters decided to cancel the attack and sent the team back to Japan.

top left
Men of the 187th Regimental Combat Team waiting alongside their C-119s for the start of the combat jump at Munsan-ni. *U.S. Army Center of Military History.*

top right
Interior of a 314th Troop Carrier Group C-119 on the flight to Munsan-ni. Equipment bundles are rigged on the monorail running down the center of the compartment. *National Archives.*

top left
Landing in the rice paddies at Munsan-ni.
Department of Defense.

top right
Closer view of 187th troopers smacking into the rice paddies at Munsan-ni.
U.S. Army Center of Military History.

bottom right
Company E, 187th Airborne Infantry covering Company F's attack on Hill 299, east of Munsan-ni, Korea.
Department of Defense.

The 187th's third tour in Korea began on June 22, 1953, and did not involve airborne operations. It entered the line on July 16 alongside the 3d Infantry Division and fought on the ground to help restore the UN defensive line. The armistice (July 27) found it still in place.

ARMISTICE

The UN and North Korea signed an armistice at Panmunjom on July 27, 1953, bringing an end to the fighting in Korea. Because this was only a cease-fire and not a peace treaty, two armies still sat uneasily along the demilitarized zone. That fact, plus deep concerns about the Soviet threat to Western Europe, prevented the typical postwar demobilization seen after every other American war.

President Dwight D. Eisenhower took office on January 20, 1953, committed to cutting defense spending by focusing it on the main threat to democracy. Congress supported this program. By 1956 Army strength dropped to only a million men, two-thirds the size at the peak of the Korean War. Airborne forces now had to define their role in terms of the Cold War.

Chapter 8
Cold War, 1946–65

PEACETIME

As soon as the ink dried on the World War II surrender documents, the American people wanted to "bring the boys home." And they wanted to slash the enormous defense budget to cut taxes. Given that the United States had a monopoly on nuclear weapons, political leaders in Washington saw no reason not to start drawing down. Most of the men and women in uniform went back to civilian life, but others remained on occupation duty in Europe and Japan until new democratic governments emerged.

By the end of 1947, when the demobilization process finally ceased, the Army had only 12 divisions still on active duty: four at home and eight overseas. Three of the five airborne divisions stood down almost at once—the 13th, 17th, and 101st—while the 11th remained in Japan as part of the occupation. The 82d at Fort Bragg, North Carolina, formed part of the strategic General Reserve along with one armored and two infantry divisions, but was the only airborne division kept at full strength. Within a few years only 10 divisions remained on active duty, including both the 82d and the 11th which had moved from Japan to Camp Campbell, Kentucky.

Four nominal airborne divisions were included within the postwar reserve components—the 80th, 84th, 100th, and 108th. All were located east of the Mississippi River. They converted to infantry divisions in April 1952 when leaders in Washington concluded that it was too difficult to sustain the necessary special airborne skills and training. The Army also experimented briefly with using divisions as training organizations as a way to build morale among the new recruits and peacetime draftees. Two airborne divisions served in this capacity in

1948–49: the 17th at Camp Pickett, Virginia, and the 101st at Camp Breckinridge, Kentucky.

A NEW ENEMY EMERGES

At the end of World War II there had been widespread belief that the victorious Allies would continue to have good relations, and that the brand-new United Nations (UN) ensured that war could be avoided in the future. Dividing Europe and other occupied territory into distinct English, French, Soviet, and American zones promised to speed up the recovery process without causing friction.

The era of good feelings deteriorated rather rapidly into hostility. Josef Stalin's Soviet Union imposed a much harsher rule over her share of the former Axis homeland. Stalin also took increasingly brazen steps to choke off dissent in liberated nations in Eastern Europe such as Poland, and puppet Communist parties swiftly took control. Winston Churchill proclaimed of Stalin's actions in a speech given at Westminster College in Fulton, Missouri,

in May 1946: "From Stettin in the Baltic to Trieste in the Adriatic an iron curtain has descended across the Continent."

In June 1948, Stalin attempted to chase his former Allies out of Berlin by imposing a blockade to cut off all food and fuel. By 1949, Chinese Communists led by Mao Zedong gained control of that huge country, naming it the People's Republic of China. Because none of these actions involved armed conflict among the former World War II Allies, the postwar years of confrontation became known as the Cold War.

American leaders, regardless of party, reacted swiftly, particularly when they discovered extensive Soviet spying including the theft of the secret of the atomic bomb. Diplomats pursued a foreign policy known as "containment" because it sought to erect a barrier around Stalin through a series of alliances. Holding that line still required military muscle capable of turning back any armed incursion. Preventing Communist expansion in Western Europe led to establishment in 1949 of the most important of the postwar military alliances—the North Atlantic Treaty Organization (NATO).

Obviously the threat of using nuclear weapons played a major role in America's strategy. Its Allies, however, still wanted to be sure that Washington leaders would actually come to their defense by having American troops located where they would be a "tripwire" in the event of an enemy attack. The United States satisfied them by keeping forces at overseas bases after the initial occupation needs passed. Allies in Australia and the Far East were supported not only by the units in Japan that had reacted to the invasion of Korea but also by units in Hawaii and Alaska. Forces committed to NATO grew as the Cold War intensified with more units moving to stations in Europe.

A second type of instability in the years following World War II came from the turmoil caused when former colonies of European nations gained independence. Those in the Middle East made the transition with relatively little violence directed against their former rulers, but then became embroiled in long-term conflict among religious groups. Independence in the Asian region resulted in fighting between pro-Western and Communist elements, often with ethnic overtones. As a rule, the Europeans held on to African colonies longer than those elsewhere and fought against rebels until finally departing, often leaving tribal groups fighting each other for control of the new nations.

DEFINING THE NEW MISSION

Washington leaders had to deal with two types of threats posed by the postwar world situation. First and foremost, they needed to build nuclear and conventional forces to contain the Soviets, their European satellite states, and Communist China. But they also had to react to assorted crises in the rest of the world. Because the majority of countries in Asia, Africa, and the Middle East chose to remain outside the military alliances formed by the two superpowers, they came to be called the Third World.

Each basic mission called for different kinds of Army units. Heavy armored and infantry divisions were required in Europe to engage the Soviets. Not all of the forces needed could stay in forward bases so the Army had to be ready to send reinforcements if trouble broke out. Third World interventions, however, tended to reach critical levels quickly and therefore put a premium on swiftness of movement and agility. The paratroops played a part in both missions. Thanks to new aircraft entering the Air Force inventory during the 1950s, airborne

C-82A PACKET

A new type of transport plane entered service just after World War II ended. The C-82A Packet significantly surpassed the range and capacity of the C-46s and C-47s thanks to an innovative twin boom design. Not only did it carry 42 paratroopers, but with doors on each side it could put out two sticks simultaneously, completing a drop faster and more accurately than before. Additional clamshell doors in the rear permitted carrying a much larger amount of equipment to accompany the troops. A monorail down the passenger compartment allowed the loadmaster to drop fifteen 350-pound bundles in addition to two kicked out the old way. The Fairchild C-119 Flying Boxcar with similar design and more power succeeded the C-82 beginning in 1950.

Paratroopers jumping from a Fairchild C-82 Packet. The jump doors, at 6 feet high by 3 feet wide, were easier to use than the C-47's doors at 5.5 feet high by 2.5 feet wide. The C-82's utility led to development of its look-alike successor, the C-119 Flying Boxcar. *U.S. Air Force.*

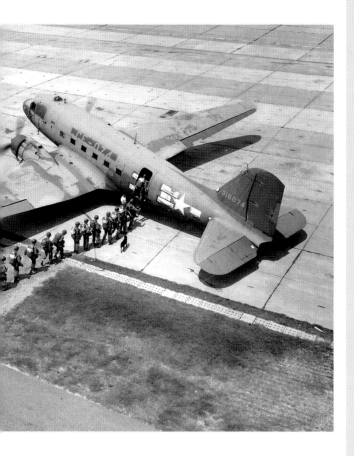

Airborne school trainees follow their jumpmaster's orders to board a C-47 for a practice jump at Lawson Field, Fort Benning, Georgia, August 1946. Even during demobilization, a steady influx of new paratroopers was needed to keep two airborne divisions manned. *U.S. Army.*

divisions and regimental combat teams could be the first reinforcements to reach Europe or bases in the Far East. Paratroops at overseas bases or home stations took on the mission of in-theater reaction force.

FINDING A DESIGN

Immediately after World War II came to an end, Gen. Dwight D. Eisenhower convened a series of boards to evaluate the Army's performance in the European Theater of Operations (ETO). One of the so-called ETO boards reviewed the use of airborne forces and recommended changes in unit organization. This started the Army on a search for the best configuration to perform the often-competing missions. It lasted into the 1960s.

The first examination, which took place in 1946, looked at the way in which airborne divisions in both theaters had actually been used and recognized that they frequently had to fight in the line for extended periods. Practical reality therefore required that an airborne division should be capable of either attacking from the air or carrying out sustained fighting on the ground.

Trying to take a basic infantry division, augmented with pathfinders and parachute maintenance personnel, and simply put the entire group on jump status didn't work. Not only did dual missions require different sets of equipment but such a division would be too large and bulky to be moved by existing aircraft. A different approach improved on the original notion of using parachute units to secure a drop zone (DZ) and bringing in heavier weap-

Paratroopers from the 505th Airborne Infantry boarding a C-82 for a jump during Exercise Snowdrop in northern New York.
National Archives.

ons by glider. The division would still operate this way, but it would also have its own heavier element to form the spearhead of the ground forces that would link up with the airhead.

Washington leaders ordered the 82d Airborne Division to conduct tests in 1948, which led to more tinkering. Finally, in 1950, the Army settled on an organization it believed retained strategic mobility yet was large enough for sustained ground combat. It remained triangular—that is, it had three infantry regiments as the basic elements for creating combat teams—but limited jump status to only 11,000 of its 17,500 men.

PROFICIENCY

Real-world readiness could not slide during this period of experimentation. Large-scale exercises formed the most visible type of training and revealed that the airborne community still had the basic missions as identified in 1943 and validated by the Swing Board. The Army paid particular attention to missions that had been critically important during the war. It continued to look at conducting vertical envelopments that were quickly reinforced by elements landing by glider or airplane on a landing area captured during the parachute assault, and then linking with approaching heavy ground forces. And because there had been serious problems, such as those in Sicily where the different armed services were not used to working with the airborne, the exercises were, in most cases, jointly conducted.

Exercise Combine in 1947 marked the beginning of the series. In the scenario part of this exercise the 82d Airborne Division acted as the aggressor force near Fort Benning. The 316th Troop Carrier Group employed the new C-82 transport for the first time. Next came a winter operation, Exercise Snowdrop, in which part of the 505th Airborne Infantry captured an airhead at Wheeler-Sack Air Force Base (AFB) near Fort Drum, New York.

During 1948 the 82d carried out two more important field exercises. In the spring it sent Task Force Lucky 500 miles to Fort Campbell in a major operation using the primary seizure of an airhead and reinforcement tactics of World War II. Some 2,200 jumpers formed the first wave using 72 C-82s. A dozen more C-82s followed in a second wave, each towing a pair of gliders. Then, on D+1, 60 planes landed in the airhead with reinforcements.

Late in the year the 505th Airborne Infantry carried out a jump near Eglin AFB, Florida, during Exercise Combine. This time a second group of C-82s, coming in three minutes behind the infantry, dropped artillery pieces. The gliders used during this mission brought in supplies, but were retrieved using the snatch technique suggested by the air commandos in the China-Burma-India theater. A second experiment involved laying communications wire from a low-flying airplane. Gliders would formally be declared obsolete in April 1952 when actual combat and major exercises proved that the new generation of transports could perform all of the gliders' missions better.

top right
Members of a battalion combat team of the 82d Airborne Division descend from a C-82 transport in 1947 as part of the training to maintain combat readiness. Troopers from an earlier aircraft descend in the foreground.
National Archives.

bottom right
Three riggers of the Parachute Maintenance Company, 82d Airborne Division, complete repacking a reserve parachute, left, and two T-7 main parachutes during Exercise Longhorn in Texas, March 1952.
National Archives.

Swarmer, another large exercise carried out before the Korean War in the spring of 1950, involved two divisions. Four thousand men from the 82d carried out two separate drops in a single day around Camp Mackall using C-82s and some of the brand-new C-119s. Part of the 11th Airborne Division then air landed. A third jump two days later brought in an additional 1,700 paratroopers. In this second round the airborne forces registered another first: two artillery batteries each dropped four howitzers and four Jeeps on pallets.

THE FIRST CRISIS

When the Korean War broke out, officials in Washington felt that it might be intended as a distraction and that Stalin's real objective was a Soviet attack in Germany. Sending troops to Korea stripped out most of the forces stationed in the United States. Other than an understrength armored division, all that remained were the 82d Airborne Division which was almost at full wartime manning and the 11th Airborne

Division which had sent one of its regimental combat teams to Gen. Douglas MacArthur.

While the Army did build up to a total of 20 combat divisions by 1953, sending many to Europe and Korea, it needed tens of thousands of draftees and volunteers to fill them and keep them manned. Five other regular Army divisions activated to operate new training centers. One of the five was the 101st Airborne Division at Camp Breckinridge, Kentucky. Despite the

T-10 PARACHUTE

The T-10 parachute system (a main parachute and reserve) served the airborne forces for more than 50 years. Nearly every paratrooper who has jumped since soon after the Korean War has used the T-10. Longevity is proof of its sound design and manufacture. It remained "good to go" even as paratroopers' combat loads grew. In the 1950s a jumper with weapons, ammunition, pack, and the parachutes themselves weighed around 300 pounds. By Operation JUST CAUSE in Panama (December 1989) the total jump weight was more than 350 pounds. The soldiers who jumped in Operation ENDURING FREEDOM in Afghanistan in 2001 reached a total jump weight of nearly 400 pounds. But greater weight increases the rate of descent. Dropping faster in turn means hitting the ground harder; and that means more jump injuries.

Paratroopers of 2d Battalion, 325th Airborne Infantry, 82d Airborne Division, use T-10 parachutes to descend onto Holland Drop Zone at Fort Bragg, North Carolina, on May 26, 1955, to begin the battalion's annual Army Training Test. *325th Airborne Infantry.*

designation, it was not on jump status nor did it train paratroopers. That function continued to be performed by the airborne school which moved to Fort Lee, Virginia, to make room at Fort Benning. The 101st had an on-again, off-again career as a training division, inactivating in 1953 when the war ended, but then coming back on duty in 1954.

The second change wrought by the wartime expansion involved the corps headquarters maintained at Fort Bragg. V Corps left as part of the buildup in Germany and on May 21, 1951, the XVIII Airborne Corps took up residence—a home that it still occupies after more than a half century. For most of the 1950s it controlled the airborne elements forming the heart of the Army's strategic deployment combat power. At one time or another all three of the active airborne divisions (11th, 82d, and 101st) and the separate 508th Regimental Combat Team (RCT) trained and exercised under its supervision. Because the Joint Airborne Troop Board also called Fort Bragg home, the corps was able to work with it as well.

The armistice ending the Korean War allowed the Army to cut down

Constant training kept the airborne units prepared for the contingency missions they could expect. Paratroopers of 2d Battalion, 325th Airborne Infantry, jump from a U.S. Air Force C-119 Flying Boxcar over Holland Drop Zone, Fort Bragg, North Carolina, in the annual Army Training Test, May 26, 1955. *325th Airborne Infantry.*

on the number of new recruits and close some training centers. Attention turned to improving the General Reserve in the United States to meet the conditions arising from Soviet activities around the world. Most of the resources went to the divisions earmarked for early deployment to Europe. But in October 1953 Washington leaders assigned the most mobile unit it had, the 82d Airborne Division, a new mission as the Western Hemisphere's designated contingency force.

ROTATIONS

No matter what steps the peacetime Army took to emphasize its vital role in defending the free world, it still had a great deal of trouble convincing the Defense Department and Congress to provide necessary funds. Both the Air Force and the Navy successfully garnered the lion's share because their nuclear capabilities fit a new national strategy. The United States' economy and political traditions guaranteed that it would not attempt to match the huge conventional armies of the Soviet Union and Communist China. Instead it developed the concept of Mutually Assured Destruction to hold down the size of conventional forces by convincing those nations that in the event of conventional attack, the United States was prepared to immediately resort to all-out nuclear war, even if it meant suffering enormous destruction from the Soviets.

The Army had to search for ways to cut expenses while at the same time maintaining readiness and building up morale. Retaining experienced officers and noncommissioned officers would go a long way to meeting these needs and also provide cadres in the event of future expansion. The staff developed a plan to trim costs by making better use of manpower, while at the same time enhancing unit esprit

REGIMENTAL COMBAT TEAM

During the 1950s the airborne regimental combat team (RCT) served as the basic combined arms element capable of independent action, even if only for a few days, and contained more than 3,000 men. The airborne infantry regiment of this period was significantly more powerful than the parachute or glider regiments of World War II. In addition to regimental headquarters, medical, and service elements it had a support company armed with antitank guns and heavy mortars. Each of the three battalions contained a headquarters company, three rifle companies, and a heavy weapons company. They employed recoilless rifles, mortars, and .30-caliber machine guns, giving it significant firepower. Other airborne elements rounded out the RCT: a field artillery battalion with 105-mm howitzers, an automatic weapons battery, a combat engineer company, and a quartermaster company.

de corps and taking better care of dependents. Traditional reliance on individual replacements changed to a program of unit rotations.

Under the new concept, divisions and other large units in the United States would exchange places with comparable overseas units every three years. Gyroscope, as it was called, had several additional features. Before rotating, each stateside division conducted its own basic and advanced individual training, and by moving entire units a soldier and his family would have a "home" during his career. In theory, practicing the Gyroscope cycle also tested ways to replace an entire division destroyed by nuclear weapons.

Beginning in 1955 divisions and a number of smaller formations "Gyroscoped." In May of that year the 508th RCT went to Japan and relieved the 187th RCT which then came back to Fort Bragg. This rotation preserved the air-

C-130 AND C-123

Two new transports important to the evolution of the airborne force entered service in the second half of the 1950s bringing better range and cruising speed. These were the medium-range four-engine C-130 Hercules and the short-range twin-engine C-123 Provider. They were specifically designed to operate on unimproved airstrips. Both retained airdrop advantages from a rear tailgate door and ability to put two sticks of jumpers simultaneously from side doors. The larger Hercules could carry up to 64 paratroopers, and proved to be such a good basic design that it went through many upgrades and continued in production into the 21st century.

borne capability that had existed in the Pacific since the start of the occupation. The European Command (EUCOM) had wanted to gain a similar strike potential and finally achieved it in 1956 when the 11th Airborne Division from Fort Campbell replaced the 5th Infantry Division. This exchange of dissimilar divisions also helped the U.S. Continental Army Command (CONARC) by opening up Fort Campbell for other uses.

The first increment of 11th Airborne Division troops and dependents reached Germany on January 23, 1956, and the last landed on April 1 of that year. United States Army, Europe (USAREUR) quickly discovered that an airborne division was a very different creature than a normal infantry division. For example, maintaining jump qualifications required the construction of jump towers, rigging sheds, and other facilities; cost more money; and actually reduced the division's ability to perform normal European infantry missions. Washington officials and USAREUR wrestled with these issues, even considering keeping only one of the three RCTs in airborne status. In the end conventional needs and pressure to hold down expenses won out. Washington officials ruled that the division would only conduct individual jump proficiency training although everyone hoped that it would still be possible to retain some unit capability without compro-

mising its new primary mission. Therefore, it allowed the division to bring only a third of its special airborne equipment overseas.

USAREUR then discovered a second personnel problem. Airborne divisions were almost entirely filled with volunteers, not draftees like the rest of the Army. Expiration of enlistments took place at a constant rate and could only be filled by a steady stream of qualified replacements. Gyroscope had been designed to save money by eliminating this phenomenon. The difficulties encountered in moving large units eventually led the Army to terminate the program in 1959.

CAPABILITY GROWS

Airborne commanders moved into high positions in the Army starting in the mid-1950s. Gen. Matthew Ridgway and Gen. Maxwell Taylor became chiefs of staff and Lt. Gen. James Gavin served as the G-3. Each had learned important lessons about flexibility and leadership during World War II, and all exerted their influence to obtain the funds necessary to keep the Army moving forward. They also used XVIII Airborne Corps to conduct a series of large exercises that identified potential problems and looked into ways to take advantage of new Air Force transports.

Exercise Test Drop employed 40 C-119s to examine various heavy-drop rigging concepts up to 21,000 pounds at Fort Bragg. Once on the ground it then used that equipment to see if airborne forces could still construct a hasty airstrip and bring in reinforcements by landing. They found that this mission, set in 1943 by the Swing Board, still worked even with the large 200-man C-124 Globemaster II. It also carried almost every type of equipment in the Army in-

Tactical Air Command C-119s fly in a V of Vs formation over Sewart Air Force Base, Tennessee, while working with the 101st Airborne Division during its transition to a combat division in 1956. *National Archives.*

ventory, and with front clamshell doors loaded and unloaded it with unprecedented speed.

Two other transports complemented the long-range Globemaster and proved their worth during other exercises. Both the medium-range C-130 Hercules and the C-123 Provider were designed to use dirt landing strips and drop paratroopers, supplies, and equipment on pallets. The 64-man capacity of the Hercules in particular marked another step forward in the airborne assault by increasing the speed and accuracy of a drop. That created a smaller DZ, which made the ground commander's job of collecting his men and taking objectives much easier.

Major exercises grew in size and complexity. More than 140,000 soldiers and airmen participated in the joint Exercise Sage Brush in 1955. The Strategic Army Corps (STRAC) engaged 40,000 men in Exercise Swift Strike in 1961 and 60,000 in Swift Strike II the next year. Both exercises provided realistic tests of STRAC units' ability to deploy. Other exercises, with exotic names like Banyan Tree or Towers Moon, sent troops on drops as far away as Alaska, Panama, and Greenland.

A SHARE OF THE BUDGET

All the testing had a purpose. When Taylor became chief of staff he decided to use a new division structure to win the Army a larger share of Pentagon resources. During Ridgway's tenure the Army looked into what would be needed to win on an atomic battlefield where survival required spreading out without losing the ability to wage a conventional war. Two new ideas came out at this time—divisions fighting in five battle groups instead of three RCTs, and making divisions nuclear-capable by giving them the new Honest John rocket. Taylor continued this work while also looking for a way to make the most of the new weapons and equipment starting to enter service. He chose his former unit, the 101st Airborne Division, to start practical field tests. On April 30, 1956, the 101st ceased serving as trainers and transferred its flag from Fort Jackson to Fort Campbell. There it reorganized as a combat division by taking men from the 187th and 508th RCTs and using the equipment left behind when the 11th went to Germany.

Taylor started on the paratroops because he thought that their current state needed the most work. An existing division could not be airlifted, which eroded the ability to perform traditional airborne missions identified back in 1943. At the same time it lacked balance and power necessary to fight on the ground for an extended period. The 101st began testing a small division with 10,000-12,000 men divided into the five battle groups. Specific tests included validating the capability to perform basic airborne missions such as airborne raids, assaults ahead of a ground advance, and even extraction.

It succeeded in energizing thinkers to work on further improvements and new airborne doctrine. While it took several rounds of adjustments, the Army finally settled on a structure that seemed to meet both requirements. Taylor, wanting to convince the civilian leaders to give the Army a larger share of funds, called the new division "Pentomic." The label was a combination of "pentagonal" and "atomic." It was intended to counter the arguments by the other services in the Washington budget battles.

During the second half of 1958 both the 82d and 101st Airborne Divisions reorganized. They now had five airborne battle groups. Each battle group contained five rifle companies, a heavy weapons company, and organic engineer, signal, supply, maintenance, reconnaissance, and medical resources. Division artillery consisted of five batteries, each with five 105-mm howitzers, plus some cumbersome 762-mm Honest John rockets with tactical nuclear warheads. In addition to the usual array of supporting elements, the division's small engineer battalion had the resources needed to construct an airstrip within 48 hours. For the first time it was possible to airlift everything except the Honest Johns in existing transport airplanes.

Taylor also used the transition to give the Army a new generation of equipment. For paratroopers this meant replacing the World War II-era rifles, carbines, submachine guns, Browning Automatic Rifles, and heavy and light machine guns with just two weapons: the M-14 rifle and the M-60 machine gun. The M-14 could fire in either semiautomatic or automatic mode. Both the M-14 and the M-60 fired the same standard NATO 7.62-mm round. This one change simplified everything from production to training and logistics. Centralizing basic parachute training at Fort Benning was another cost-reducing step, although it resulted in closing the 82d's basic airborne school on February 9, 1962, soon after it had graduated its 50,000th student.

STRATEGIC ARMY CORPS

When the turmoil caused first by demobilization and then by the Korean War subsided, the Army had developed a stationing scheme to position its airborne forces where they would be the most valuable. The majority remained in stateside bases where strategic mobility made them able to deploy faster than other types of units to anywhere trouble might break out. A smaller number of units served in overseas locations where theater commanders identified special requirements.

Europe needed heavy conventional forces in Germany and only obtained paratroopers when the 11th Airborne Division arrived. The airborne capability passed on to the 24th Infantry Division in the next rotation, but now only in two battle groups at Augsburg. The next reorganization moved it yet again, this time to a brigade of the 8th Infantry Division at Bad Kreuznach.

In the Pacific huge distances and the absence of direct confrontation other than in Korea made theater airborne capability more important. After the 11th Airborne Division had departed, a separate RCT remained on duty. In June 1960 during the Pentomic era the mission passed from Japan to the reinforced 2d Airborne Battle Group, 503d Infantry, in Okinawa. It was briefly assigned to the Hawaii-based 25th Infantry Division and then became a separate entity. In 1963 the 1st Airborne Battle Group, 503d Infantry, arrived from Fort Bragg and the two became the maneuver elements of the 173d Airborne Brigade activated in Okinawa March 26, 1963. The battle groups reorganized in June as the new-style battalions.

Alaska was the other Pacific basin location with a need for airborne troops. It was near Siberia and sparsely populated, which made infiltration a real danger. Primary responsibility for patrolling the wilderness and detecting penetrations rested with the National Guard's Eskimo scouts. But in case they made contact the only way to bring in a reaction force was by parachute or air landing. Although the configuration of the Alaskan regular garrison fluctuated over the years, it always kept at least one airborne battalion.

When the Soviet Union started using surrogates in the Third World the strategic requirement for reaction forces emerged from the shadow of the conventional containment strategy. Ballistic missiles and the doctrine of Mutually Assured Destruction had effectively reduced the threat of a general nuclear war and reduced the chances of an incident escalating into a full-blown conventional war in Europe. President John F. Kennedy's assessment concluded that the possibility of brushfire wars had increased and he responded by announcing a strategy of "flexible response."

By this time the Army had split its home-based troops into two major groups. One would deploy while the other provided the capability to mobilize and train additional units. In May 1958 it identified part of the former group as STRAC and required it to be ready to deploy immediately, like the minutemen during the Revolution. This force assumed two specific missions—serving as the first reinforcement in case of a general war, and dealing with "limited wars." Because the units had to maintain the highest possible standards, a whole generation of soldiers used the term "strac" to mean being squared away.

The commanding general of XVIII Airborne Corps initially served as the commanding general of STRAC. As expected, the heart of his combat power came from his airborne divisions. In 1962 the Army added III Corps with heavier divisions. The Army intended to deploy using the "fire brigade" concept by sending out the lighter half to any location in the world within 50 days, and the other half within 60 more days.

Because the Joint Chiefs of Staff (JCS) did not approve that Army plan, neither the Air Force nor the Navy agreed to provide the transportation required to move the troops. Instead, the JCS told each overseas theater commander to develop his own plans for the various situations his command could face. After reviewing these plans, Washington leaders tasked the services to earmark the necessary units. At the end of 1961 it improved the process by creating U.S. Strike Command (STRICOM) as a joint headquarters at MacDill AFB, Florida, and gave it the mission to react to crises breaking out anywhere in the world. (U.S. Central Command of the 21st century is the lineal descendant of Strike Command.)

Although the high-readiness forces did not deploy during either the Berlin Crisis of 1961 or the Cuban Missile Crisis the following year, both times the airborne units proved their readiness by quickly going on full alert.

FLEXIBLE RESPONSE

The Army abandoned Pentomic structures, which had turned out to be too cumbersome, in order to meet the various challenges under President Kennedy's new vision of flexible response. In a period when decision-makers valued the ability to fight small wars the Army no longer needed to hide behind a name. It now turned to finding a divisional organization that could be tailored to meet any situation by altering its maneuver elements. In theory any division could contain infantry, mechanized infantry, airborne infantry, and armor battalions. As with the previous transformation, reorganization brought with it more new equipment including tanks, armored personnel carriers, and helicopters.

In practice the airborne division actually needed to be somewhat different from the others. When the new tables of organization were published in September 1961 they called for maneuver elements consisting of nine airborne infantry battalions and a light tank battalion. The latter temporarily used self-propelled guns until the new M-551 Sheridan armored reconnaissance airborne assault vehicles arrived. Division artillery consisted of three 105-mm howitzer battalions, and a two-battery battalion armed with 318-mm Little John rockets that had replaced the larger Honest John. The rest of the division consisted of somewhat lighter airborne versions of reconnaissance, signal, engineer, medical, and assorted support units. After completing the transformation the 82d and 101st Airborne Divisions fielded about 13,500 men each.

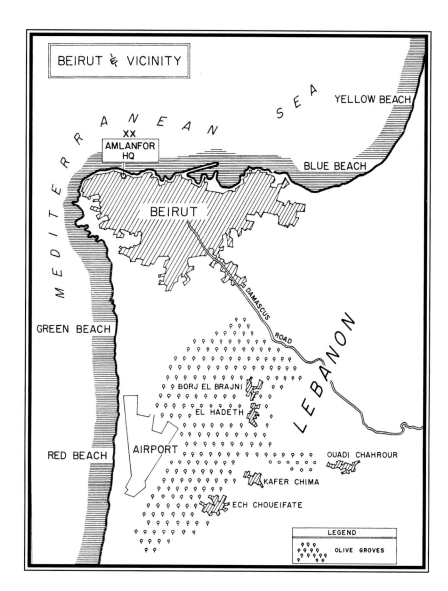

Key locations in the Beirut
area, October 1958.
*U.S. Army Center of
Military History.*

Flexible response also required combined arms units smaller than divisions: brigades. The airborne brigade designed at this time had the ability to control and support between two and five maneuver battalions, a 105-mm howitzer battalion, a support battalion, and company-sized reconnaissance, light tank, and engineer units. Under normal circumstances all of these components were airborne-qualified. While the division and brigade were highly deployable, they were not given enough vehicles to make them very mobile once they were on the ground.

LEBANON

The first major test of using the airborne as a theater contingency force came, ironically, in the last theater to get the capability. European Command (EUCOM) responsibilities included Africa and the Middle East. In 1958 pro-Western Lebanon charged Syria with stirring up a

rebellion and asked for American help. President Eisenhower directed EUCOM to respond. The theater then tasked each of the services to furnish contingents to make up a force of 14,000 to stabilize Beirut.

USAREUR's contribution consisted of a task force with both combat and logistical components. Fortunately the previous December a three-day war game held at 11th Airborne Division headquarters had worked out a contingency plan for such an operation. Paratroopers would conduct one of the basic airborne missions and seize an airport through which other troops would air land. The war game decided that USAREUR would need 110 C-119 aircraft or their equivalent to carry it out.

Shortly thereafter the division rotated back to the United States under Gyroscope and handed off responsibility to the incoming 24th Infantry Division. Although primarily a ground combat force, it still controlled two of the 11th

Airborne's battle groups that had not yet rotated and which still remained as the theater's crisis responders.

The actual Lebanon operation used Marines to carry out an amphibious landing and focus on the port. Army Task Force 201 would concentrate on securing the Beirut International Airport, a few miles south of the city. Logistical elements would flow in by sea. At the end of the deployment the Marines would re-embark and then the Army would redeploy in increments. Under USAREUR's Operation BLUE BAT plan, its two airborne battle groups were to be inserted along with minimum essential support elements, but it had built-in flexibility to adjust to a fluid situation. The task force would move to Lebanon in four echelons while a fifth operated the European end of the lines of communications.

While both Army and Marine forces received deployment orders on July 15, 1958, only the Marines who were on board ships offshore made assault landings the following day. Because they were able to secure the airport almost immediately, the parachute assault was canceled. Army forces air landed on July 19, executing the reinforcement part of the mission. The lead echelon consisted of the reinforced 1st Airborne Battle Group, 187th Infantry, commanded by Lt. Col. Thomas W. Sharkey and the task force command group. These 1,720 personnel left Fürstenfeldbruck air base aboard 19 C-119s, plus some of the new aircraft—11 C-124s and 30 C-130s. Other sorties brought in additional troops or equipment and handled resupply until a sea route began operating.

Combat did not develop so the 2d Airborne Battle Group, 503d Infantry, never left its station in Germany and stood down. The rest of the division's contribution to the third echelon had been intended to include two howitzer batteries, a reconnaissance troop, a section of the Honest Johns, and engineer and support personnel. Follow-on sealift moved sustainment forces and even a battalion of tanks, but the lack of hostilities allowed other combat units to be left behind. By August 5 the last of Army Task Force 201 arrived in Lebanon.

Paratroopers of 1st Airborne Battle Group, 187th Infantry, soon after its arrival in Beirut. The group had not yet received the new generation of weapons. The near trooper still carries the World War II-era Browning Automatic Rifle. *National Archives.*

A senior noncommissioned officer, right, briefs paratroopers of 1st Airborne Battle Group, 187th Infantry, as they arrive at Beirut International Airport. *National Archives.*

The paratroops left their heavy equipment, still rigged for possible airborne operations, on one of the two runways and moved into the nearby olive grove, where they established their bivouac area. Many of the airborne-qualified personnel had not had an opportunity to make their proficiency jumps so headquarters immediately laid out a training program. A suitable spot was found just north of the Beirut International Airport which the men promptly dubbed DZ Sahara. It began operation on August 27 for proficiency jump training. The battle group covered the phased withdrawal of American forces and finally departed in late October.

The mission was accomplished according to plan. American forces apparently averted a coup d'etat and kept things stable until a new government took office. However, the services did find that aspects of responding to contingencies needed fixing if a forced entry rather than this permissive one was required in the future. On the Army side, transports landing in the airhead clearly continued to work.

The real question was whether it made sense to have USAREUR or STRAC responsible for Middle Eastern contingencies. USAREUR didn't want the mission because Lebanon had shown that contingency deployments seriously weakened infantry strength needed for its containment responsibility against the Warsaw Pact. And it could save costs if it no longer needed to maintain forward-deployed airborne troops.

USAREUR's argument did not persuade the JCS so it retained its contingent. During the winter of 1958–59 the two battle groups exchanged places with the 1st Airborne Battle Group, 504th Infantry, and 1st Airborne Battle Group, 505th Infantry, from the 82d Airborne Division at Fort Bragg. When the 8th Infantry Division replaced the 24th several years later, it continued to maintain a brigade-sized force of paratroopers.

THE CONGO

The second European contingency experience originated in 1960 when Belgium abruptly granted independence to its former African colony in 1960. Anarchy broke out, requiring the UN to commit a multinational task force within two weeks to restore order. Air Force planes helped in that deployment and on several subsequent occasions over the next four years. Teams from the 82d Airborne Division sometimes went along to provide security while the aircraft were on the ground. USAREUR had placed an airborne task force on alert at the start of the crisis but it was not needed.

In 1964, when the UN forces left, a new round of open fighting broke out between the government and rebels in the outer provinces. This time traditional tribal rivalries had an overlay of Cold War tensions. It became a crisis in November. The rebels rounded up a large number of Americans and Belgians to use as hostages in Stanleyville. Stories of atrocities began to circulate and then, on November 16, the rebels announced that an American medical missionary would be executed as a spy.

By then American and Belgian representatives were already making secret plans to take military action and rescue their citizens. EUCOM would furnish the C-130 aircraft, but not the troops. Belgium committed its Parachute Commando Regiment. Together they would conduct a Los Baños-style airborne raid and extraction. The need to strike swiftly mandated that planning be done "on the fly" while the forces moved into position. Operation DRAGON ROUGE dealt with Stanleyville while a series of other color-named "dragon" operations provided for the most probable follow-on actions.

In the first stage of the raid, 320 of the Belgian paratroopers conducted a classic airfield seizure at 0400 on November 24 followed by the rest who air landed. American airplanes were used throughout, including two B-26s with markings removed which orbited overhead in case the Belgians needed fire support. A heavy drop delivered armored Jeeps that were immediately used for the dash into town to free the civilians. They arrived just as the rebels were beginning a massacre and limited the deaths to 28. Other troops established blocking positions and guarded the airstrip. The first of the hostages arrived at the airfield at 0630 and 2,000 flew out over a period of two days on the C-130s. The same planes extracted the paratroopers who repulsed one counterattack. A second raid at Paulis (Operation DRAGON NOIRE) on November 26 went equally well.

Three heavy drop platforms rigged for Exercise Deep Furrow. Two Jeeps rigged on each platform testify to the ingenuity of the Quartermaster riggers in advancing aerial delivery techniques by 1965.
U.S. Army Center of Military History.

The task force returned to Brussels on December 1. Two Belgian soldiers had been killed and 11 wounded. Several of the C-130s were hit by ground fire, but none seriously. Although American paratroopers did not carry out this mission, it had been executed in the same manner as they would have used. EUCOM reviewed it closely and made appropriate adjustments to its training and plans.

TURKEY

Before the Congo rescue operation took place Washington officials and EUCOM continued discussing options for shifting responsibility for contingencies outside the central front in Europe. The Berlin Wall crisis focused the Pentagon's attention on the importance of not weakening USAREUR's ability to carry out its no-notice defensive mission. It considered and rejected stationing an airborne brigade permanently in Europe just to retain the theater's contingency capability with battalions from the United States rotating in and out. Then, on December 1, 1963, the JCS officially shifted

responsibility for the Middle East, eastern Asia, and Africa over to STRICOM.

A series of exercises followed in Iran, Greece, and Turkey to rehearse the ability of STRICOM to perform its new responsibilities. All of these took place along the southern arc of the containment line where American ground forces were not stationed. Exercise Deep Furrow 1964 simulated NATO repelling an invasion of Greece but was canceled for diplomatic reasons. STRICOM would have deployed an airborne task force to test contingency plans and carried out joint training with Italian, Greek, and Turkish paratroopers.

The following year, 1965, a revised Deep Furrow did take place which used a scenario of simultaneous invasions of Greece and Turkey. Although the Americans were unable to furnish a large logistical contingent, the Secretary of Defense directed that an airborne division participate for a valid test of rapid deployment capability. Participation by an entire airborne division proved impractical, so a brigade-size force was designated.

The 3d Brigade, 82d Airborne Division, jumping into Adapazari, Turkey, on September 21, 1965. *U.S. Army Center of Military History.*

The 82d was the division chosen to provide the brigade. It had been reorganized into a smaller and lighter configuration, better adapted to fighting in undeveloped parts of the world. It had replaced its M-14 rifles with the 5.56-mm M-16 which saved each paratrooper several pounds of weight. The structural changes cut the number of airplanes needed to deploy the division to 620, half as many as in the Pentomic era.

Participants in the exercise fell under the 3d Brigade headquarters, and used two battalion task forces—1st Battalion, 505th Infantry and 1st Battalion, 508th Infantry. The artillery component consisted of most of the 1st Battalion, 319th Artillery, and together with a small support element provided the pieces necessary to make this a realistic test.

The brigade flew from Pope AFB, North Carolina, to Incirlik Air Base in Turkey which became its temporary home. The exercise scenario called for the Americans and the Turkish

Presidential Airborne Battalion to make a parachute assault, secure an airhead, and conduct a linkup with the Turkish First Army in order to capture a series of objectives. Tactics and capabilities had improved considerably since the 82d had tried this type of mission in Sicily, so the plan was complex but not so complicated that it would fail if things started to go wrong.

On September 21, 1965, the C-130s took off from Incirlik and headed for Adapazari. Jumpers and equipment filled 69 aircraft (four of which would have to turn back); one carried the Turks' heavy drop. Along the way they were joined by eight more aircraft from Ankara with the Presidential Airborne Battalion. The first echelon included an Air Force Combat Control Team among the jumpers. The first man of the first wave jumped out the door on schedule at 0730 to capture the DZ. With the first wave controlling the DZ, the 38 heavy drop planes came in next and released 96 platforms. The final wave carried the rest of the paratroopers. By 1200 the airhead was secure and the

Turkish ground forces had arrived. Follow-on maneuvers lasted several more days.

The daylight jump had been precisely executed by well-trained soldiers and airmen. Part of the success came from a special C-130 configured to carry an aerial command post called Jackpot. Manning it with Army and Air Force representatives created joint command and control and allowed inter-service problems to be resolved on the spot. The drop also stood out because there were only five jump injuries, mostly minor sprains. None of the Turkish paratroopers reported being hurt. Success extended to the heavy drop as well, with only one of the platforms suffering a parachute malfunction.

LEANING FORWARD

Deep Furrow marked a transition in thinking. Instead of every theater commander needing a robust airborne presence, the JCS would allocate those resources as needed. Availability of transport planes with longer ranges, higher speeds, and greater capacity played a major part in the process. Because it was increasingly possible to move airborne assault forces great distances and have them arrive able to go into action almost at once, concentrating assets in STRICOM made sense. Airborne training and jump proficiency cost less when it only had to be conducted at a few posts. Frequent interaction between Army units and the Air Force crews who flew them built mutual confidence just as it had in World War II.

Ridgway, Taylor and many others from World War II had ensured that the airborne force remained a significant part of the Army. They kept pushing for better training, better arms and equipment, and better doctrine to keep pace with a changing world. As a result of their leadership the airborne division of 1965 was

a much more lethal weapon than it had been 20 years earlier. It still focused on being able to carry out the basic missions identified by the Swing Board because those missions still needed to be done. Airfield seizures, raids, taking and holding key terrain to support a ground advance or to cut off retreating enemy troops, and creating chaos in enemy rear areas continued to make sense. So too did the tactics of swiftly bringing in reinforcements via air landing.

Soldiers and scholars often overlook a very important intangible of the Cold War years—the influence that the airborne community had on future leaders. During the era of a peacetime draft the paratroops remained all-volunteer. Quality soldiers and high standards, not better pay or adventure, attracted young officers and noncommissioned officers thinking about an Army career. Pride, confidence, and esprit de corps tended to set them apart from their peers. Years later a surprising number held senior leadership positions and were training a new generation to follow in their footsteps.

These years also witnessed the addition of another mission for the airborne. Once again it came because airborne units were light and easily transported, but when on the ground had a relatively large number of infantrymen. In 1957 racial violence erupted in Little Rock, Arkansas, when the high school tried to integrate. President Eisenhower used the 101st Airborne Division to restore order. Hereafter all of the airborne units had to expect to be sent to deal with serious domestic disturbances. They were committed to restore order during rioting in the 1960s in several major cities, including Washington, D.C., in 1968.

Chapter 9
Vietnam War, 1961–75

Bringing Them In (Battle in the Sky), by John Potter Wheat. The terrain faced by the 173d Airborne Brigade and the paratroopers who followed severely limited parachute operations in Vietnam. *Army Art Collection, U.S. Army Center of Military History.*

PUTTING OUT BRUSHFIRES

During the Cold War, airborne forces had been held in reserve in the United States to react to crises or swiftly reinforce overseas theaters. Smaller contingents of paratroopers performed like functions in Europe and the Pacific to give those commanders a similar capability. Airborne units were easier to move rapidly than conventional ones, but lightness made them vulnerable to counterattack. During World War II the War Department attempted to offset that problem by bringing heavier weapons into an airhead in gliders or transports, or by keeping the drops close for rapid linkup with ground forces.

The defensive problem of the airborne once on the ground had not been solved by the time of President John F. Kennedy's flexible response doctrine. The country now placed a premium on putting out "brushfires," small conflicts popping up worldwide. Units capable of reacting rapidly were required, and that meant paratroopers. The extra attention had a profound impact on the airborne community by stimulating the most extensive experimentation since the original Airborne Command days.

The Army converted from the cumbersome Pentomic structure at the same time that it responded to Kennedy's directive. When the dust settled, the airborne force was still stationed at home and abroad. The XVIII Airborne Corps with the 82d Airborne Division at Fort Bragg, North Carolina, and the 101st Airborne Division at Fort Campbell, Kentucky, served inside the United States. In Europe one brigade of the 8th Infantry Division served on jump status, while the 173d Airborne Brigade with two battalions in Okinawa gave a forward-based presence in the Pacific. Smaller elements also served in Alaska and Panama. Making them more powerful became a priority.

A VISION

During the Korean War the Army learned to use helicopters to evacuate the wounded. In the years that followed a number of leaders became aviators and started questioning how the Army could use them, and other aircraft, in additional ways.

The movement began in 1960 with two separate actions. The Chief of Staff created the Army Aircraft Requirements Board to study how to obtain more aircraft. Meanwhile, Maj. Gen. William Westmoreland, commander of the 101st Airborne Division and a former commander of the 187th Regimental Combat Team in Korea, centralized the aviation assets of the division under a battalion headquarters. Other individuals like Lt. Gen. James Gavin started calling for a more mobile way to attack from the air, adding the notion of the Army having helicopters and fixed-wing airplanes to perform such tasks in addition to the more traditional parachute assaults.

Secretary of Defense Robert McNamara's review of the issue reflected his concern that the Army focused too much on firepower and not enough on mobility. On April 19, 1962, he told the Army to think "outside the box" and come up with recommendations. The Army responded by creating the Tactical Mobility Requirements Board with Lt. Gen. Hamilton H. Howze, commanding general of XVIII Airborne Corps, as its president. Both he and the board's secretary, Col. John Norton, were qualified aviators and parachutists. Howze had been a cavalryman and armor officer during World War II before gaining his jump wings in 1951; Norton had been the G-3 of the 82d. The board had the broad mission to look ahead to 1975 and see how to use aircraft. It also was

Lt. Gen. Hamilton H. Howze, commander of XVIII Airborne Corps, chaired the Army's Tactical Mobility Requirements Board. Its recommendations in 1962 sparked a revolution in Army air mobility. *National Archives.*

told to consider tactics and organization as well as equipment, and to consult with the Air Force and industry.

Howze took his mandate seriously and ran a series of 40 separate tests that led to suitably radical recommendations. The key one was the notion of an airmobile division, which would be small and light so that it could deploy almost as easily as an airborne division. In action more than 450 organic aircraft let it lift one of the three brigade teams, and provide it with armed aviation fire support. During the action all of the aircraft would be directly controlled by the ground commander. One basic mission of the division would be seizing and reinforcing an airhead, as the airborne did. The difference lay in the helicopters giving the troops greater mobility once on the ground. In

fact, the board felt that such a division could be flexible enough to replace the airborne division if all the men were on jump status.

The Howze Board also called for two kinds of separate brigades. An air transport brigade of Army airplanes working in the forward area would augment the division when it needed additional lift. Even more radical was the board's notion of separate air combat cavalry brigades to carry out reconnaissance, screening, and delaying actions. Each of these would have more than 300 aircraft, about half of which would be armed helicopters and small fixed-wing airplanes. Unlike the airmobile division, this type of unit would fight exclusively from the air. The board presented its report on August 20, 1962. Howze noted that these were preliminary thoughts and more work was needed to finalize the concepts.

TESTING

Inevitably, critics swarmed out of the woodwork—led by the Air Force. Traditionalists objected to committing such a large share of the Army's resources to helicopters. The Air Force feared chaos in the crowded air over a battlefield unless it could control all of the assets and allocate them to missions. Advocates of the aerial approach saw the need for extensive testing, especially force-on-force maneuvers to work out the best tactics and organization of units.

The Department of the Army decided to carry out those vigorous tests without interfering with the existing combat divisions. Therefore the 11th Airborne Division was put back on the active rolls on February 1, 1963, as the 11th Air Assault Division. It was assigned to Fort Benning, Georgia, with an experimental air transport brigade to test that part of the board's vision. Selecting the 11th as the test bed signaled that the Army's senior leadership clearly viewed airmobile as a companion to airborne. The same message was sent when Maj. Gen. Harry W. O. Kinnard, the World War II G-3 of the 101st, became division commander. One infantry brigade was filled using the 1st battalions of the division's original World War II regiments: 187th, 188th, and 511th. A second brigade for maneuvers came from the 2d Infantry Division, also at Fort Benning. Division artillery grew to include three full battalions of aerial rocket artillery.

During the next 21 months, the 11th carried out the most intense tests across the southeast with both Kinnard and Howze aggressively seeking innovation. It tested a full range of tactics as well as air assaults. At the same time the Army fended off Air Force complaints that it was encroaching on their roles. The idea of armed helicopters survived the challenge as did the improved cargo helicopter, while the Air Force carried the point in most instances with fixed-wing planes. These decisions put the air cavalry brigade back on the shelf.

In October and November 1964 the evaluation culminated in Exercise Air Assault II pitting the 11th against the 82d in high-tempo offensive and defensive maneuvers. Both Kinnard and Maj. Gen. Robert York of the 82d agreed that the concept was valid. A positive report went up to the Department of the Army to form a permanent airmobile division and supporting air transport brigade. Like the airborne

C-7 CARIBOU

The fixed-wing twin-engine deHavilland C-7 Caribou entered Army service in 1959. It used a rear ramp to load and unload cargo or up to 32 passengers. It also was a capable jump platform for 24 parachutists. The first one arrived in Vietnam in 1961 and was used to resupply isolated Special Forces camps and other units near short, unimproved runways. By 1963 several companies had arrived in Vietnam. The Air Force contended that Army possession and employment of the Caribou infringed upon its roles and missions. Ultimately, an April 1966 agreement between the two services' chiefs of staffs transferred all Caribous to the Air Force.

CH-47 CHINOOK

The Boeing CH-47 Chinook, a cargo helicopter also capable of dropping 28 fully equipped paratroopers, entered service in 1961. It became a larger, faster, but less maneuverable complement to the Huey. The Chinook progressed through many versions, each of which increased its capabilities. It remains the Army's primary cargo helicopter. A rear ramp is convenient for loading and unloading cargo, and a suitable platform for paratroopers to make "tailgate" jumps.

division, the 11th had validated that a light combat unit could in fact take to the air, hit the enemy in close combat, and destroy him while at the same time retaining both strategic and theater mobility. McNamara mediated the resulting inter-service argument and approved the division but not the transport brigade. Ironically, Howze and Kinnard had looked at using air mobility in a high-tempo war in Europe. Now the Army saw it as a weapon for brushfire wars.

NEW MISSIONS

Without having the two kinds of separate brigades available, the airmobile division had to take a more restricted approach to mobility and tactics. Rather than retain the 11th, the Army chose to carry out a very complicated shuffling of flags. It sent the colors of the 2d Infantry Division to Korea and inactivated the 11th Air Assault Division. The 1st Cavalry Division, then in Korea, sent its colors from Korea to Fort Benning. The personnel and equipment from the 2d Infantry and 11th Air Assault divisions became the cadre for the new 1st Cavalry Division (Airmobile).

The division's maneuver battalions, although being airmobile infantry, carried cavalry designations. The official conversion came on July 1, 1965.

The entire Army scrambled to fill the new airmobile division and make it combat ready in a matter of weeks. All of the jump-qualified paratroopers went into Col. Elvy B. Roberts's 1st Brigade where they formed the 1st and 2d Battalions of the 8th Cavalry and the 1st Battalion, 12th Cavalry. Men not already parachutists went through the Basic Airborne Course as units. Other soldiers who had participated in the development tests moved on to new assignments, particularly in the 82d and 101st Airborne Divisions. Once there, the similarity of missions guaranteed the spread of ideas.

By July 1965, while the Cold War Army still focused its attention on Europe, it had increased the strength of its power projection forces. In the United States it retained the XVIII Airborne Corps's two robust parachute divisions and now added the 1st Cavalry Division (Airmobile) with its other style of vertical attack. The various theaters had smaller airborne forces, but only the small airmobile capability found in the expanded helicopter fleet in the standard divisions.

The first challenge to the mixed force came in Southeast Asia. After years of fighting, the French gave up their colony of Indochina in 1954. Vietnam split into a Communist north and a non-Communist south. But southern Communists, the Viet Cong (VC), carried out an escalating guerrilla campaign against the Army of the Republic of Vietnam (ARVN). Kennedy began furnishing military assistance in 1961, including aviation units and Special Forces. By 1965 the situation had degenerated to the point that Army combat troops had to be committed to protect several bases in the southern part of the country.

top left
Immediately after arrival at Bien Hoa Air Base near Saigon, "Sky Soldiers" of the 173d Airborne Brigade move out on a security mission, May 5, 1965. *National Archives.*

top right
173d Airborne Brigade "Sky Soldiers" shoulder sleeve insignia. *U.S. Army Center of Military History.*

AIRBORNE FORCES AT WAR | 146

Brig. Gen. John Norton, right, welcomes Maj. Gen. Harry W.O. Kinnard to Vietnam. Kinnard landed August 2, 1965, to prepare for the arrival of his 1st Cavalry Division in September. A year later, Norton would succeed him in command. *National Archives.*

DEPLOYMENT AND BUILDUP

Following Army doctrine, the first unit sent to Vietnam was the Pacific region's paratroopers, the 173d Airborne Brigade on Okinawa. At this time Brig. Gen. Ellis Williamson's "Sky Soldiers" included two infantry battalions (1st and 2d Battalions, 503d Infantry) and the 3d Battalion, 319th Artillery. C-130s flew the first men into Bien Hoa air base on May 5, 1965. The brigade immediately moved into the jungles to create bases and began airmobile training even as it started operations.

Additional large units followed. In July 1965 the 1st Brigade, 101st Airborne Division, arrived at Cam Ranh Bay. It had originally been considered as a replacement to allow the 173d to return to Okinawa as the theater reaction force, but the situation on the ground kept the 173d in Vietnam. Like its predecessor, the 1st Brigade of the 101st consisted of true paratroopers. The rest of the division would follow by the end of 1967. By then it was no longer able to jump as a unit. At the end of 1968 the 101st completed transition into the second airmobile division.

In late August 1965 the 1st Cavalry Division, recently reorganized as an airmobile unit, reported in-country as the first full division to be committed to the fight. It disembarked at Qui Nhon, then set up its base at An Khe. It

had eight infantry battalions, one short, but with its 1st Brigade qualified as paratroopers. At that point Westmoreland, now serving as the joint commander in Vietnam, had three full airborne brigades in United States Army, Vietnam (USARV).

The Communists had also been increasing their own forces beyond the VC. Large contingents of North Vietnamese Army (NVA) regulars moved down the Ho Chi Minh Trail to gradually take over the heavy fighting from the VC. Both sides kept building up. Then, in 1968, the Communists launched surprise attacks all across the country during the Tet religious holidays. In response, the final airborne brigade—again selected because it was the most strategically mobile—deployed to Chu Lai. The 3d Brigade, 82d Airborne Division, had trouble finding enough qualified paratroopers before it left Fort Bragg.

In early 1968 there should have been four full airborne brigades in Vietnam. The demand for qualified paratroopers worldwide outstripped the number available, so the 101st and 1st Cavalry Division stopped receiving replacement jumpers as men rotated home, turning those units into airmobile forces.

LAPES

The Low Altitude Parachute Extraction System (LAPES) was a significant aerial resupply innovation of the Vietnam era. The U.S. Air Force developed it for the C-130. The load is mounted on a platform atop rollers on the floor of the aircraft. The pilot approaches the extraction zone at slow speed, descending to about five feet above the ground in level flight. During final approach, the copilot releases a reefed (undeployed) 28-foot ringslot parachute. It is towed behind the aircraft until the right moment. The copilot electrically deploys the extraction chute, which pulls the load along the rollers and out the level ramp. The platform contacts the ground, decelerates, and stops, ready for derigging and use.

A U.S. Air Force C-130 Hercules uses LAPES to deliver a load of supplies to the 1st Cavalry Division at An Khe. *National Archives.*

ADDING COMBAT POWER

Tactical conditions in Vietnam rarely called for large operations after the early period. To increase firepower, and to cover larger sectors with multiple smaller attacks, required additional infantry, artillery, and dedicated supporting forces. The 1st Cavalry Division and the 173d Airborne Brigade each gained another infantry battalion in 1966. The following year the 173d was assigned a fourth, giving it the 1st through 4th Battalions of the 503d Infantry.

Artillery also underwent modifications in Vietnam. Once the 1st Cavalry Division proved that it was possible to move the 155-mm howitzer by slinging it under a CH-47, each of the airmobile divisions gained a battalion with those weapons. The 173d Airborne Brigade picked up a fourth battery to match the number of infantry battalions. And the introduction of the Low Altitude Parachute Extraction System (LAPES) designed for airborne operations allowed very large equipment and pallets of supplies to reach isolated positions, extending the effective reach of units.

Most importantly, the nature of combat operations changed dramatically in Vietnam. Large operations involving multiple brigades became rare after 1967. The NVA realized that, unlike the French, the Americans were too powerful to confront in open battle. When they dispersed into smaller units, U.S. actions became focused on battalion and company attacks and fending off attempts to overrun small firebases. A soldier's memories tended to be different from his World War II or Korean War counterparts. He didn't feel part of a sweeping campaign like Normandy; his moment in history might be in a nameless platoon firefight on a jungle trail or coming into a hot landing zone (LZ).

Paratroopers jump from an Army Caribou transport on July 29, 1965. The jump was part of arrival ceremonies for the 1st Brigade, 101st Airborne Division, at Cam Ranh Bay. Ambassador Maxwell D. Taylor, the World War II division commander, helped to welcome them. *National Archives.*

BRIGADE EXAMPLES

TO THE READER

No single book can tell the story of the airborne units in Vietnam adequately without unfairly omitting someone. Every airborne element that served in the war, from individual to division, built an exemplary record of achievements and service.

A laundry list of actions for each unit would be just that—a list. Therefore, the following pages present examples of skill and courage for each of the units. The recounting of a unit's actions represents the service of all its brethren. One example is presented for each brigade.

173D AIRBORNE BRIGADE

The 173d Airborne Brigade saw action in the area north of Saigon during the first part of its deployment and then in 1967 went up to the central highlands. While in the south, the brigade routinely carried out search and destroy operations in the three fortified areas known as War Zones C and D and the Iron Triangle, the latter only 20 kilometers west of Saigon and a base that the VC had occupied for 20 years.

By the end of 1966 the Americans had built up to large multidivision sweeps lasting several months, some in reaction to enemy moves and others the result of deliberate planning. The most significant of these for the brigade was Operation JUNCTION CITY designed to clear War Zone C up to the Cambodian border and to knock out the Central Office of South Vietnam, which was the controlling headquarters for the VC and NVA. It would employ two division task forces, an armored cavalry regiment, ARVN units, and the 173d. The plan was to form a horseshoe around the zone and then sweep north, driving the enemy into the waiting brigades.

In the original vision both the 173d and the 1st Brigade of the 101st were to conduct combat jumps, but by the time it was actually launched on February 22—D-Day—the other brigade was no longer available. Brig. Gen. John R. Deane, Jr., selected a task force built around Lt. Col. Robert Sigholtz's 2d Battalion, 503d Infantry, supported by Battery A, 3d Battalion, 319th Artillery to carry out the drop.

The target was Drop Zone (DZ) Charlie, only three kilometers from the border. The task force boarded 16 C-130s at Bien Hoa and took off at 0825 on February 22, 1967. It arrived over the DZ on schedule, and the first men went out the door at 0900 from an altitude of 1,000 feet. The airborne standard was followed: Deane was jumper one of Chalk One going out the right door while Sigholtz went out the left door as first in his stick. CWO Howard Melvin held the distinction of making his fifth combat jump this day; the other four were with the 82d during World War II. It took two passes to get everyone into the small DZ, but the last man was on the ground in about ten minutes. Ten more C-130s started the heavy drop at 0925. The battalion team had only 11 jump injuries, all minor.

By 1000 Deane's command post was operational and the airhead secured. At the same time, the other two battalions conducted four air assaults nearby to complete the brigade's sector of the horseshoe. Although often criticized for jumping into a secure DZ (it had taken no ground fire), the 173d carried out a true airborne assault, seizing an airhead to prevent an enemy escape and rapidly reinforcing it. Thereafter it conducted a series of sweeps marked by small firefights. On April 13 it returned to Bien Hoa.

The brigade accumulated streamers for 14 campaigns, a Presidential Unit Citation for its fight at Dak To, a Meritorious Unit Commendation, the Republic of Vietnam Cross of Gallantry with Palm, and the Civic Action Honor Medal.

Helicopter Pickup by Paul Rickert. Soldiers of the 1st Brigade, 101st Airborne Division, evacuate a wounded comrade by UH-1 "Huey" in 1966. *Army Art Collection, U.S. Army Center of Military History.*

1ST BRIGADE, 101ST AIRBORNE DIVISION

The 1st Brigade, 101st Airborne Division, arrived in Vietnam in July 1965 and habitually worked in the country's central highlands in some of the worst terrain possible. Brig. Gen. Willard Pearson's men quickly learned to deal with the heavy jungle that prevented parachute jumps from being a viable option. They adapted airborne tactics of sending pathfinders in ahead of the main force and bringing engineers into the airhead to create a landing strip to airmobile conditions. The brigade trained teams to rappel into the forests from helicopters. Then it brought in equipment by airdrop or sling load and cleared LZs for the main body.

In June 1966 the brigade received the mission to relieve the outpost of Tou Morong, which was the target of the 24th NVA Regiment. It completed the task by late afternoon on June 6 with the 1st Battalion, 327th Infantry, remaining nearby. They were supported by a hasty fire support base four kilometers west.

Battery B, 2d Battalion, 320th Artillery, and Company A, 2d Battalion, 502d Infantry, occupied it, and were hit by an enemy battalion at 0200 on June 7. The battle raged on at point-blank range until 0845. One 105-mm howitzer was overrun, recaptured, overrun a second time, and finally had to be destroyed by the fire of the other pieces. The morning after, enemy bodies were found within the gun positions.

Pearson immediately began exploiting the contact by sending 1st Battalion, 327th Infantry, in pursuit along with several Vietnamese elements. They pushed north while the 2d Battalion, 502d Infantry, carried out an airmobile insertion and started south. Heavy fighting brought additional American and Vietnamese forces into the battle, gradually encircling the NVA regiment.

On June 10 an enemy counterattack hit Company C, 2d Battalion, 502d Infantry, which was already understrength and casualties mounted. As Lt. Col. Henry Emerson tried to push relief forces forward, the company's position became critical. Capt. William S. Carpenter, Jr., realized that his company was about to be completely overrun. Rather than accept defeat, he called in an air strike on the perimeter. The napalm hit so close that some of the paratroopers suffered burns, but this broke the back of the attack and at 2330 Company A finally got through.

The battle of Tuo Morong continued until June 17 and included an Arc Light mission on June 13 by 24 B-52 heavy bombers that pounded the NVA positions from 0800 to 0847. Within 30 minutes Carpenter's company led the way into the target area and began collecting dazed prisoners. The 1st Brigade showed that an airborne force could react swiftly to a changing tactical situation and hit hard. By fighting on when surrounded and outnumbered, its men followed the example set by the division at Bastogne.

During its Vietnam service the brigade received a Presidential Unit Citation for Dak To, a Valorous Unit Award for Tuy Hoa, a Meritorious Unit Commendation, two Vietnamese Crosses of Gallantry, and a Civic Action Honor Medal. It displays 15 of the war's 16 campaign participation streamers.

1ST BRIGADE, 1ST CAVALRY DIVISION

The 1st Cavalry Division (Airmobile), "The First Team," became fully operational in Vietnam on September 28, 1965, only 90 days after unfurling its colors at Fort Benning. Its 1st Brigade (Airborne) had arrived eight days earlier on board the USNS *Geiger*. In less than a month it carried out Operation ALL THE WAY as part of the complex campaign to relieve the Special Forces camp at Plei Me. The brigade used helicopters for a basic airborne mission to cut off the 33d NVA Regiment trying to retreat across the Cambodian border. Although it had to cover 1,200 square miles of jungle, the paratroopers' airmobile tactics maintained pressure and created a series of pitched fights up to battalion size. They made good use of fire support by having CH-47s leapfrog artillery batteries forward, and by using aerial rocket artillery for the first time.

In mid-May 1966 the 1st Brigade (Airborne) was at An Khe where it kept an eye on a civilian irregular defense group (CIDG) camp in the Vinh Thanh Valley. The enemy had wanted to capture the CIDG camp on Ho Chi Minh's birthday (May 19), but their plan fell apart. When the camp reported contact on May 16 Company B, 2d Battalion, 8th Cavalry responded. It landed on LZ Hereford and worked its way to the top of the adjacent ridge where it collided with an NVA battalion. Operation CRAZY HORSE evolved from this firefight as the new division commander, Maj. Gen. John Norton (formerly the Howze Board's secretary) committed additional forces to exploit the situation. Within three days the brigade had five battalions slugging it out with two full regiments—the 2d VC and the 12th NVA.

1st Cavalry Division shoulder sleeve insignia. *U.S. Army Center of Military History.*

Soldiers of the 1st Cavalry Division (Airmobile) stride to their new encampment near An Khe, Vietnam, September 17, 1965. *National Archives.*

CRAZY HORSE ended on June 5. Along the way the paratroopers had overrun an important base and captured documents that allowed the South Vietnamese to eliminate most of the VC leadership in Binh Dinh Province. Ironically one of the key qualities of an airborne force, its ability to react rapidly to take advantage of an opening, prevented the brigade from making a combat jump. CRAZY HORSE took precedence over a major sweep around Tuy Hoa that was in the planning stage. The brigade was going to undertake a multi-battalion operation including a battalion jump. The sweep took place later in June, but without the airborne phase.

By the time it left Vietnam the 1st Brigade, 1st Cavalry Division, had added 13 battle streamers to its colors along with five unit decorations: a Presidential Unit Citation, a Valorous Unit Award, three Vietnamese Crosses of Gallantry, and a Civic Action Honor Medal.

3D BRIGADE, 82D AIRBORNE DIVISION

Flying the 3d Brigade, 82d Airborne Division, from Fort Bragg to Vietnam required 140 transport aircraft sorties via the northern route via Alaska and Japan. Once in Vietnam, Col. Alexander Bolling's "Golden Brigade" immediately coped with serious personnel turbulence as well as the enemy. The Army discovered that many of the men did not have enough time left on their enlistments to be sent overseas, and they had to return home.

However, in less than a month after arriving on February 14, 1968, the paratroopers from the 82d went into combat alongside the 101st in Quang Tri and Thua Thien provinces. Operations CARENTAN I and II were named to commemorate Normandy where the divisions had served in combat together for the first time. The ties carried on in the decades that followed when they formed the heart of XVIII Airborne Corps, and would extend into the 21st century during the two wars with Iraq.

The brigade's tour of duty came at a time when large-scale operations were rare. USARV now assigned each command its own area of operations where it focused on local actions. The brigade drew a sector in the highlands around Phu Loi and spent nearly all of its energy there.

These paratroopers operated most of the time during their tour of duty as part of battalion- or company-sized task forces. They carried out innumerable search and destroy missions, airmobile assaults, and ambush patrols too small to have names. And, of course, they occupied small fire support bases.

The troopers also supported a variety of civic action projects such as "medcaps" where medical teams visited villages to care for the inhabitants with other soldiers furnishing security. While not as visible to the American public or to historians writing well after the fact, those missions were actually central to the national strategy of "winning the hearts and minds of the people" at the grassroots level.

During its time in-country the brigade would receive two unit decorations—the Vietnamese Cross of Gallantry and Civic Action Honor Medal—and six campaign streamers. But it never had a chance to make a combat jump.

REDEPLOYMENT

In 1968 the stress of deployments to Vietnam and the need to stay strong in Europe and Korea "just in case" forced reductions and reorganizations elsewhere. These hit the airborne community especially hard because the number of qualified parachutists had already been stretched to support an expanded Special Forces component. To preserve the 82d's ability to serve as the strategic reserve ready reaction force, it gained a 4th Brigade during the period when the 3d was in Vietnam. To help fill these spaces Panama lost its airborne battalion.

In June 1969 President Richard Nixon began "Vietnamization," gradually turning the war back to ARVN and reducing USARV. One of the first units home was the 3d Brigade, 82d Airborne Division, which replaced the 4th Brigade at Fort Bragg that December. The return of the other airborne unit, the 173d Airborne Brigade, was more complex.

Troopers of 3d Brigade, 82d Airborne Division, arrive at Chu Lai, South Vietnam, on February 14, 1968, en route to deployment northward near Hue-Phu Bai. First elements of the brigade began leaving Fort Bragg within 24 hours after being alerted. *National Archives.*

Dates of Service

Unit	Date Arrived	Date Departed
173D AIRBORNE BRIGADE	MAY 1965	AUGUST 1971
1ST BRIGADE, 101ST AIRBORNE DIVISION	JULY 1965	JANUARY 1972
1ST CAVALRY DIVISION (LESS 3D BRIGADE)	AUGUST 1965	APRIL 1971
3D BRIGADE, 1ST CAVALRY DIVISION	AUGUST 1965	JUNE 1972
2D BRIGADE, 101ST AIRBORNE DIVISION	DECEMBER 1967	FEBRUARY 1972
3D BRIGADE, 101ST AIRBORNE DIVISION	DECEMBER 1967	DECEMBER 1971
3D BRIGADE, 82D AIRBORNE DIVISION	FEBRUARY 1968	DECEMBER 1969

Paratroopers of the 3d Brigade, 82d Airborne Division, returning enemy fire a month after arriving in Vietnam. Training and physical conditioning of airborne soldiers helped them adjust quickly to combat in the jungles and rice paddies.
National Archives.

It couldn't go back to Okinawa but the Army wanted to keep it active because it had been the first large unit sent to Vietnam. Westmoreland—now the Army Chief of Staff—decided to station it at Fort Campbell until the 101st returned. The 173d arrived in September 1971. In January 1972 the brigade headquarters stood down and some elements transferred to the 101st to honor its Vietnam combat. The time from the first plane arriving at Bien Hoa in May 1965 until the last one took off for the States, the 173d had spent six years, three months, and 20 days in Vietnam.

Both airmobile divisions came back in stages. The 101st Airborne Division returned to Fort Campbell over a period of four months. Its 3d Brigade arrived in December 1971, the 1st in January 1972, the 2d in February, and the rest of the division closed in March. It was kept as the Army's lone airmobile division, but with the original configuration that made one of the brigades airborne and capable of deploying separately. In 1974 that brigade came off jump status and the division formally became air assault instead of airmobile. The 1st Cavalry Division went to Fort Hood, Texas, in April 1971 with the 3d Brigade following in 1972. It would become an armored force and lose its association with the airborne community.

Vietnam had been a test for the airborne community. Large numbers of paratroopers otherwise used for strategic and theater rapid reaction forces were diverted to fill Special Forces and advisory teams. Others were assigned as individual replacements to non-airborne units and stopped jumping. Now, as the Army adjusted to a smaller peacetime size, it had to make further cuts in the theaters' airborne spaces. Alaska's would eventually shrink to three companies. Europe cut down to a single battalion stationed in Italy, intended to work as part of a multinational mobile force.

Chapter 10

Nation's Contingency Force, 1965–2000

NEW VISION

The unique capabilities of airborne forces led Pentagon leaders gradually to develop a new vision of vertical envelopment. This interest played a part in the modernization of weapons, organization, and doctrine initiated by Gens. Matthew B. Ridgway and Maxwell Taylor. Modernization was put on hold as nearly the entire Army became committed to Vietnam and containing the Soviets and the People's Republic of China.

The Army always tries to apply lessons learned in war. By 1965 parachute and the new airmobile variety divisions had made vertical attack more lethal. Over the next 30 years the range and size of effective airborne operations led to further evolution.

THE CHALLENGE

President John F. Kennedy's introduction of flexible response as a new component of national strategy tasked the Army to provide forces to react to small conflicts around the globe with little notice. The requirement grew out of a new Communist tactic that used surrogates to open up new fronts in the Cold War. As the deployment to Lebanon demonstrated, the nature of parachute assaults made airborne units the best choice to project force.

Basing airborne units in the United States made more sense than scattering them among regional overseas commands. Stateside basing allowed more intense training and resulted in better unit readiness and closer relationships with the Air Force.

THE RESPONSE

Steps to overcome identified problems took the Army in several directions. The more obvious led to the Howze Board's vision of air mobility with its multiple uses. But equally important innovations emerged from the review of missions studied in 1943 by the Swing Board. In time, planners found a way to anticipate crises in the Western Hemisphere and started looking at global applications.

Speed in tactical deployment had always been the hallmark of airborne divisions. The need to apply combat power evolved into the use of mass jumps. The drawback came once forces reached the ground. In World War II and Korea it was impossible to bring in bulky items, like vehicles and heavy weapons, needed to hold off counterattack. The light airborne forces were vulnerable until they were relieved by ground troops. However, the threat posed by the mere existence of an airborne capability compelled the enemy to divert forces to protect his rear areas.

Airborne units also had a second innate characteristic that received less public attention but was just as important. Using only volunteers and a system of training that retained only the most motivated men naturally produced the paratrooper's hallmark aggressive nature and ability to think on his feet. Senior commanders tried to keep them in the fight even after the ground linkup, attaching heavier units and support troops as required. The Battle of the Bulge demonstrated that airborne units could quickly enter combat on the ground provided that they were given enough trucks.

XVIII Airborne Corps and its divisions based in the continental United States became the Army's strategic reserve in the 1950s. Readiness and rapid deployment were its hallmarks.

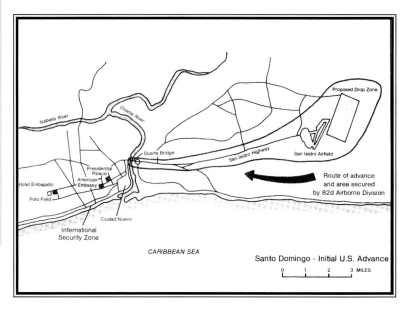

Santo Domingo Area of Operations, 1965. *U.S. Army Center of Military History.*

The Caribbean basin lay within its reach and became a focal area. Over time, exercises and a series of real-world deployments transformed the corps into the nation's contingency force. It was flexible and well-rounded to meet large and small challenges. Without losing its fundamental identity as paratroopers, the XVIII Airborne Corps became the most sophisticated strike force the Army ever had.

POWER PACK

The Dominican Republic in 1965 generated the Army's first experience in moving a significant force within the hemisphere to deal with a crisis. America saw Fidel Castro's support of insurgents as a real threat. When the government of the nearby Dominican Republic lost effective control and the country lurched toward civil war, President Lyndon B. Johnson acted to prevent a Communist takeover.

On the morning of April 25, 1965, the president ordered the Joint Chiefs of Staff (JCS) to plan to evacuate Americans living in the capital of Santo Domingo. State Department diplomats asked the Organization of American States (OAS) to negotiate a political settlement. Events over the next few days left no doubt in Washington leaders' minds that unless unilateral action was taken soon, it might be too late. On April 28 President Johnson ordered Marines ashore to protect the embassy and those Americans remaining in the city.

Protection was the first mission. Restoring stability was a much larger task that began by imposing a cease-fire. The only way to achieve stability in time was to send in the 82d Airborne Division. President Johnson made that decision at 1930 on April 29. Maj. Gen. Robert York, the division commander, immediately encountered problems. Trying to communicate with a complicated chain of command stretching all the way to Washington was difficult. This was never resolved during the operation.

Paratroopers from the 3d Brigade of the 82d soon began flying from Pope Air Force Base (AFB), adjacent to Fort Bragg, North Carolina, to a staging point in Puerto Rico. At this point the operation was only a show of force intended to prevent combat. The next day York was ordered to move POWER PACK I to San Isidro airport, east of the capital city. The brigade prepared to conduct an airfield seizure mission in part because the aircraft were already rigged for airdrop but also because experience in exercises made it clear that the airstrip would become overcrowded. The JCS, however, directed air landing. This caused massive problems. However, it was a lucky break for the paratroopers because the drop zone (DZ) was covered with sharp coral outcroppings that would have caused many injuries.

At 2130 on April 29 the Commander in Chief, Atlantic (CINCLANT) sent his aide and two Marine captains to the airfield, where they found friendly Dominicans in charge. They succeeded in getting the control tower and runway lights operational and talked in the first

Members of the 82d Airborne Division's band performing in Santo Domingo while providing their own security. *82d Airborne Division War Memorial Museum.*

planes. This was the second unexpected stroke of luck because the initial POWER PACK force did not include an Air Force airlift control element.

York in Chalk One (the first plane) touched down at 0216 on April 30. The following 46 aircraft delivered two battalion combat teams within a few hours. Because no materiel handling equipment was sent, the paratroopers lost time unloading rigged equipment by hand and dodging arriving C-130s. Others established a perimeter around the airhead and pushed patrols toward the city. Company C, 1st Battalion, 508th Infantry, crossed the key bridge over the Ozama River and secured ground for a staging area.

For the rest of the day, York's 2,500 men encountered sporadic heavy fighting that continued through May 2. He requested four additional battalion combat teams from the 2d Brigade (POWER PACK II) and support units to deal with his expanding mission. By the time the Army received permission to link up with the Marines at the embassy Lt. Gen. Bruce Palmer, Jr., took charge.

About to become Commanding General, XVIII Airborne Corps, Palmer brought down the headquarters to provide command and control. JCS put the rest of the corps on alert to follow. Although only two more increments (POWER PACK III and IV) deployed, Palmer's joint forces grew to 24,000 including nine infantry battalions and three of Marines.

During the mission the corridor between the airfield and the embassy, for obvious reasons, gained the nickname "All American Expressway." In just three weeks U.S. armed forces changed the entire outlook of the Dominican rebellion. Overwhelming American combat forces had separated the combatants and forced a military stalemate which gave the OAS time to broker a political settlement. As normalcy returned, the Inter-American Peace Force assumed more and more of the mission. By autumn only a single brigade remained, and it soon departed. American casualties included 27 killed in action, 20 died of non-combat causes, and 127 wounded.

THE VOLUNTEER ARMY

The end of the Vietnam War returned the nation's focus to the Soviet Union's direct threat to the North Atlantic Treaty Organization (NATO) in the event of a conventional war. The Army had to ensure that it could carry out the mission in Europe at the same time that yet another demobilization shrank the available force to a mere 13 active divisions. The most important barrier that had to be overcome during the 1970s, however, grew out of the antiwar sentiment held by so many civilians.

Politicians in Washington reacted to the demands of voters and the media by abolishing the draft. While the airborne community suffered less direct impact because it had always relied on volunteers, the transition to the All-Volunteer Army (VOLAR) caused great pain to the Army at large. It took time to raise pay and quality of life enough to attract the necessary kind of men—and women—and to find the right way to appeal to their patriotism. The national emphasis on achieving equality between the sexes opened up many more career fields to women.

For example, on December 14, 1973, Pvts. Rita Johnson and Joyce Kutsch graduated from the Basic Airborne Course at the Infantry School and pinned on the Parachutist Badge. They be-

came parachute riggers, a vital skill in airborne units. Pvt. Reita Lewis Los, the 100th woman to graduate from the course (April 18, 1975), thrived in her airborne career. She became the first female "Black Hat" instructor in the Basic Airborne Course. She was the first woman qualified as a pathfinder and jumpmaster.

Behind the scenes, planners looked at the long-term implications of these changes and made a conscious decision to alter the very nature of the Army. Not only did VOLAR leave a much smaller force, active and reserve components, but also it guaranteed that there would not be enough of them available to train new units in the event of a rapid expansion. However, the Army leaders knew that the evolution would lead to more highly motivated, better educated soldiers serving longer. With that force they could build an Army that won by having more sophisticated weapons and equipment and a better way of fighting than any potential enemy. The paratrooper's advantage that came from putting quality ahead of quantity became the Army standard.

Much of the effort went into producing heavy divisions to carry out the high-tempo warfare needed in Europe. Weapons like M-1 Abrams main battle tanks, M-2 infantry fighting vehicles, and AH-64 Apache attack helicopters came into service during the 1980s. The

Beginning in December 1973, women joined the airborne community. In this 1979 painting by Janet Fitzgerald a female rigger in the red hat performs pre-jump checks on another trooper. *Army Art Collection, U.S. Army Center of Military History.*

rise of officers with Vietnam experience into senior leadership positions went further. They demanded that soldiers be given the best possible training and doctrine to prevent needless combat casualties. The capstone of that commitment came in the form of the first real war games carried out under stressful conditions intended to be worse than actual war. The National Training Center (NTC) in California's Mojave Desert became the graduate school for a unit's training cycle.

The contingency force also gained significant new capabilities. Although the only forward-deployed paratroopers were small units in northern Italy and Alaska, XVIII Airborne Corps started growing. When the 101st Airborne Division returned to Fort Campbell, Kentucky, it had two airmobile brigades and one airborne brigade. In order to make it more lethal, the Pentagon streamlined the 101st's organization and in 1974 took the brigade off jump status. New scout, utility, and attack helicopters in development would need new tactics. The resulting doctrine created the true offensive power that the Howze Board had wanted. And because the skills had become distinct enough, the Army added a special air assault badge to take a place beside the parachute wings.

Changes in the combat power of the 82d Airborne Division were harder for the outsider to notice, but just as profound. For example, in the fall of 1974 it gained an air defense artillery battalion for the first time since World War II and expanded support capability. It would also receive a share of the new helicopters. An airborne armor battalion gave

the division a tank capability for the first time using air-droppable Sheridans. Each addition, including the pilots, served on jump status.

The heart of the 82d's combat power came from three flexible brigade combat teams built around nine infantry and three field artillery battalions. Each of those teams had a full array of "slices" from other division assets and could be tailored to each specific mission. It also refined a readiness system in which the three brigades rotated through a training, alert, and reconstitution cycle. The division ready brigade (DRB) had its three battalions working with a similar rotation pattern to maintain the ability to keep the division ready force (DRF) battalion combat team able to go "wheels up"—take off from Pope AFB—within 18 hours of first alert.

URGENT FURY

Once the Army completed its difficult transformation to an all-volunteer status and the nation regained its self-confidence, the contingency forces had to deal with a series of new Cold War crises. In May 1978 another round of trouble in Zaire (formerly the Congo) required western intervention. The Air Force supported a joint Franco-Belgian task force, but although it had been on alert to carry out a combat drop, the 82d did not go. Communist leaders wondered if the withdrawal from Vietnam and the overthrow of the pro-American Shah of Iran meant that America was weak. The Kremlin didn't want to risk nuclear war. But proxies offered a chance to test the nation's will by taking small nibbles in the Caribbean again.

In 1979 the island of Grenada elected a government with Marxist ties. It formed alliances with Castro and brought in Cuban paramilitary engineers to expand the Point Salines airport to a size that would allow the Soviets to have a potential base that threatened the entire region. On October 12, 1983, more extreme elements staged a coup which added to Washington's concerns because more than 400 Americans attending medical school there were suddenly potential hostages—like those recently seized at the embassy in Tehran.

On October 19 the JCS tasked CINCLANT, headquartered in Norfolk, Virginia, to develop options in the event that a force had to be sent to rescue the medical students and neutralize the Cubans and Grenadian armed forces. CINCLANT had no experience with ground operations, especially airborne ones. With so little time, all planning had to be done on the fly. The forces it selected came from the Special Operations community, the Navy, and the Marines who had a task group just departing for Lebanon that could be diverted. However, these elements had never worked together before; because the mission was so highly classified, coordination and planning at subordinate levels became difficult.

In its final form Operation URGENT FURY called for a simultaneous attack on multiple targets just before dawn on October 25. The complicated plan assigned each participant objectives that ranged from Special Operations teams securing key individuals before they could be harmed to the Marines sweeping across half the island. The primary assault would take place on Point Salines where two battalions of Rangers would carry out an airfield seizure with part of the 82d Airborne Division following. These forces had the task of rescuing the medical students and neutralizing the Cubans.

The division started out at a disadvantage because it did not learn of the operation until October 22. This was compounded by the fact that CINCLANT didn't understand how the Army was structured and bypassed XVIII Airborne Corps, which was left in the dark. Maj. Gen. Edward Trobaugh, the 82d's commanding general, also didn't get a decision on whether they would jump in or air land. No one in Norfolk understood that each option required different preparations, and assumed that a change could be made at the last second.

Coordination of the attack suffered when a series of problems cropped up at the last minute. The Rangers encountered a problem when the

A member of XVIII Airborne Corps's 16th Military Police Brigade guarding a group of Cuban engineers captured during Operation URGENT FURY. *Department of Defense.*

Paratrooper from the 82d Airborne Division applying camouflage. These men are on a ridge overlooking the Point Salines airfield secured by the division during Operation URGENT FURY. *Department of Defense.*

navigational aids failed on the lead C-130 flying them in from Barbados. The resulting scramble of the aerial stream brought them in 36 minutes late and in daylight. They jumped at a height of only 500 feet and paid the price in jump injuries. But the airport was secured by 0715 and their follow-on rescue took place without incident. However, intelligence activities had failed to discover that American students actually were in different places on the island and had badly underestimated the size of the Cuban and Grenadian forces.

These revelations resulted in the division being ordered to send in two battalions much earlier than expected, and to air land. It had only two hours to prepare load plans before planes started taking off from Pope AFB at around 1000. This haste allowed only 35 logistical personnel to go, and they took no materiel handling equipment to unload planes upon arrival. The first C-141s touched down at 1400. By then the exhaustion of the initial forces had led to calling forward two additional battalions and the 2d Brigade headquarters. Because all of the Army elements were airborne qualified, they recognized the stages of a seizure and the 82d quickly pushed out to expand the airhead and engaged in five hours of fighting before opposition became sporadic.

Clearing the island exposed more coordination problems. The services couldn't communicate with each other. Marines clearing the northern half of the island moved faster than the paratroopers moving up from the south leading

to inter-service arguments. This was partly because the Army had a much more densely settled area that took longer to clear properly but also because each force had different tactical doctrine. There were friendly fire incidents, the most serious of which took place on October 27 a half-mile east of Frequente when Navy A-7 attack aircraft mistakenly bombed the 2d Brigade command post, causing 17 casualties.

The Rangers started departing on October 28. The Marines resumed their voyage to Lebanon on November 2 when combat operations formally ended. The strength of the 82d peaked the next day at more than 6,000 men from seven infantry and three artillery battalions, plus a proportion of the rest of the division. The drawdown started almost immediately. By December 12 the last battalion arrived back at Fort Bragg. Operation URGENT FURY rescued more than 700 civilians, including 564 medical students, and removed the island from Cuban-Soviet influence. It had cost 19 men killed in action and 116 wounded. But many of the participants gained critical experience that would serve them well when they faced crises in later years.

URGENT FURY's success also revealed terrible weaknesses in the different services' ability to work together. New equipment and new doctrine resulted. For the airborne, that led to closer ties to the Air Force; permanent liaison with the Marines; and seamless integration with air assault, light infantry, and mechanized units. Training concentrated on developing a sophisticated airfield seizure package compatible with Special Operations Forces.

In the years immediately following URGENT FURY, the Army created a new light division capable of being air landed and adjusted the 82d and 101st to make them smaller but more powerful. Each gained an aviation brigade to control an air-ground reconnaissance squadron as well as helicopters. That of the 101st was markedly different, much larger, and actually served as a fourth combat brigade. The division's ground power revolved around nine airmobile infantry battalions and three artillery battalions specifically trained to move entirely by helicopter if necessary. XVIII Airborne Corps found itself controlling airborne, air assault, mechanized infantry, and light infantry divisions and grew to include a complete range of forces, all of which had units on jump status: artillery, engineer, signal, military police, military intelligence, and aviation brigades, plus finance and administrative groups. Given the range of different contingency plans it faced, the corps needed a wider array of available units than the Army's other corps.

GOLDEN PHEASANT

The first test of the post-Grenada reforms came in Honduras in 1988. Nicaraguan President Daniel Ortega's Sandinistas had seized power by force in 1979. After years of civil war, the Sandinistas prevailed over the contras. Elections in 1984 kept Ortega in office. Encouraged by Cuba's Fidel Castro, he strove to expand his influence within Central America. In March 1988 the Sandinistas began moving large forces toward Honduras with the clear intention of crossing the border in pursuit of the remaining contras.

On March 16, within an hour from start to finish, the JCS set in motion an American military response to a Honduran request for support. By now it was possible to carry out impromptu planning without the problems of earlier years. Working through the normal chain of command, the JCS could initiate a no-notice emergency deployment readiness exercise (EDRE), now a frequent training event in the contingency force. Ready alert units would receive their alert notification—N-Hour—and immediately begin performing established procedures that could have leading elements in the air in only 18 hours. Because these preparations were automatic, top Defense Department leaders had time to make deliberate decisions before the president gave the execution order. If the deployment was canceled the exercise still proceeded as a training event, and the effort was not wasted.

In this case the corps received orders to send a four-battalion force under Brig. Gen. Daniel Schroeder, the XVIII Airborne Corps chief of staff, and Brig. Gen. James Johnson, one of the assistant division commanders of the 82d Airborne. Two battalions (1st and 2d Battalions, 504th Infantry) would come from the 82d at Fort Bragg, plus most of the 1st Battalion, 319th Field Artillery. The other two (2d and 3d Battalions, 27th Infantry) were light infantry combat teams from the 7th Infantry Division at Fort Ord, California. In classic fashion, the concept called for paratroopers to jump on an airfield with the light infantry landing on transports as reinforcements. Because many airborne officers and noncommissioned officers served tours of duty in the light infantry, the two divisions used many of the same techniques which made cooperation simple.

Things went smoothly in part because the corps and division staffs had learned to assume

Paratroopers from the 82d Airborne Division jumping from C-141 Starlifters during Operation GOLDEN PHEASANT. *Department of Defense.*

that there would never be as many airplanes available as they requested. The 82d during late 1986 had worked out a radically different way to form its force packages. Instead of starting with units and then trying to work out what to cut based on available aircraft, standard packets were built around weapons systems. A decision now involved only choosing the type and number of systems to send, which were plugged into standard load plans.

President Ronald Reagan decided at 2145 on March 16 to send the task force to Honduras. The JCS issued its deployment order at 0010 on March 17. The first plane took off from Pope AFB at 0703. The 7th Infantry Division's contingent started departing from Travis AFB, California, a few hours later. The first C-141 landed at Palmerola Air Base in Honduras at 1124. For the next 26 hours, another plane landed about every 30 minutes until nearly 3,000 troops had closed in. The last team to arrive, 2d Battalion, 504th Infantry, made the

jump in front of dignitaries and the press. Two more jumps alongside the 2d Honduran Airborne Battalion followed.

Redeployment began after 10 days including a jump back into Sicily DZ at Fort Bragg. The mission ended at 0740 on March 31 when the final plane from Honduras landed. The contrast between GOLDEN PHEASANT and the earlier Dominican Republic and Grenada deployments was remarkable. Refined planning, better equipment and training, and experienced personnel created the confidence and skills that took every glitch in stride and made the necessary adjustments smoothly.

JUST CAUSE

The crowning achievement of XVIII Airborne Corps contingency operations at the end of the decade came in Panama. While the collapse of the Soviet Union removed the immediate Communist threat in Latin America, the

Soldiers paid a heavy price to be the nation's contingency force. Airborne operations depend on maintaining the highest proficiency possible, and that demands constant practice and global travel.

The 101st Airborne Division lost 248 members of 2d Battalion, 502d Infantry, in an airplane crash. The troopers were returning from a tour of duty in the Sinai Field Mission. The DC-8 transport carrying them crashed on December 12, 1985, near Gander, Newfoundland.

Eight and one-half years later, tragedy struck the Fort Bragg airborne community. Paratroopers passed through Pope Air Force Base's Green Ramp passenger shed area during training as well as when they deployed. On March 23, 1994, two Air Force planes collided while trying to land at the same time. Their collision sent a huge fireball through the area where men and women from the 82d Airborne Division and other XVIII Airborne Corps units were preparing for two routine practice jumps. Twenty-four soldiers died and 106 others were seriously burned in the 82d's worst peacetime disaster.

region's heavily armed drug rings became a major concern. Gen. Manuel Noriega, the head of Panama's armed forces, became a willing ally. Two Florida federal grand juries indicted him as a drug trafficker during 1988.

This situation had much wider implications than just the drugs. The Carter-Torrijos Treaties of 1977 committed the United States to turn over the Panama Canal to Panama on December 31, 1999, and would abolish the Panama Canal Zone. Southern Command (SOUTHCOM) retained bases to guard the vital waterway, but had started a slow process of transferring them. The fear in Washington was that Panamanian control of the Canal could become a severe threat to national security.

By early 1988 Noriega's hold on the country made the civilian government irrelevant. He used violence in May 1989 to halt an election poised to defeat his puppet candidate. Washington leaders considered the situation serious enough to take military action and ordered a temporary increase in the garrison to be performed by a rotation of units. United States Army, South (USARSO), which had only the small 193d Infantry Brigade as combat troops, received the most help. Besides being augmented with military police and aviation units, USARSO gained a mechanized infantry battalion and a light infantry brigade task force from the 7th Infantry Division. Procedures within the country increased security, moved most of the military families onto bases, and returned many families to the United States.

SOUTHCOM had plans to deal with a military crisis in Panama, but these called for a slow buildup of defensive forces. Called proportional response (or tit-for-tat by critics), the technique had been a staple of the Cold War and was used in Vietnam. When things kept getting worse, the Pentagon decided to take a new approach. Gen. Maxwell Thurman, a former artillery commander in the 82d Airborne Division, put off his planned retirement and became the new SOUTHCOM commander in chief.

Thurman then turned to his old friend Lt. Gen. Carl Stiner and designated him to lead Joint Task Force South (JTF South). Stiner, who had significant Special Operations experience, had just been promoted from commanding the 82d to commanding general of XVIII Airborne Corps. Thurman tasked the corps to create an entirely new plan for a worst-case scenario. Instead of slow escalation, Thurman and the JCS allowed those with experience in contingency operations to make the case for applying overwhelming force at the outset of a crisis.

Madden Dam controls the Chagres River, creating Madden Lake. It is the source of the water for the Panama Canal, filling during the rainy season and ensuring a water supply for the canal locks year-round. Madden Dam was one of the H-Hour objectives secured by the 3d Battalion, 504th Infantry. *XVIII Airborne Corps.*

Stiner and his plans chief, Lt. Col. Timothy McMahon, arranged for a massive attack striking so swiftly that it would immediately crush resistance. At the same time, troops would be available to protect vital installations and several large communities housing American employees of the Panama Canal Commission and dependents of military forces.

The plan designated the U.S. troops stationed in Panama to deal with defense of the Canal. They also would have to neutralize the country's two largest cities. Panama City (the capital) lies at the Pacific end of the Canal and was assigned to the nearby 193d. Colon, on the Atlantic side, fell to the augmentation brigade stationed close by. Most of the Panamanian troops occupied small bases called cuartels that were outside the immediate Canal area but from which they could swiftly join a fight. Only a surprise airborne attack would neutralize them. Because Panamanian Defense Force (PDF) heavy mortars could prevent using Howard Air Base, the plan called for using an airfield seizure mission to capture Torrijos-Tocumen airport and air land follow-on forces.

On October 5, 1989, Noriega survived a second attempted coup, helped by two loyal companies who flew to Panama City from their base at Rio Hato. Stiner revised the plan to include seizing the airfield at Rio Hato. Stiner and McMahon designated 27 separate D-Day targets for JTF South. Learning from previous contingency operations, Thurman had made the task force truly joint for the first time. Placing every asset, including Special Operations Forces, under Stiner's direct command fixed one of the worst defects of URGENT FURY.

Special circumstances let XVIII Airborne Corps create the most sophisticated operations plan that the Army had ever seen. American troops had been serving in the objective area for nearly a century, which provided exceptionally detailed intelligence. A deliberate planning process allowed the JTF to identify nearly every critical point or potential problem in the entire scenario. And the Pentagon gave Thurman anything that Stiner needed.

The plan broke the operation into a series of missions to be carried out by each major headquarters, assigned clear responsibilities, and allocated forces needed to deal with every target. In this way the JTF could avoid compromising the overall secrecy of the plan and still rehearse intensively enough to identify and resolve problems. The process culminated with full-dress rehearsals of the airborne assaults by the Rangers and the 82d.

Months of training by every element involved in the operation provided the same confidence and ability to take the unexpected in stride. Because nearly all of the key players belonged to the same tight community—airborne, Special Operations, and light infantry—they had worked together before and trusted each other. The two division commanders— Maj. Gen. James Johnson (82d) and Maj. Gen. Carmen Cavezza (7th)—had been Stiner's assistant division commanders when he led the 82d, which gave both divisions essentially the same approach to rapid deployment.

Operation JUST CAUSE, the name selected by the JCS, involved a total of eight airborne battalions (three of which were Rangers) among its 27,000 participants. Two were already in Panama—the 1st Battalion, 509th Infantry, as part of the 193d Infantry Brigade; and the 3d Battalion, 504th Infantry, from the 82d which was attending the Jungle Operations Training Center and fell under the 3d Brigade, 7th Infantry Division. The other six made the first nighttime combat jumps since Normandy.

The 75th Ranger Regiment had both of the airfield seizure missions. Most of the Rangers landed at Rio Hato to take out the two PDF companies there along with the PDF military schools. One reinforced battalion jumped outside Panama City to capture and hold Omar Torrijos International Airport and the adjacent Tocumen military complex.

The 82d Airborne Division would follow 45 minutes later in a second wave of transports. DRB-1's mission to prevent PDF units from moving into Panama City demanded that it attack three major cuartels as fast as possible. Stiner directed that the brigade jump rather than air land because that was the only way to put reinforcements on the ground quickly— one of the airborne missions that hadn't been used since World War II. Army helicopter units already in Panama would fly in, pick up the paratroopers, and carry out a succession of three air assaults. On November 29 the 3d Brigade conducted a rehearsal of the plan during an EDRE code-named Black Knight, using Sicily DZ at Fort Bragg to simulate the airport and the three targets.

Noriega declared on December 15, 1989, that a "state of war" existed between Panama and the United States. The next day a series of incidents took place where the PDF confronted American personnel, including killing a marine lieutenant. This triggered action in Washington. At 2000 on December 17 the JCS ordered Stiner to carry out Operations Plan 90-2 using an EDRE as a cover story and designated 0100 on December 20 as H-Hour. The individual assault units began receiving their N-Hour alerts at 0900 on December 18 and immediately went into lockdown. Stiner departed Fort Bragg for Panama with a small command group. Four hours later he set up the JTF headquarters at Fort Clayton.

INTO ACTION

Actual execution of the mission followed the complex and coordinated timeline. Units in place in Panama took up their assigned jump-off locations by appearing to be carrying out another round of test alerts. A contingent of helicopters, Sheridans, and Special Opera-

The Panamanian Defense Force 5th Infantry Company's Building 4 at Fort Amador captured by the 1st Battalion, 508th Infantry. The second floor shows battle damage caused by a 105-mm howitzer on December 20, 1989. *XVIII Airborne Corps History Office.*

tions personnel already infiltrated into Panama undetected got into position for H-Hour. The additional forces came from the United States in three large groups. The Ranger Regiment assembled and its two assault groups flew to Panama as planned, using C-130s for the Rio Hato jump and C-141s for the airport. The 7th Infantry Division at Fort Ord staged through Travis AFB, California, and began moving as soon as the airport and Howard Air Base were secure enough for transports to land. The 16th Military Police Brigade and other supporting units from Fort Bragg followed the same way.

The one major deployment problem came at Pope AFB where bad weather created havoc for the 82d Airborne Division. The 1st Brigade had just assumed the DRB-1 mission. It and the rest of the division task force, a total of about 1,850 jumpers, went through their deployment preparations without incident. The Air Force loaded 31 C-141s with heavy drop platforms and containerized delivery system (CDS) pallets and sent them on to Charleston AFB, South Carolina. However, 21 more C-141s that would carry the paratroopers encountered freezing rain as they tried to load late on December 19. Instead of flying down as a single formation, the 82d had to take off as fast as individual planes' wings could be de-iced and hope that they could link up in the air. The first seven finally took off from Pope at 2130, roughly an hour late.

In Panama, the 1st Battalion, 508th Infantry, from Fort Kobbe boarded UH-60 Blackhawk helicopters and flew across the Canal to Fort Amador. The PDF and the Americans shared that installation. The paratroopers had to land, secure the family housing area, and isolate the PDF military police company barracks. After daylight they began systematically capturing one building at a time, trying to talk the defenders into surrendering rather than shoot them. The battalion had one 105-mm howitzer (the only field artillery piece in the entire operation that fired at a target) and set it up at point-blank range to "convince" holdouts to give up. The battalion also provided a company to the mechanized task force attacking Noriega's headquarters building, La Comandancia, in downtown Panama City. AH-64 Apache attack helicopters from the 1st Battalion, 82d Aviation, supporting that attack marked a little-noticed combat "first" when they launched two Hellfire missiles.

Elsewhere in Panama, the 3d Battalion, 504th Infantry, simultaneously executed a series of different missions along the Canal. The vehicles from Company D, the antitank company, secured Madden Dam—gateway to Madden Lake and the source of water for the Canal—and several additional points. Company B captured the Cerro Tigre depot by air assault. Company A flew into Gamboa at the mouth of the Chagres River to protect a housing area and capture the PDF women's training center. But the most challenging assign-

ment fell to Company C. They had to capture El Renacer Prison on the banks of the Canal and liberate the political prisoners there before guards could kill them. Their unique attack plan worked. The inner courtyard of the prison could only hold two helicopters, and even then the pilots had only feet to spare. Part of the company went in that way while the remainder used four LCM-8s (Landing Craft, Mechanized) from the 1097th Transportation Company to carry out the Army's first amphibious assault in decades.

The DZ for the paratroopers arriving from Fort Bragg extended alongside the main runway at Torrijos-Tocumen. Precision would be needed to avoid injuries from landing on the hard concrete. Everything started reasonably well. Heavy drop finished at 0205 and the personnel started jumping between five and ten minutes later with Johnson, in airborne tradition, going out the door as jumper one of Chalk One on schedule. He landed exactly on target, but few of the other 2,200 men did. The final jumpers only landed at 0545 an hour and a quarter after the division's assault command post was in operation.

Minor navigational issues, the straggling arrival of the planes, and pilots trying to ensure the soldiers' safety spread out the drop pattern. Distances from the assembly areas were no more than several kilometers in most cases, but what had appeared to be a field turned out to be marshy ground under high razor-sharp kunai grass with a tall chain-link fence that most men had to scale. Johnson's troops rediscovered the basic problems in every

nighttime combat jump. Fortunately their instincts and training produced the correct response. Instead of becoming disoriented, they "moved to the sound of the guns," as their World War II predecessors had done.

ACCOMPLISHING MISSIONS

The delay in assembling threw off the timing of the three air assaults. Instead of launching at 0230 they couldn't begin until after first light, which allowed many of the PDF troops to run away before they could be trapped. The 2d Battalion, 504th Infantry task group attacked Panama Viejo (Old Panama) on the outskirts of the city. The cuartel there located along the shore was home to the PDF cavalry squadron and special operations personnel. Despite ground fire and some of the men getting stuck in mud, the overwhelming force secured the objective by 1050.

The 1st Battalion, 504th Infantry, attacked the PDF heavy mortar company at Tinajitas. Its cuartel was located on the top of a steep hill, requiring the infantrymen to use a landing zone (LZ) at the foot and then climb to the objective. Intense ground fire caused casualties while the battalion was still in the air, and a number of the aviators (including the commander) were wounded. It took longer than planned and cost several lives, but this attack also succeeded and the objective was declared secure at 1433.

The target of the 4th Battalion, 325th Infantry, was Fort Cimarron where the PDF's Battalion 2000 was based. Unlike the other two air

Air Assault, Tinajitas by Al Sprague. The 1st Battalion, 504th Infantry, captured the base of the Panamanian Defense Force's 1st Infantry Company on December 20 after parachuting into Torrijos-Tocumen airport and boarding helicopters. *Army Art Collection, U.S. Army Center of Military History.*

assaults, in this case the airfield was actually between the fort and Panama City, which made time less critical, especially because a Special Forces team had blocked a key bridge. Once the battalion cleared the objective, it became available for other missions.

December 20 marked the only day of significant fighting for JTF South. After the initial round of assaults the paratroopers, like the rest of the JTF, moved on to a series of follow-on missions most of which involved stabilizing conditions in the two major cities and rounding up Noriega loyalists. The most exciting of these missions came after dark on December 20 when Washington officials told the JTF that American civilians were trapped in the Panama City Marriott Hotel. Lt. Col. Harry Axson and Company B, 2d Battalion, 504th Infantry, ran several miles from Panama Viejo in the dark and secured the hotel at 0004 on December 21 before anyone was harmed.

The JUST CAUSE plan worked as designed. Simultaneous precise strikes on multiple targets effectively eliminated all PDF command and control. Overwhelming force ended resistance quickly without causing substantial casualties or collateral damage. A sophisticated psychological operations campaign enabled the Rangers and the 7th Infantry Division (which started air landing as soon as the airport was secure) to persuade every PDF detachment in the rest of the country to surrender without firing a shot. Noriega sought refuge in the Vatican Embassy. When he finally surrendered on January 3, 1990, the operation was essentially complete. Combat units began redeploying as fast as possible. Stiner and Johnson led the main group back to Fort Bragg on January 13, making a symbolic mass jump on Sicily DZ.

Operation JUST CAUSE officially ended on January 31, 1990. It cost the lives of 23 American servicemen and left another 324 wounded. It made a powerful statement about the United

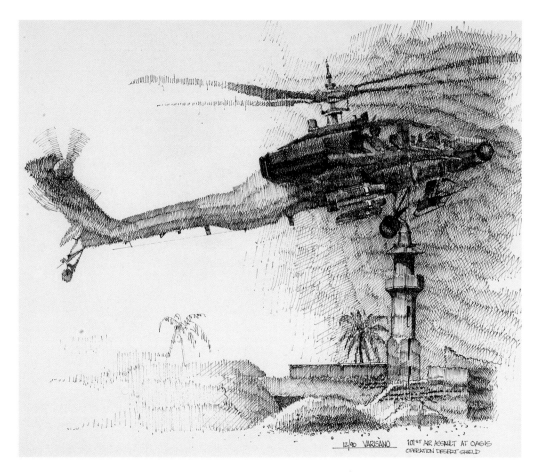

12/90 VARISANO   101ST AIR ASSAULT AT OASIS
OPERATION DESERT SHIELD

States' ability to deal with contingencies literally at the very moment that the Cold War was ending—soldiers in Panama watched on television as joyous Germans continued knocking down the Berlin Wall.

DESERT SHIELD INITIATED

Even before the cheers stopped, the commanders of XVIII Airborne Corps's divisions and separate brigades began reviewing the experience in Panama. Most had already seen that rapid deployment was an absolute necessity. Also, the corps realized that not every opponent would be lightly armed. Airborne operations historically had trouble if they ran into enemy armor. The corps began finding ways to cope, making that issue the focus of a spring 1990 NTC training rotation and fully integrating into its plans the heavy element built around the mechanized 24th Infantry Division. The corps also started to look at possible missions outside the Western Hemisphere.

When Lt. Gen. Gary Luck took command a few months later, the corps staff and subordinate units were capable of building and deploying much stronger task forces than they had been in 1989. The entire team completed a command post exercise for Central Command (CENTCOM) in July to update plans for dealing with a Middle East crisis. This was a stroke of good fortune because on August 2, 1990, Saddam Hussein invaded Kuwait and threatened Saudi Arabia.

The United Nations (UN) condemned Iraq and authorized collective action to restore Kuwait's independence. When the Saudis asked for support, Washington initiated an immediate deployment. Army ground forces came from the full XVIII Airborne Corps, the contingency force, augmented with additional aviation and heavy units. The other armed services sent equally strong forces.

Luck passed the deployment orders to the corps on August 7, 1990. Eighteen hours later, at 0357 August 9, the corps tactical command post and the first elements of Lt. Col. John Vines's 4th Battalion, 325th Infantry (the 82d's DRF-1), took off from Pope AFB. By August 14 the lead elements of the 101st Airborne and 24th Infantry Divisions were on their way. Dhahran, the main city in the Eastern Province and the site of a large modern air base and its port, Ad Damam, served as the points through which nearly all Army forces passed.

101st Air Assault at Oasis by Peter Varisano. An AH-64 Apache attack helicopter from the 101st Airborne Division hovering as Task Force Normandy did when firing to open the war. *Army Art Collection, U.S. Army Center of Military History.*

Col. Ronald Rokosz, kneeling, commander of the 2d Brigade, 82d Airborne Division, and Command Sgt. Maj. Steven Slocum with French liaison officers on February 23, the day before the ground attack. *XVIII Airborne Corps History Office.*

It soon became clear that the Iraqis would not immediately invade the kingdom, allowing the Pentagon to shift from the combat-ready deployment to the much more efficient normal mode. XVIII Airborne Corps established headquarters just outside the air base in a Saudi air defense headquarters compound which immediately became "Dragon City," reflecting the shoulder patch of the corps. Both Johnson's 82d and Maj. Gen. J. H. Binford Peay's 101st set up farther north. Each used code names based on their World War II histories. The 82d headquarters became "Champion Main" while the 101st at the not-yet-opened King Fahd International Airport used "Camp Eagle II."

By October the full corps had deployed some 125,000 troops and worked out its defensive plan to repel a full invasion by Saddam. The most mobile division, the 101st, reinforced with additional attack helicopters, and the 2d Armored Cavalry Regiment would make the initial contact and slowly fall back. Their mission with the coalition air forces was to destroy Iraqi tanks and damage Saddam's logistics. They would then hand off the battle to the heavy 24th Infantry Division which would bring the invasion to a halt. Then the corps would counterattack using the armored 1st Cavalry Division, 82d, and the refreshed 101st. The corps's drive would halt only after regaining control of Kuwait. On the east flank Marines, a British brigade, and Saudi-led Islamic forces would match those movements.

UN resolutions enabled the coalition to add more forces. This would apply pressure on Iraq to withdraw from Kuwait or allow a massive offensive to drive them out. Although the forces arrived from several nations, Saddam remained defiant and Iraqi forces remained in Kuwait.

DESERT STORM BEGINS

At 0238 on January 18, 1991, the coalition struck. Task Force Normandy, eight AH-64 Apache helicopters of the 101st led by Lt. Col. Richard A. Cody, fired the first shots of the war. Their Hellfire missiles took out Iraqi early warning radars. Massive air strikes roared through that open door, and an extensive bombing campaign began.

Under the cover of the air campaign, the Army executed one of the most complex maneuvers in its history. VII Corps slid west to a position where it could turn the Iraqi flank. XVIII Airborne Corps leapfrogged hundreds of miles past its sister corps and went far to the west where Saddam had almost no troops. The harsh desert conditions there limited even Bedouins to moving only in small numbers.

The corps's offensive assignment was to sweep north to the Euphrates River and hook east to seal off an Iraqi retreat, and then reinforce VII Corps in destruction of the Republican Guard. Thanks to its focus on contingencies the corps possessed a unique ability to move rapidly across large distances without encountering crippling supply problems. While the 1st Cavalry Division remained behind to reinforce the central battle, XVIII Airborne Corps picked up "Force Daguet," the French contingent, which included the Foreign Legion's parachute regiment.

Luck placed his heavy forces on the right. They tied in with VII Corps and had less ground to cover. He used the French on the left. Their mission: push forward and prevent any Iraqis from trying to move toward the corps and attack it from the rear. The 82d reinforced would go with the French push north. Then Col. Ronald Rokosz's 2d Brigade and the 4th Battalion, 325th Infantry, would take the point. The 82d would then turn right and race across the entire sector, reaching a point where it could dig the enemy out of his extensive fortification. That task would be much more difficult for Maj. Gen. Barry McCaffrey's heavy 24th Infantry Division and attached 2d Armored Cavalry Regiment. McCaffrey had few riflemen who could dismount from their Bradley fighting vehicles.

The 101st drew the center of the corps area and a mission behind enemy lines like that given to the airborne in Europe during World War II or to the 187th Regimental Combat Team in Korea. It would conduct a series of brigade-sized air assaults deep behind the lines. Unlike the earlier era, these insertions were not intended to block an enemy withdrawal but rather had the offensive role envisioned by the Howze Board. In each leap the brigade secured a forward operating base from which attack helicopters could strike from an unexpected direction. The division also wheeled to the east as it advanced and expected to be sent across the Euphrates to prevent any Iraqi remnants from escaping over bridges still standing.

THE 100-HOUR WAR

At 0400 on G-Day (for Ground Attack Day), February 24, 1991, the corps attack kicked off. In keeping with the great wheel analogy, the western units started forward sooner than those on the east. Col. James "Tom" Hill's 1st Brigade, 101st Airborne Division, with four infantry battalions was supposed to take off at the same time, but was delayed by fog until 0727. The Blackhawks and CH-47 Chinooks, with Apaches out in front, began touching down in Forward Operating Base (FOB) Cobra at 0815. The infantry fanned out to set up a perimeter around the very large area while the artillery and support troops set up and prepared to begin attack helicopter operations. Unknown to intelligence officers, the Iraqi 2d Battalion, 843d Brigade, 45th Infantry Division, held positions within the FOB but close air support, attack helicopters, and 105-mm artillery fire forced them to surrender to Company A, 1st Battalion, 327th Infantry. The Americans did not have to fire a single round from their rifles.

Thereafter the attack went as planned but faster on the left flank. The French secured their final objective, the As Salman air base and surrounding area, at 1750, February 25. The 24th Infantry Division and the 2d Armored Cavalry Regiment were about 27 miles from Basrah, with the 82d closing in to join them. And after leapfrogging east to set up more FOBs, the 101st had Hill's force waiting to go north of the Euphrates and cut off the last remaining Iraqi escape route. The division helicopters had been conducting battalion-size

Refueling operations "on the fly" during the movement from defensive positions to offensive ones hundreds of miles away. Painting by Jim Dietz. *Army Art Collection, U.S. Army Center of Military History.*

top left
Members of 3d Platoon, Company A, 1st Battalion, 327th Infantry, 1st Brigade, 101st Airborne Division, pose with their guidon at Forward Operating Base Cobra. These men captured the Iraqi defenders on G-Day. *Department of Defense.*

top right
A member of Battery C, 1st Battalion, 319th Field Artillery, prepares to attach a 105-mm M-102 howitzer to an 82d Airborne Division UH-60 Blackhawk during Operation DESERT STORM. *Department of Defense.*

bottom right
On G-Day, February 24, 1991, an M-551A1 Sheridan of the 3d Battalion, 73d Armor, advances as part of the 2d Brigade Task Force, 82d Airborne Division. The M-198 howitzers from the corps's 18th Field Artillery Brigade are firing in support of the French. *XVIII Airborne Corps History Office.*

sweeps through the area, destroying every vehicle that moved. VII Corps and the Marines on the extreme right flank made similar progress. At 0800, February 28, a cease-fire halted movement. Iraq had given up in just 100 hours.

The corps spent March clearing its zone of weapons, equipment, and ammunition and starting the homeward journey. The final group of the 82d, except for rear detachments loading equipment, left on April 6, and the 101st on April 13. The final members of the corps main command post left the incomplete Rafha airport, restoring it to the condition it was in when Americans arrived. Luck and the main body lifted off from Dhahran in a 747 airliner two days later.

Operation DESERT SHIELD-DESERT STORM validated the ability of XVIII Airborne Corps to carry out a contingency operation anywhere in the world with more than 120,000 soldiers. On scene, they could crush even armored forces, and then return home rapidly to resume alert status.

UPHOLD DEMOCRACY

Soon after the victorious divisions returned from the Gulf, the nation began implementing major cuts in military strength made possible by the end of the Cold War. The dissolution of the former Soviet Union and its Warsaw Pact alliance reduced the need to maintain large conventional forces in Europe, and the size of forces deployed in other forward locations. The Army at home returned to an approximation of the Strategic Army Forces of the early 1960s—a light force built around XVIII Airborne Corps for contingencies and a heavier one if more power was needed.

The United States carried out a number of different deployments during the 1990s. Army elements based in the United States served in the multinational relief force sent to Somalia. Units from the United States Army, Europe (USAREUR) carried out several different missions in the Balkans. When another crisis erupted in the Caribbean in 1994, the airborne community participated in Operation UPHOLD DEMOCRACY.

DISASTER OPERATIONS

The same qualities that make airborne forces ideal for contingency operations—the ability to deploy rapidly, the high state of training, and a flexible approach to dealing with problems—made them the logical choice when the Army began carrying out emergency relief in the wake of natural disasters. In October 1989 Hurricane Hugo pounded St. Croix in the Virgin Islands. The resulting loss of power let inmates escape from the prison. XVIII Airborne Corps sent out its assault command post with parts of the 16th Military Police Brigade and the 1st Support Command to restore order in Operation HAWKEYE, the first mission of this kind. The much larger devastation caused to south Florida in 1992 by Hurricane Andrew involved more troops. Such deployments are part of operations other than war.

Gen. Gordon R. Sullivan, U.S. Army Chief of Staff, speaks with members of the XVIII Airborne Corps during their relief efforts in the aftermath of Hurricane Andrew, which struck the south Florida area on August 24, 1992. *Department of Defense.*

The island of Hispaniola is divided between two nations, the Dominican Republic on the east and Haiti on the west. Fort Bragg's paratroopers had gone to the Dominican Republic. In 1994, they turned to Haiti. On September 30, 1991, a military coup had ousted President Jean Baptiste Aristide. Two years later when its treatment of the civilian population started to become intolerable, the JCS directed XVIII Airborne Corps to begin planning for a possible intervention to restore the legal government. Subsequently the 10th Mountain Division, a corps subordinate element, was told to develop an alternate approach to give the president several different options. The corps's assignment authorized the use of direct force, the division's phrase for a "permissive entry."

Lt. Gen. Henry Hugh Shelton's staff built upon the lessons of previous Caribbean contingencies. It provided for overpowering force in a lightning strike to neutralize the junta's troops, protect civilian lives and property, and restore order. During the four days prior to H-Hour corps troops would stage to advance bases. Over the next three days they would gain effective control of Haiti. Other units would assume the nation-building task, allowing the combat troops to return home within a month to a month and a half. Simply put, the corps would kick in the door and then get out quickly.

Maj. Gen. David Meade's innovative plan called for moving into position on an aircraft carrier and then executing a show of force. These measures would persuade the junta to accept Americans and contingents from other Caribbean nations landing to preserve order during a transition back to the Aristide government. The selection of 10th Mountain Division was natural as it had recently performed two other non-combat missions—relief efforts in Florida in the aftermath of Hurricane Andrew and Operation RESTORE HOPE in Somalia.

The Navy, Air Force, and Marines fully integrated into the planning, which proved how far the Department of Defense had progressed in the years since Grenada. As in Panama, involving the corps ensured that a headquarters trained and equipped to furnish a wide array of support and service elements was used. Although not explicitly directed by the JCS, the corps and division also worked out an intermediate version with a much quicker transition from one to the other.

XVIII Airborne Corps's concept of operations developed during the summer of 1994 also took the use of force to a new level. For the first time since World War II a division would make a nighttime combat jump, but all at once rather than in waves over several days. Its mission was the airhead seizure at Port-

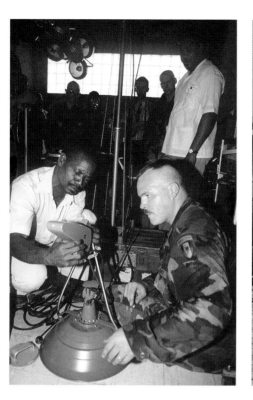

au-Prince coupled with a Marine amphibious assault on Cap Haitien, the other major city. Four infantry battalion combat teams were to capture the international airport before it could be destroyed, while another used nearby DZ Pegasus to bring in more combat power that could fit on the primary. Special Operations Forces who already infiltrated would mark the DZs in the manner used in the war. Because heavy firepower would be counterproductive (like Panama), division artillery would have the challenging responsibility of pushing out an assault group much larger than Fort Bragg ever used before.

The most innovative part of the plan called for the division aviation brigade to fly in from a staging base at Great Inagua Island with one battalion. At dawn the final brigade combat team would air land on the secure airport. Every effort would be made to talk the Haitians into surrendering in the same way that JTF South had used. The 10th Mountain Division's troops would be on USS *Eisenhower* (CVN 69) and would follow later. Timing of D-Day in September kept changing as diplomatic negotiations tried to persuade the junta to leave on its own. This led to chaos in setting the airflow, but the Army and Air Force had the training and flexibility to adjust. It had also carried out a full rehearsal—Exercise Big Drop.

Forty specific targets had been identified and the most detailed intelligence in history furnished to the units assigned to each. There were to be 8,000 jumpers plus 175 heavy drop platforms and 800 CDS loads. C-130s were allocated to the airport to ensure a focused landing with C-141s assigned to the drop at DZ Pegasus.

The 82d began taking off from Pope AFB according to plan, heading for Haiti. However, Gen. Raoul Cedras had a spy near Pope. He correctly guessed that the abnormal activity indicated a forthcoming assault and called the junta to report that the 82d Airborne Division was on the way. This caused immediate Haitian agreement with a three-man negotiating team in Port-au-Prince, led by former President Jimmy Carter, for a cease-fire, and the armada of planes turned around.

The U.S. forces entered Haiti peacefully, and spread teams out across the country. Maintaining order was a familiar task. Being able to assist the inhabitants getting back on their feet was a new mission that the Army mastered in the 1990s. As soon as conditions permitted the combat troops turned control over to the UN and returned home.

Chapter 11
Into the 21st Century

left
Sgt. Tim Bowen, a team leader in Company A, 1st Battalion, 325th Infantry, pauses on April 8, 2003, during the 82d Airborne Division's drive toward As Samawah, Iraq. *82d Airborne Division.*

bottom right
Waiting for the loadmaster to give the "Go" sign, Sgt. 1st Class Dennis Lanum, a platoon sergeant in 1st Battalion, 508th Infantry, prepares to jump from a C-130 over Kosovo in 2001. The 173d Airborne Brigade was participating in a multinational exercise in the Balkans. *Department of Defense.*

THE MILLENNIUM ARRIVES

As the millennium turned, the U.S. Army possessed a significant contingency force. Approximately 85,000 troops served in the XVIII Airborne Corps, which was a versatile organization that included the 82d Airborne Division and the 101st Airborne Division (Air Assault), plus the 3d Infantry Division and the 10th Mountain Division. A complete range of combat support and combat service support personnel on jump status rounded out its capabilities for worldwide action. Both the European and Pacific theaters were building large forward-deployed contingents. The 173d Airborne Brigade activated in Vicenza, Italy, in 2000, while Alaska's force expanded to a full brigade.

Those men and women were the Army's cutting edge. They maintained the ability to launch their first element into the air within 18 hours of receiving a mission. They trained incessantly to sustain their readiness. But they also carried out their share of the continuing commitments around the world, sending battalion task forces out on six-month rotations such as the Multinational Force and Observers in the Sinai or the Balkans. Other troops deployed to places like the Bitterroot National Forest in Montana to fight forest fires, or trained to carry out other disaster relief activities.

They also were part of the service's most profound change in 40 years. During the 1990s leaders in the Pentagon concluded that with the end of the Cold War, the services no longer needed to focus on fighting large conventional wars. The Army realized that it had to become more agile and mobile—in other words, more like the contingency corps.

The Army in 1999 began a multistage transition into a force built around brigade combat teams (BCTs). Division and corps headquarters would shift to more flexible command and control organizations instead of focusing just on their own units. This approach allowed a subordinate element to deploy without disrupting the combat readiness of the whole. The changeover caused some confusion because many battalions exchanged places, were inactivated, or were brought back on the active rolls. In 2007, the alignment of units within the divisions and separate brigades echoes that of World War II.

The transformation process continues to unfold. Technology produces new weapons, communications, and intelligence systems; better vehicles and aircraft; and a host of less visible items like better canteens. All must be incorporated into doctrine and deployed to the field.

By 2006 a normal BCT included six battalions—two of infantry, one each of field artillery and armor, plus one support, and one for special troops. Each brigade is capable of controlling far more elements when necessary. Under this configuration both the 82d Airborne and 101st Air Assault have four BCTs. The two other Airborne BCTs are the 173d in Italy and 4th Brigade Combat Team, 25th Infantry Division, in Alaska. Several airborne cavalry brigades began entering the force structure in 2005. Each is lighter than a normal team and is designed for rapid movement rather than parachute operations.

American life changed forever on the morning of September 11, 2001. Al Qaeda hijacked four airliners and used them as suicide weapons. Two flew into New York's World Trade Center and destroyed the twin towers as a horrified nation watched on live television. A third struck the Pentagon. The fourth airplane failed to strike its target in Washington because the passengers heroically overpowered the terrorists on board.

More than 3,000 Americans died that day. A unified America declared war on terrorists everywhere on the planet.

For the Army, the Global War on Terrorism (GWOT) involved the entire regular force, and brought reserve component forces on active duty for extended periods of time.

OPERATION ENDURING FREEDOM

The extremist Taliban regime had gained control of most of Afghanistan following years of civil war. They welcomed al Qaeda and furnished a sanctuary for its bases. This was a profound miscalculation. America, supported by allies, held the Taliban equally responsible for the sneak attack and retaliated swiftly.

top
Troopers of Company B, 2d Battalion, 504th Infantry, clear a cave in the mountains of southern Afghanistan in 2003. They were searching for terrorists near Spin Buldak.
82d Airborne Division.

bottom
A paratrooper from the 82d Airborne Division's 307th Engineer Battalion finishes searching a house for weapons in Afghanistan in 2003.
Department of Defense.

top left

Capt. Jeffrey Giltzow of the 1st Battalion, 325th Infantry, shakes hands with a young Afghan boy in Wardak. This 2005 Medical Civic Action Project is an example of the efforts made by paratroopers during the Global War on Terrorism.
82d Airborne Division.

top right

1st Lt. Bertis McMillan, from the 3d Battalion, 319th Field Artillery, treats an Afghan child at Kakaran during 2003.
Department of Defense.

The campaign that resulted, Operation ENDURING FREEDOM, demonstrated the military's new capabilities. Relatively small Special Operations Forces moved in to assist Afghan opponents of the Taliban beginning in early October 2001. In 60 days they overthrew the Taliban regime and closed down the sanctuary. The United States then helped them drive al Qaeda into retreat.

Conventional units moved into the Kandahar region in support of the Special Forces and Ranger teams. They were taken, as usual, from the contingency force. In this case, an element of the 10th Mountain Division led the deployment. This contingent secured the forward base and provided a small Quick Reaction Force that could move to support irregulars. Meanwhile, Gen. Tommy Franks at U.S. Central Command (CENTCOM) opened a forward headquarters in Kuwait to coordinate land operations and to begin humanitarian assistance to help Afghanistan form a stable government.

The buildup in Central Asia led to the deployment of the full 10th Mountain Division as the year ended, except for units serving in the Balkans. From Kuwait it could send troops whenever needed. The 3d Brigade, 101st Airborne Division, went directly to Kandahar airport where its mobility could be employed to find and neutralize the residual al Qaeda and Taliban terrorists.

Early in 2002 Operation ANACONDA employed Col. Frank Wiercinski's Task Force RAKKASAN with two of its three battalions as a blocking force along the eastern side of the Shahi Kowt Valley. Special Forces and Afghans swept toward them to flush out the guerrillas. Air assault moved the lead troops from the 1st Battalion, 87th Infantry, into position on D-Day, March 2. They immediately started taking heavy fire and could not be reinforced because bad weather blocked a second lift until nightfall. Enemy fire also hit the Apache helicopters providing most of the fire support.

The 2d Battalion, 187th Infantry, came in to help clear the high-altitude ridges. 1st Battalion followed into a landing zone (LZ) farther north, and early on March 4 started moving toward the rest of the task force, clearing positions as it went. Additional troops from the 10th Mountain Division, plus Canada's 3d Battalion, Princess Patricia's Canadian Light Infantry, soon joined the fighting. ANACONDA officially ended on March 19. This was the first time that al Qaeda had stood and fought.

Multinational military operations persist in Afghanistan into 2008. This has added another commitment to the Army's global missions. The troops also continue hunting down Taliban and al Qaeda bands. The mission is handled by deploying units from home stations for 15-month tours of duty.

Under the Army's "transformed" organization, corps and division headquarters are capable of leading task forces. XVIII Airborne Corps performed this duty in the second half of 2002 from Bagram Air Base north of Kabul, with the 3d Brigade of the 82d providing the bulk of the maneuver force. It was followed by the 82d's tactical command post and 1st Brigade. Corps logistical assets perform support functions from locations in Uzbekistan. These operations still continue. In 2005, XVIII Airborne Corps headquarters, under command of Lt. Gen. John R. Vines, led the Multi-National Corps-Iraq from January 2005 to January 2006.

OPERATION IRAQI FREEDOM

A second front in GWOT opened in 2003. Operation IRAQI FREEDOM brought the 82d and 101st Airborne Divisions back to places along the Euphrates Valley that they had seen during Operation DESERT STORM, and the 173d Airborne Brigade into action for the first time since Vietnam.

The campaign ended the oppressive regime of Saddam Hussein and his Ba'ath Party. As in the first Gulf War, Americans led a multi-national coalition and carried out joint and combined operations. The Army and Marines each contributed a corps-sized ground force to CENTCOM. Franks assigned the former to the left flank where it would advance in the Euphrates Valley and the latter to the Tigris Valley on the right. They would converge on Baghdad.

The V Corps from Europe served as the Army's combat headquarters with its three divisions coming from XVIII Airborne Corps. The plan put the heavy 3d Infantry Division in the lead, backed up by the 101st which would swing out using air assault tactics to push its attack

helicopters forward to take the Iraqis from the flank. The 82d, which could bring only its 2d Brigade, provided an airborne capability for an airfield seizure as well as dismounted infantry to clear bypassed urban areas. As in the earlier war, the allies enjoyed total air domination.

The Army staged in Kuwait before the air campaign began on March 19, 2003. It crossed into Iraq the next day. The 101st's first move was to swing out and create two Forward Operating Bases (FOBs). The 3d Battalion, 187th Infantry, conducted the air assault which established one FOB while ground movement was used for the other. Its operations were particularly difficult due to bad dust storms that interfered with efficient use of helicopters.

The 82d had remained in Kuwait, rigged for a jump into the Karbala Gap. Its airborne mission was scrubbed when speeding ground units overran the objective, as happened during the breakout from Normandy in 1944. It was sent forward to secure the lines of communications along Highway 8 to Baghdad. The route had come under attack by the paramilitary Fedayeen loyalists, local militia, and armed Ba'athist irregulars.

Franks had intended to contain and bypass the cities in order to conserve strength for the decisive battle, but unexpected resistance made him employ an increasing number of troops. When the heavy force slowed down at As Samawah and Najaf, two brigades had to be committed to relieve them. 1st Brigade of the 101st initially sealed off Najaf on the west, spent March 29–30 completing the isolation, and the next three weeks blocking Iraqi reinforcements to avoid having to fight house-to-house. Meanwhile the 82d had come forward from Camp Champion to neutralize As Samawah, using Tallil air base for its new headquarters.

It gained operational control of the 2d Armored Cavalry Regiment as that unit arrived in the theater, letting the division cover the length of the lines of communications. Freeing up the 3d Infantry Division allowed it to regroup for the final push into Baghdad.

The 101st launched its first deep attack on March 28. Following the vision of the Howze Board, its armed helicopters struck the Republican Guard's Medina Division near Karbala. This strike took place at extreme range. When it then committed the 2d Brigade to take over the fighting at Karbala, it began with an air assault that established a new FOB from which attack helicopters ranged from the lake region on the west to isolating Al Hillah on the east.

On April 8, while the 1st Brigade was still fighting in Najaf and the 2d at Karbala, the 101st committed its 3d Brigade to take down a "hornet's nest" at Al Hillah on the far side of the Euphrates. The division attached an armored battalion to assist with that difficult, but important, attack. Helicopters worked over the area for several days before the ground advance. Opposition collapsed the next day and 3d Brigade swung north and pushed on toward Baghdad.

The 82d finished off An Nasiriyah and then came forward to take over As Samawah from the 101st. From there it repeated the relief in place at Najaf before attacking Ad Diwaniyah on April 9 to make contact with Iraqi freedom fighters. The next day it again relieved elements of the 101st, this time at Karbala. Then, on April 11, it started humanitarian operations. Because Arba'in (near Najaf) was an important Shia holy site, the division would also undertake the important mission of providing security for a pilgrimage later in the month.

The 101st continued its advance on the capital, supporting the drives of the 3d Infantry

Division and the Marines closing in from the Tigris Valley. Its 2d Brigade cleared the highways and entered the southwest outskirts of Baghdad on April 13. The next day the division carried out air assaults which cleared Al Mamadiyah and Iskandariyah. Clearing operations and aggressive patrolling continued. A major new responsibility accrued on April 20 when the 1st Battalion, 502d Infantry task force, relieved the Rangers at the Haditha Dam. The same day, I Marine Expeditionary Force carried out a relief in place of the 82d and assumed responsibility for Ad Diwaniyah and As Samawah.

After Baghdad fell on April 9, operations shifted focus from liberation to occupation.

SKY SOLDIERS JUMP

While much attention was directed on the advance on Baghdad, the coalition opened a second front in the north. When it proved impossible to use heavy forces, Franks assigned this area to his theater Special Operations Command. As in Afghanistan, small teams working with the friendly Kurd Peshmerga would carry out most of the action. But there still remained a need for regular troops to seal off any movement of loyal troops to the south where they could join the main fighting.

The unit selected for this mission was the only one available to conduct a forced entry—the 173d Airborne Brigade in Italy. Its target was Bashur air base, a field capable of handling extensive C-17 flights to bring in an armored battalion task force. This was a fundamental airborne mission: seizing an airhead and airlanding reinforcements.

The brigade sent in a small Army-Air Force drop zone (DZ) support team on March 25 who

C-17

The Boeing C-17 Globemaster III is capable of rapid strategic delivery of troops and all types of cargo to main operating bases or directly to forward bases in the deployment area. The aircraft performs tactical airlift and heavy airdrop missions. It carries 202 fully equipped paratroops for jumps.

The C-17 meets the most demanding air-mobility requirements, particularly in the area of large or heavy outsized cargo.

The C-17 made its maiden flight on September 15, 1991. The first production model was delivered to Charleston Air Force Base, South Carolina, on June 14, 1993. The first squadron became operationally ready on January 17, 1995.

The C-17 Globemaster III conducting a dual-row heavy drop in July 2005. One platform's extraction chute has deployed while a second platform is about to emerge off the rear ramp. *U.S. Air Force.*

FEATURES

Length:	174 feet
Wingspan:	169 feet, 10 inches
Height:	12 feet, 4 inches
Maximum payload:	170,900 pounds
Unrefueled range:	2,400 nautical miles
(In-flight refueling extends its range.)	
Cruise speed:	450 knots (.76 Mach)

parachuted in and made contact with Special Operations Forces positioned near the base. The DZ selected for the attack was about 4,500 meters long and 1,450 wide—large enough to take the 959 paratroopers. The jump force was built around the 2d Battalion, 503d Infantry; 1st Battalion, 508th Infantry; Battery D, 319th Field Artillery; and the 74th Infantry Detachment (long-range surveillance). It took off from Aviano Air Base in C-17s and spent about four and one-half hours in the air before beginning the night drop at 2000 on March 26 and finishing at 2037.

Between then and the early morning of April 9 a total of 87 C-17 sorties delivered more than 1,500 troops including the armor and mechanized elements from Germany along with their equipment and supplies. The brigade itself started south on April 2 once it became clear that the Kurds and Special Operations teams were in control and captured Irbil airfield. They conducted a series of raids on targets located to the west of the Greater Zab River. The final operation consisted of a follow-on push south to secure Kirkuk and its surrounding oil fields.

CONTINUING PRESENCE

The occupation phase in Iraq continues into 2008. As in Afghanistan the Army's forces are built around rotating BCTs serving 15-month deployments, with division and corps headquarters performing command and control in the three geographical areas of operations assigned to the Army.

Initially the 101st stationed its 2d Brigade to the north of Baghdad in part to provide a buffer between the Kurds and the Sunni and Shia. It remained until February 2004. 3d Brigade, 82d Airborne Division, continued in its sector until January 2004 when the 1st Brigade arrived. The 173d Airborne Brigade patrolled in its sector until departing for Vicenza in February 2004.

Rotations continue in Iraq and Afghanistan utilizing soldiers from the Regular Army, Army National Guard, and Army Reserve. As always, the airborne community continues to perform its basic mission of being America's first line for contingencies anywhere.

Reflections and Anticipation

WHERE WE HAVE BEEN

Bill Lee and a few other visionaries in 1940 initiated a new way for the U.S. Army to enter battle. Their successors have continued to innovate, to learn, and to be the best. The desire to learn and to apply the lessons are epitomized by the Swing Board and Training Circular No. 113 (TC 113) of 1943, and by the Howze Board of 1962. Innovations flowed from those deliberations—innovations that continue to flower in the 21st century.

(Note: The following paragraphs provide examples of correlations between the concepts and actual operations. Pairs of photos demonstrate that, although equipment may change, procedures and standards are remarkably consistent.)

Maj. Gen. William C. Lee, "Father of the Airborne" and first commanding general of the 101st Airborne Division. Fort Bragg, North Carolina, 1943. *National Archives.*

TC 113 AND THE SWING BOARD

In 1943, Training Circular No. 113 appeared and the Swing Board carried out its study of World War II's initial airborne operations. Both envisioned paratroopers working with heavier troops coming in by glider or landing on an airhead in transports. Both believed that airborne operations would always be conducted to support ground forces. From that point the Army considered a specific group of missions to be appropriate for the use of vertical envelopment. These missions have remained valid, as evidenced by the examples that follow.

The use of parachutists or gliders to conduct raids made sense. The 511th Parachute Infantry's liberation of the Los Baños internment camp was such a mission, as was the 3d Battalion, 504th Infantry's capture of El Renacer Prison in Panama. One specialized variant of raid-type mission is the capture or destruction of a specific installation. In North Africa, Edson Raff sent a detachment of his 509th Parachute

Infantry to destroy the El Djem Bridge as such a strike. The targeting of Operation JUST CAUSE included many specific installations.

Capturing enemy airfields was the initial mission performed in combat and has been the most important in the years since Vietnam. At La Senia and Youks-les-Bains during Operation TORCH and at Nadzab in New Guinea, airfield seizure packages were the first airborne strikes in both the European and Pacific theaters. This same variety of aerial assault was conducted at Grenada and twice in Panama during forced entries, and during permissive ones in the Dominican Republic, Honduras, and Haiti.

Another type of airborne operation identified in 1943 was capturing an island that was either lightly defended or would be very difficult for the enemy to reinforce. This is exactly what the 503d Parachute Infantry accomplished at Corregidor. Performing a similar task is still within the capabilities of today's paratroopers.

top left
Paratroopers of
the 2d Battalion,
503d Parachute Infantry,
in a C-47 en route to the
drop zone in England,
October 2, 1942.
National Archives.

bottom left
Paratroopers from the
82d Airborne Division
loaded into a C-17 wait
for the doors to close
and to take off for a
jump on Sicily Drop
Zone at Fort Bragg, 1995.
Department of Defense.

The original theorists considered airborne forces suited for capturing important terrain features and holding them against all counterattacks. Based on the German experiences, the thinking tended to focus on capturing bridges and other crossings of rivers and canals to create a bridgehead through which ground troops could advance. Operation MARKET was a corps-sized operation of this type, and so was VARSITY. The jump onto Tagaytay Ridge was intended to do the same: to seize control of a choke point in the way of a land advance.

A comparable mission envisioned seizing key terrain to deny it to the enemy. In 1943 the most likely way that paratroops and gliders would be used in this manner was in crippling lines of communications or taking out enemy command centers. Operation DRAGOON was executed in part to interdict German supply lines in southern France. Knocking out command and control nodes in practice has become a part of nearly every major operation such as the planned jump on Haiti or in Panama, where an important goal of the H-Hour targeting was to "decapitate the PDF."

Attacking defended positions from the flank or rear by airborne attack represented a type of operation which ranged in size from relatively small objectives to multibattalion jumps. During World War II Operation HUSKY employed Jim Gavin's 505th Parachute Infantry and Rube Tucker's 504th this way. Shortly thereafter, Doyle Yardley's 509th tried to do the same at Avellino on the Italian mainland and took very heavy casualties. In more recent times it is hard to find an example of an operation specifically designed this way because the tactic is now so fundamental to every plan.

The Swing Board and the authors of TC 113 believed strongly that large airborne operations would be particularly valuable not just by taking ground themselves but by being able to reinforce a success faster than anyone else. They thought that paratroopers and glider-borne forces would land in support of fast-moving armor spearheads and allow them to exploit the situation. In practice it has turned out to be primarily a function of bringing paratroopers into an occupied DZ. Noemfoor, Altavilla, and Manarawat were conducted this way. So was the 173d Airborne Brigade's jump in Vietnam and the 82d's at Torrijos-Tocumen Airport in Panama. They would have entered Grenada that way had it been needed. This is actually the most difficult mission for other forces to understand. A drop of this type is usually criticized as being unnecessary "because the DZ was already secured." In reality, only paratroops can immediately fly in from a distance and get into action without having to wait for an airfield to be cleared and equipment landed to unload transport planes.

Speed of insertion accounted for another original mission. Putting airborne forces into blocking positions from which they could assist tactical airpower in delaying an enemy retreat would allow the main force to close in and destroy it. Operation DRAGOON, the capture of Camalaniugan Airfield on Luzon, both of the 187th Regimental Combat Team's Korea jumps, and the 173d's most recent one during IRAQI FREEDOM are all examples. So was the 101st's final air assault during DESERT STORM, the one that was scrubbed because Saddam surrendered first—the 1st Brigade's move across the Euphrates River to block the last escape route of the Republican Guard.

Another mission identified in World War II was to create diversions to distract the enemy from concentrating on the main effort. No actual operation was ever specifically designed for this purpose. However, nearly every single airborne operation in every single conflict has produced this result as a side effect. It was especially true during night jumps where sticks dropped in the wrong place confused the defenders.

The final value did not come from performing an actual operation. Commanders and their planners discovered that simply having a powerful airborne force in existence posed a constant threat and forced every enemy to disperse his forces in an attempt to defend every possible target. This was true at the strategic level during the Cold War and underlies the doctrine of contingency operations. It also works at the theater level, which is why airborne forces are kept forward-deployed in Europe and the Pacific.

Airborne leaders following World War II devised innovations that were not foreseen by the Swing Board. They learned that carrying out an airborne exercise as a show of force can prevent fighting. Lebanon in 1958, GOLDEN PHEASANT in Honduras, and Haiti (just by taking off) are prime examples. They also learned that night drops are inherently difficult. By long practice in innumerable emergency deployment readiness exercises (EDREs) the modern paratroopers have learned to take a confused drop in stride and use their initiative to get into action. Also, by working as part of an Army-Air Force team new equipment and new techniques have largely eliminated potential problems, which made the jump at Bashur, Iraq, so successful.

top right
Paratroopers walking out to board their C-53 Skytrooper transport on November 28, 1941, during maneuvers in the Carolinas. *National Archives.*

bottom right
Members of the 82d Airborne Division participating in Exercise Joint Forcible Entry line up to board a C-17 at Pope Air Force Base, North Carolina, August 24, 2005. *Department of Defense.*

THE HOWZE BOARD

New technology let the airborne community expand its thinking about aerial attack. The helicopter provided a better alternative to the vulnerable gliders of World War II. Hamilton Howze, Harry Kinnard, John Tolson, and other experienced paratroopers displayed the ability to be innovative when they developed the air-mobility concept.

Howze's Tactical Mobility Requirements Board came up with a group of basic and radical ideas. Their conclusions and recommendations were based on extensive practical tests between 1962 and early 1965. The best-known product of this board is the airmobile division that proved its worth in Vietnam. As a result of the airmobile units' successes in Vietnam, the value of air mobility spread across the entire Army.

The range of the Huey helicopters' generation kept the Howze Board's vision focused on action at about the same distances from the front lines as the airborne operations in World War II and Korea. The need to use transport planes to go farther obviously restricted deep attacks to paratroopers. But an airmobile force could be particularly useful in reinforcing an airhead, just as the glider and air-landed units did in Europe and the Pacific.

The board made other important recommendations that had to be set aside at the time because of the pressing need for forces in Vietnam. They saw that armed helicopters provided an airmobile commander with a unified command that was absent in more traditional airborne operations. This factor enabled a divi-sion to insert its ground component into an air-head and then base attack helicopters within it, which greatly expanded their range. Therefore, these forces would be well-suited for screening operations, reconnaissance work, delaying actions, and similar tasks normally thought of as cavalry functions.

In the 1980s the 101st Airborne Division finally achieved the full capability envisioned in 1962. Now an air assault force, not merely one using helicopters for mobility, it proved itself fully capable of that entire range of missions. Twice in combat against Iraq the 101st has struck by using attack helicopters as its main weapon and deploying its BCTs to "leapfrog" forward to carve out new operating bases. The Army has seen that the 82d and 101st are a team, just as they were in Normandy and Holland. They complement each other in a way that has made the XVIII Airborne Corps's concept of contingency operations across the entire spectrum of conflict the nation's most lethal weapon.

LEADERS AND THE LED

Airborne planning from the start was characterized by the phrase, "thinking outside the box." The paratroopers and their glider counterparts took the novel view of considering combat organization as creating a task force designed to execute the immediate specific mission. They also recognized that permanent units were the most efficient approach to administration and training. Combining the two approaches kept every successful leader very flexible. This concept has spread across the Army, creating an important development—we now train as we will fight.

top right
Gen. Douglas MacArthur
encouraging Lt. Col. John
J. Tolson III, before Tolson
and his men of 3d Battalion,
503d Parachute Infantry,
took off for the capture
of Nadzab, New Guinea,
September 5, 1943.
National Archives.

bottom right
Lt. Gen. John M. Keane,
commander,
XVIII Airborne Corps,
leads the corps on a
morning run at
Fort Bragg, 1998.
*XVIII Airborne Corps
Historian.*

The Airborne is particularly successful in "thinking on its feet" and reacting quickly to any crisis because it is a tightly knit community. Career officers and noncommissioned officers keep returning to Fort Bragg for multiple tours. Each time they return, they build on experience gained during a previous tour. Every improvement in organization, tactics, and equipment occurs because the contributors have a background of repeat assignments.

Bill Lee's vision grew from a test platoon to a group of battalions, then regiments, and finally a corps and five full divisions. Looking at the leadership of World War II's force, one sees men rising in rank and growing in ability. Matt Ridgway went from division commander to corps commander, and Bud Miley from commanding the first parachute battalion to leading a division. The same can be said about Jim Gavin or Bob Sink or a host of others.

The airborne school of experience keeps right on building its leaders. The Korean War's William Westmoreland will later be seen as the XVIII Airborne Corps's commanding general. Vietnam's John Deane will lead the 82d. Jim Lindsay, John Foss, Carl Stiner in Panama, and

Gary Luck in DESERT STORM all rose to corps command via multiple airborne assignments. So did Jack Keane, Buck Kernan, Dan McNeill, John Vines, and Lloyd Austin. This phenomenon holds true in the enlisted ranks, too. Not only are first sergeants and sergeants major the product of years spent passing through Green Ramp; being a paratrooper is a family profession. Look in any battalion and you are apt to find a young soldier whose forebears also knew how to "stand up, hook up, and shuffle to the door."

top left
Members of the
504th Parachute Infantry
respond to the com-
mands to "stand up and
hook up." Fort Benning,
Georgia, May 1, 1942.
National Archives.

bottom left
The commands to
"stand up and hook
up" remain unchanged
over the decades. These
paratroopers from the
82d Airborne Division
are ready to make a
nighttime line jump
from a C-17 in 2005.
Department of Defense.

This photograph of PFC Vernon L. Haught of the 325th Glider Infantry taken near Odrimont, Belgium, on January 6, 1945, was used on a famous 82d Airborne Division poster. Its title, "I'm the 82d Airborne, and this is as far as the bastards are going," quotes S/Sgt. Frank L. Martin, another trooper of the 325th.
National Archives.

WHERE WE ARE GOING

ALWAYS NEEDED

In the 21st-century military there are only volunteers: men and women who think of others before themselves and who want to give back to their nation. The Airborne will always be held to the highest standards for they are double volunteers; they joined and then they earned their wings. The United States will always need such soldiers. They will always ask for the best to step forward, and paratroopers will take point.

The Airborne will always be composed of those who challenge themselves to take on the hardest tasks. It will always have only those who desire to be the best, to push themselves further than they think they can go.

The Airborne will always need those who can think for themselves. They will not only follow orders, but they will want to know how they fit into the larger plan so that they can make the right decisions. They will see the big picture and know that the mission comes first, and they will always look to take care of their soldiers before themselves.

As they have done since North Africa, paratroopers will never be defeated by the unexpected. They will always know that it is their duty to move to the sound of the guns.

ALWAYS GET THE BEST

The Airborne will always receive the best the nation can provide because the American people will always want to see them home safe. Their weapons will be the newest. They will receive new systems to improve command and control. New uniforms, new equipment, even new rations—all will come just as surely as the sun will rise.

The Airborne will always work to find new ways to carry out their distinctive missions. They will look to new techniques, new air items, new training programs. They know that the Air Force is working with the Army to design better planes or improve on the old reliables. They know that there will be better cooperation, better doctrine.

ALWAYS TRAIN HARD

The airborne soldiers will always keep themselves honed to the sharpest edge. Training wins wars, not gadgets. They will practice squad drills with the same focus that they would give to combat. They will seek to test themselves as individuals and as teams at training centers, and will expect the rotations to be harder than actual combat.

The Airborne will always count themselves fortunate to have each other. They will always push each other to excel. They will always turn to the next paratrooper and extend a hand to help because working together is training for the time when you share a foxhole. Airborne soldiers will always check each others' parachutes and will always try to excel in every practice jump to remain proficient.

ALWAYS PART OF A TEAM

The Airborne will never work alone. It will always rely on the Air Force to reach the objective, to be brought in at the right speed and altitude for a safe jump, and to come right down on the DZ so that the stick can roll up easily. Paratroopers will always count on the loadmasters and pilots to bring in the heavy weapons, ammunition, supplies, and equipment to sustain the fight.

Airborne troopers will always count on the Navy to move the trail parties, the heavy forces to reinforce them, and the sustainment supplies. It will look to the sea service to deliver fire support from offshore and to naval aviation to help with close air support.

The Airborne will always be ready to stand in line with the Marines. They will look to sharing forced entry or humanitarian relief responsibilities with Marines whether they come ashore as an amphibious force or arrive configured for conventional land action.

The Airborne will always act as part of the Army. It will expect to see a heavy relief column when holding the airhead. It will count on "leg" aviators, artillerymen, engineers, and all of the combat support and combat service support providers. They will always—always— see Rangers and those who wear Air Assault wings as family.

Airborne forces will begin receiving the Advanced Tactical Parachute System T-11 in 2008. Operational testing at Fort Bragg was supervised by Program Executive Office Soldier and Airborne and Special Operations Test Directorate. The Airdrop/ Aerial Delivery Director-ate of the Soldier System Center at Natick, Massachusetts, performed major tasks in development of the system. More than 3,200 successful live jumps were made during testing. *Project Manager Clothing and Individual Equipment of the Program Executive Office (PEO) Soldier at Fort Belvoir, Virginia.*

top
In World War II the only way to bring vehicles and heavy weapons into the drop zone was by glider, which severely limited the size of a load. Troopers of Battery B, 320th Glider Field Artillery Battalion, back a Jeep into the nose of a CG-4A Waco at Oujda, Morocco, June 16, 1943, while training for the invasion of Sicily. *National Archives.*

bottom
By the 1990s airborne forces could bring their vehicles and large artillery pieces into action by cargo parachute. This Humvee rigged for a drop is being loaded onto a C-141 at Pope Air Force Base, North Carolina, during an exercise in 1998. *Department of Defense.*

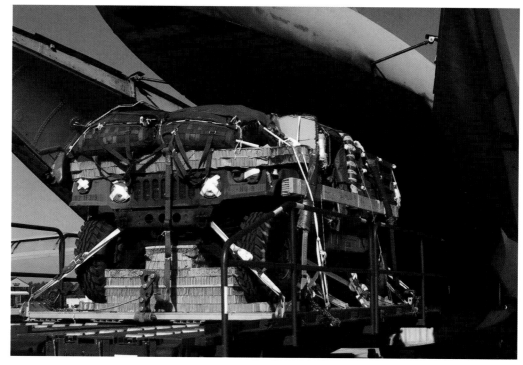

The Airborne will always be a part of an even bigger picture. They will go into action as part of a joint force—whether in a joint task force or as part of a theater commander's team. They will always know that they have a part of the mission and will always perform that part with skill and courage even though they might only be playing a supporting role. Airborne forces will know with each passing year that they have allies because they have shared the dangers and hardships.

Above all, paratroopers will always be an airborne team—men and women from every specialty in every type of unit, each performing a vital function that makes the whole much greater than just the sum of the parts.

ALWAYS READY TO HELP OTHERS

When natural disasters occur, Americans expect their soldiers to help. Hurricanes, floods, forest fires, earthquakes—these will always happen. As long as paratroopers can move faster than anyone else they will be the first choice. Infantry or artillery might not go first on such occasions. The airborne force must be ready to send its engineers, military police, quartermasters, or medics on ahead. This means everyone trains hard.

When other people around the world turn for help, they turn to the United States. Whether we are invited in, or have to force our way past those who do harm, the paratroopers must stand ready. They will always be a choice that the nation's leaders need to have in order to help in a hurry. They need to work at rebuilding ruined nations. They need to use those attitudes and skills, that quick thinking that means so much in combat, and apply it in other ways.

ALWAYS!

The Airborne will always be the nation's first choice when it needs boots on the ground as fast as possible. The N-Hour sequence will always be part of the paratrooper's way of life. Wheels up in 18 hours today; faster down the road. The EDRE is never going away.

The Airborne will always be the nation's force that stands ready to move around the globe or within a theater as the reinforcements that can get there the fastest. Parachute operations will always be the way to put combat power on the ground without having to wait for airfields or ports to be cleared.

The Airborne will always need to react to a crisis when it breaks out. Training will always focus on the contingency operation. Go anywhere, do anything. The United States will always need the ability to make a forced entry anywhere around the world.

The Airborne will always need to be ready to capture key targets. A commander will always need to be able to block an enemy's retreat, cripple the enemy's lines of communication, capture his headquarters, or carry out raids behind the lines. The fastest way to do this is by vertical envelopment whether it is with a jump or an air assault.

The Airborne will always need to fight hard once it reaches the ground. Getting there is only half the mission. Staying and prevailing is vital, as at Bastogne, for example. That has always been a hallmark of airborne operations, and it always will be.

The Airborne will always do one other thing. As long as it exists, is trained, is equipped, and is led, any potential foe will always have to think twice. If he dares to attack he will wonder where parachutes are going to open.

right
A paratrooper from the 82d Airborne Division's 82d Signal Battalion pays his respects to one of his fallen comrades at Forward Operating Base Champion Main in Ar Ramadi, Iraq, June 23, 2005.
82d Airborne Division.

"ALL THE WAY!"

What the pioneers saw in 1943 as the roles and

missions of the American airborne soldier have

never changed, and never will.

Bibliography

Anzuoni, Robert P. *"I'm the 82d Airborne Division!" A History of the All American Division in World War II After Action Reports*. Atglen, PA: Schiffer Publishing Ltd., 2005.

Arnold, Henry H. *Global Mission*. Blue Ridge Summit, PA: Tab Books, 1989. Reprint of original published by Harper & Row, New York, 1949.

Autry, Jerry, assisted by Autry, Kathryn. *General William C. Lee; Father of the Airborne*. Raleigh, NC: Airborne Press, 1995.

Barker, Geoffrey T. *A Concise History of the U.S. Airborne Corps, Divisions and Brigades*. Brandon, FL: Anglo-American Publishing Company, 1989.

Berry, F. Clifton Jr., *Milestones of the First Century of Flight*. Charlottesville, VA: Howell Press, 2002.

_____. *Air Cav; the 1st Air Cavalry Division (Airmobile) in the Vietnam War*. New York: Bantam Books, 1988.

_____. *Sky Soldiers; the 173d Airborne Brigade in the Vietnam War*. New York: Bantam Books, 1987.

Bilstein, Roger E. *Airlift and Airborne Operations in World War II*. Washington, DC: Air Force History and Museums Program, 1998.

Bradley, Francis X. and Wood, H. Glen. *Paratrooper*. Harrisburg, PA: Military Service Publishing Company, 1954.

Caraccilo, Dominic J. *The Ready Brigade of the 82d Airborne in Desert Storm*. Jefferson, NC: McFarland & Company, 1993.

Carter, Ross. *Those Devils in Baggy Pants*. Cutchogue, NY: Buccaneer Books, reprint edition, 1987.

Ciccone, Maj. Roy, MC. *A Report of Injuries Encountered in Parachute Training in Airborne Troops at Fort Benning, Georgia, During World War II*. Fort Benning, GA: Regional Hospital paper, 1946.

Cirillo, Roger. *Ardennes-Alsace (The U.S. Army Campaigns of World War II)*. Washington, DC: Office, Chief of Military History CMH Pub 72-26, 1994.

Clark, Mark W. *Calculated Risk*. New York: Harper & Brothers, 1950.

Collins, John M., with Hamerman, Frederick, and Seevers, James. *U.S. Low-Intensity Conflicts 1899–1990*. Washington, DC: Congressional Research Service study prepared for the Committee on Armed Services, House of Representatives, 1990.

Crookenden, Napier. *Airborne at War*. London: Charles Scribner's Sons, 1978.

_____. *Dropzone Normandy; the Story of the American and British Airborne Assault on D-Day 1944*. London: Charles Scribner's Sons, 1976.

Department of the Air Force. *Airborne Assault on Holland*. No. 4 in the "Wings at War" series. Washington, DC: Center for Air Force History, 1992.

Department of the Air Force. *AAF in Northwest Africa: an account of the Twelfth Air Force in the Northwest African Landings and the Battle for Tunisia*. No. 6 in the "Wings at War" series. Washington, DC: Center for Air Force History, 1992.

Department of the Army. *Airborne Operations. Office Chief of Military History Study 2-3.7 ACF*. Washington, DC: Center of Military History, 1965.

Department of the Army. *Airborne Operations; A German Appraisal. Department of the Army Pamphlet 20-232*. Washington, DC: Department of the Army, 1951.

Department of the Army. *Air Movement of Troops and Equipment; Technical Manual 57-210*. Washington, DC: Department of the Army, 1960.

Department of the Army. *Static Line Parachuting Techniques and Tactics; Field Manual 3-21.220 (FM 57-220)*. Washington, DC: Department of the Army, 2003. Acrobat PDF format.

Department of the Army. *Technical Training of Parachutists; Technical Manual 57-220*. Washington, DC: Department of the Army, 1958.

Department of History, Kansas State University. *Airborne Missions in the Mediterranean, 1942–1945. USAF Historical Studies: No. 74*. Manhattan, KS: (undated). Copy of Historical Studies No. 74, published by USAF Historical Division, Research Studies Institute, Air University, Maxwell AFB, Alabama. 1955.

Devlin, Gerard M. *Paratrooper! The Saga of U.S. Army and Marine Parachute and Glider Combat Troops During World War II.* New York: St. Martin's Press, 1979.

XVIII Corps (Airborne). *Mission Accomplished. A summary of military operations of the XVIII Corps (Airborne) in the European Theatre of Operations, 1944–1945.* Schwerin, Germany: XVIII Corps (Airborne), 1945.

Eisenhower, Dwight D. *Crusade in Europe.* Garden City, NY: Doubleday & Company, Inc., 1948.

Esvelin, Philippe. *D-Day Gliders; Les planeurs américains du Jour J.* Bayeux: Editions Heimdal, 2001.

Flanagan, Edward M. Jr. *Airborne: A Combat History of American Airborne.* New York: A Presidio Press book published by the Ballantine Publishing Group, 2002.

_____. *The Angels: A History of the 11th Airborne Division.* Novato, CA: Presidio Press, 1989.

Fontenot, Gregory, with Degen, E. J. and Tohn, David. *On Point. The United States Army in Operation Iraqi Freedom.* Annapolis, MD: Naval Institute Press, 2005.

Galvin, John R. *Air Assault; the Development of Airmobile Warfare.* New York: Hawthorn Books, 1969.

Gavin, James M. *Airborne Warfare.* Washington, DC: Infantry Journal Press, 1947.

_____. *On To Berlin; Battles of an Airborne Commander 1943–1946.* New York: The Viking Press, 1978.

_____. *War and Peace in the Space Age.* New York: Harper & Brothers, 1958.

Glantz, David M. *The Soviet Airborne Experience; Research Survey No. 4.* Fort Leavenworth, KS: Combat Studies Institute, 1984.

Hoyt, Edwin P. *Airborne; The History of American Parachute Forces.* New York: Stein and Day, 1985.

Huston, James A. *Out of the Blue: U.S. Army Airborne Operations in World War II.* West Lafayette, IN: Purdue University Press. 1999.

Lowden, John L. *Silent Wings at War; Combat Gliders in World War II.* Washington, DC, Smithsonian Institution Press. 1992.

MacDonald, Charles B. *The Last Offensive; the European Theater.* A volume in the official series, "U.S. Army in World War II." Washington, DC: Chief of Military History, first printed 1973. Minnetonka, MN: the National Historical Society edition, 1995.

Otway, T. B. H. *Airborne Forces; The Second World War 1939–1945 Army.* London: Imperial War Museum, 1990.

Rapport, Leonard and Northwood, Arthur Jr. *Rendezvous With Destiny; A History of the 101st Airborne Division.* Greenville, TX: 101st Airborne Division Association, 1948. Second edition, 1965.

Ridgway, Matthew B. *Soldier: The Memoirs of Matthew B. Ridgway as told to Harold H. Martin.* New York: Harper & Brothers, 1956.

Stouffer, Samuel A., et al. *The American Soldier—Adjustment to Army Life, Vol. I.* Princeton, NJ: Princeton University Press, 1949.

_____. *The American Soldier—Adjustment to Army Life, Vol. II.* Princeton, NJ: Princeton University Press, 1949.

Tolson, John J. III. *Airmobility 1961–1971. A volume in the Vietnam Studies series.* Washington, DC: Department of the Army, 1973.

United States Air Force Historical Division Liaison Office. *USAF Tactical Operations; World War II and Korean War.* Washington, DC: Department of the Air Force, 1962.

Walkowicz, T. F. *Future Airborne Armies; A Report Prepared for the AAF Scientific Advisory Group.* Classified SECRET. Declassified to RESTRICTED. Dayton, OH: Headquarters Air Materiel Command, 1946.

Warren, John C. *Airborne Operations in World War II, European Theater. USAF Historical Studies: No. 97.* Manhattan, KS: Sunflower University Press (undated). Copy of Historical Studies No. 97, published by USAF Historical Division, Research Studies Institute, Air University, Maxwell AFB, Alabama. 1956.

Waters, Andrew W. *All the U.S. Air Force Airplanes, 1907–1983.* New York: Hippocrene Books, 1983.

Wilson, John B. *Armies, Corps, Divisions, and Separate Brigades.* Army Lineage Series. Washington, DC: Center of Military History, United States Army, 1999.

Wolfe, Martin. *Green Light! A Troop Carrier Squadron's War from Normandy to the Rhine.* Washington, DC: Center for Air Force History, 1993 reprint of University of Pennsylvania Press edition, 1989.

Index

Italics indicate photographs or illustrations.

Shoulder sleeve insignia of the
XVIII Airborne Corps.

Parachutist, by Harvey Dunn.
Army Art Collection, U.S. Army Center of Military History.

N

Nadzab, *90, 91, 92, 93–94, 97,* 110
National Training Center (NTC), 161
Nedigate, S. F., 40, *40*
Netherlands American Cemetery, 69
Newfoundland
    101st casualties at Gander, 166
New Guinea, *91, 92, 92–94*
Nichols Field, 102
night drops
    risk, problems with in WW II, 48
Nijmegen, Holland
    bombing damage to, *67, 67*
Nimitz, Chester, 113
Ninth Air Force, 48, 49
Nixon, Richard M., 154
Noemfoor Island, 94, *96*–98
    area map, *96*
    paratroopers landing at, *95*
Noriega, Manuel, 166, 167, 168
Normandy American Cemetery and Memorial, *69, 69*
Norris, John, 113
North Africa, 21, 24, 27, 30
North Atlantic Treaty Organization (NATO), 124
North Korea
    attack on South Korea, 114
    Munsan-ni, attack on, 118–20
    Opa-ri, 117
    Sukch'on and Sunch'on, attack on, 115–16, *116,* 117
Norton, John, 143, 147, 152
Norway, 3

O

Oldfield, Barney, 87
Operation ALL THE WAY, 152
Operation ANVIL, 42, 60, 61. *See also* Operation
    DRAGOON
Operation AVALANCHE, 38
Operation BLUE BAT, 136
Operation COMET, 61
Operation COURAGEOUS, 118, *119*
Operation CRAZY HORSE, 152, 153
Operation DESERT STORM, 173–75, *174,* 188
Operation DRAGON NOIRE, 138
Operation DRAGON ROUGE, 138
Operation DRAGOON, 42, 43, 187, 188
Operation ENDURING FREEDOM, 128, 180–82
Operation GOLDEN PHEASANT, 164–65, *165,* 188
Operation HAWK, 118
Operation HAWKEYE, 176
Operation HUSKY, 21, 94, 187
    82d's role in, 33–35
    Biazza Ridge area map, *35, 35*
    casualties, 37
    lessons learned, 36–37
    planning, mission, 31–32
Operation IRAQI FREEDOM, 182–83, 188
Operation JUNCTION CITY, 149

Operation JUST CAUSE, 157, 185
    airborne forces deployed in, 168
    casualties, 171
    events preceding, 164–66
    jump weight for paratroopers, 128
    missions of, 170–72
    planning missions for, 166–68
    rescue of Americans, 170, 171
Operation MARKET-GARDEN
    82d, 101st objectives for, 63
    airborne casualties, 68
    airborne phase, 64–69
    assault area map, *61, 63, 64*
    change in tactics for, 62–64
    FAAA planning for, 61–62
    glider missions, 66–67
    ground phase of, 68
    objectives of, 64–65
    role of troop carrier wings in, 63
    taking of bridges, 65–66
Operation MERCURY, 9
Operation NEPTUNE, 49
    82d Airborne's role in, 56–58
    101st Airborne's role in, 53–56
    assault area map, *50, 51, 53*
    D-Day casualties, 58
    pathfinders' role in, 52–53
Operation OVERLORD, 42
    Cotenin Peninsula, 49
    initial airborne planning, 48–49
    organization of airborne forces for, 47–48
    revised planning for, 49–52
    Utah Beach, 49
Operation RESTORE HOPE, 176
Operations CARENTAN I, II, 153
Operation SHINGLE, 40
Operation SIDESTEP, 120
Operation TABLE TENNIS, 94
Operation THURSDAY, 110
Operation TOMAHAWK, 118, 120
Operation TORCH, 27–30, 45, 185
Operation UPHOLD DEMOCRACY, 175–77
Operation URGENT FURY, 162–64
    coordination problems, 163–64
    design flaws, 162
    impact on restructuring 82d, 101st, 164
    responsibility for designing, 162
Operation VARSITY, 80–85
    assault area map, *81*
    German POWs captured during, *85, 85*
    landing areas, drop zones, 81, *81,* 83
    Medals of Honor awarded, 85
operations other than war, 176
    for airborne forces in the 21st century, 179
    hurricane relief efforts, 176
    "medcaps," 154, 181
Organization of American States (OAS), 158, 159
Ortega, Daniel, 164

Private P. D. Hanson of Headquarters, 502d Parachute Infantry, adjusts equipment on another parachutist just before a mission at Camp Campbell, Kentucky. Tennessee maneuvers, June 16, 1943. One year later the troopers of the 502d were carrying out their missions in Normandy. *National Archives.*